MAKERS OF THE CHRISTIAN TRADITION

HARPER TORCHBOOKS

A reference-list of Harper Torchbooks, classified by subjects, is printed at the end of this volume.

MAKERS OF THE CHRISTIAN TRADITION

From Alfred the Great to Schleiermacher

John T. McNeill

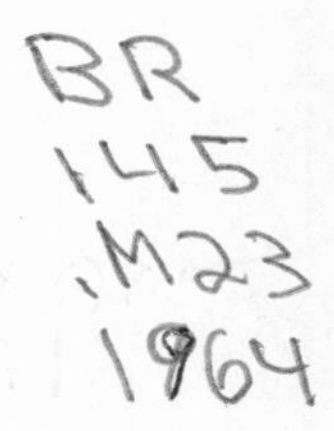

HARPER TORCHBOOKS
The Cloister Library
Harper & Row, Publishers
New York, Evanston, and London

Printed in the United States of America.

This book was originally published in 1935 under the title *Makers of Christianity* by Henry Holt and Company, Inc. It is here reprinted by arrangement.

First HARPER TORCHBOOK edition published 1964 by
Harper & Row, Publishers, Incorporated
49 East 33rd Street
New York, N.Y. 10016

CONTENTS

CONTENTS

PREFACE TO THE TORCHBOOK EDITION

This book is essentially a reproduction of *Makers of Christianity from Alfred the Great to Schleiermacher*, published by Henry Holt and Company in 1935. It appeared as the second volume in a series in which Shirley Jackson Case treated selected figures in Church History to the time of Charlemagne, and William Warren Sweet presented a selection of eminent personalities in American Christianity. I should like here to pay a deserved tribute to the pioneering scholarship of these now deceased former colleagues, whose companionship was an inspiration to me through many years.

The alterations made in the text for this edition, numbering a few more than one hundred, are relatively slight. Illustrative references to events and personalities that were in the foreground of world news twenty-five years ago but are now faded from ready remembrance, have been deleted. A few misprints, some involving dates, have been corrected, and a number of statements have been altered in the light of new evidence or for greater precision. Here and there a short passage has been inserted where clarity and proportion had been impaired by too great brevity. The Bibliography has been revised throughout, and now contains numerous selected new titles, including some on the art of biography.

Biography, conceived as the depiction of personality by means of a recital of the entire life story, is virtually a modern art. In antiquity we come nearest to it in some of the Old Testament narratives, especially those of I and II *Samuel* in which we see unfolded the career and character of David. Xenophon in his *Memorabilia of Socrates* lacks the range of satisfying biography, and he is a panegyrist who sees his subject as the faultless exemplar of all virtue and piety. Plutarch, whose work was to be vastly influential in the later literature of biography, sets his account of each life in a framework of conventional morals and so subordinates personality to moral instruction. Suetonius cares more for piquant anecdotes than for just evaluations on a broad basis of knowledge. Precious, indeed, are the elements of good biography exemplified by such authors; but they hardly glimpsed the dimensions of human personality as modern biographers have come to view it.

Similarly the medieval hagiographers often show fragments of excellent biographical material together with elementary concepts of the biographer's task. They are most satisfactory where the writer has known the subject personally and has observed his habits, attitudes, and typical utterances. Such, for example, are Bede's account of Benedict Biscop, John of Salerno's life of St. Odo, Peter Damian on St. Romuald and Thomas of Celano on St. Francis. Where there was no personal memory and the tradition was dim, a devout imagination too often took the place of fact-finding, with results more readable than reliable.

It is remarkable how far the abundant biographical writing of the Renaissance was indebted to Plutarch's pattern; but it is at the same time characteristically charged with partisanship and as a consequence with exaggeration. The Renaissance brought a fresh sense of human values and, as its currents were mingled with those of the Reformation, men saw in a new light the importance of human personality. Biography became in some hands an instrument of controversy, and some reputations unduly suffered. But we may take as typical of much that was to follow two short biographies that are wholly favorable: William Roper's *Life of Thomas More* and Theodore Beza's *Life of John Calvin.* Each is in its way a panegyric, though armed with a considerable array of easily-acquired facts. To Roper, More is "that mirrour of all honour and vertue," and for Beza, Calvin is the paragon of religious leaders and teachers. Both authors were personally well acquainted with the subjects of their writing, and both neglected that documentary research that would have led from reminiscence and casual inquiry to an adequate biographical method.

We should not forget that in some respects autobiography, though less frequently practiced, reached a more advanced stage than the heterobiography of which we have been thinking. There is no more enduring literary work than Augustine's *Confessions,* with its brilliant and unreserved revelation of the inner experience of a man of religious genius. If Augustine through anguish discovered the marvels of grace, Abailard sounded the depths of "calamity" in his narrative of success, temptation, sin and savage punishment. In later times, John Bunyan's *Grace Abounding* brings us also to the deep places; and the modern understanding of religion has been enriched by the personal memoirs of such religious men as George Fox, John Wesley, John Henry Newman, Søren Kierkegaard, Leo Tolstoy, and Albert Schweitzer.

In the seventeenth century the art of the biographer took on new vigor, as men learned to take a greater interest in their own lives and those of others. Diaries and journals, many marked by religious introspection, abounded; but it was also the age of the entertaining episodic superficiality of Samuel Pepys. There were a few labored and extensive lives of great personages; and such writers as Thomas Fuller and Isaac Walton, through their patience and conscientiousness in the search for data made their biographical sketches of permanent value, while by their qualities of style they are also of lasting attractiveness to English readers. But they differ greatly in their interests, for while Fuller seems as happy among the sinners of his *Profane State* as in the high company of his *Holy State*, Walton will not soil his pages with the history of an evil-doer.

From the time of these notables to our own day the stream of biographical writing has continued to swell, and almost all possible varieties of the genre have been explored. Industrious examination of environment and background has led to the production of a mongrel literature between biography and history. In a title even a very minor name may be followed by the swelling phrase, "and His Times." More legitimately, David Masson's *Milton* embraces an era of English history. On the other hand there has been a good deal of that penetrating examination of the inner personality which is exhibited in the more searching autobiographical works. In America Gamaliel Bradford advocated and practiced this type of writing, which he designated "psychography," the description of the soul. Certainly this is a commendable development, and it has its appeal in a generation in which many readers have some knowledge, and others a smattering, of psychology, and like to look inside the minds of others. Bradford once wrote: "Nothing interests young people, or old ones, or all men and women, so much as other men and women;" and there is proof of this opinion in the banal intimacies of journalism and radio and television entertainment, in which the personal experiences of quite ordinary people are made to seem of extraordinary importance, however badly expressed. Bradford's conception, and we may say biography itself, is for the most conscientious. It is easy to use familiarities with great men without penetrating to the soul.

It will perhaps always be true that most biographers adopt subjects whom they admire, and thus that favorable biographies outnumber the others. But Lytton Strachey has written in an intriguing style a series of biographies of exposure, designed to lower the reader's estimate of the characters described, and has thus started a new trend of irreverence for reputations. He has also denied the assumption of most moderns that ideally a biography should be comprehensive both in research and in content, partly on the ground that this is really impossible, but also in the belief that selected samplings of the mass of material will yield a more revealing picture of the person. Such a method seems, however, to lend itself too readily to subjective bias, and is likely to produce either defamatory or unduly laudatory characterizations. There is, of course, a value in what we may call corrective biography, and it may profit by the just use of previously neglected fragments of evidence and properly give to these an importance they would not deserve in a pioneering work. In the field of history generally, complete comprehensiveness is even more impossible than in biography. Yet it is wholesome to feel that we are under a moral compulsion not to be content with sample materials but to make the fullest possible use of all the data, and to draw our conclusions carefully and responsibly from these.

In the type of brief biographical sketch used in this book,

no approach to comprehensiveness of presentation can, of course, be claimed. But a serious effort has been made to read the sources and essential literature for each person treated, and to know intimately his acts and thoughts. I have tried in a restrained way to convey what I feel of a common bond with these great Christians. Surely one of the ways of fulfilling the command to love our fellowmen is to reach back into past ages for the companionship of those who in the same spirit faithfully served God and their brethren. I may be accused of some partiality for persons of the type here described, but I hope this partiality does not amount to adulation or escape the bounds of critical judgment, and that I have not played favorites within the chosen company. In some instances the documents fail to give much that could contribute toward a psychograph of the man, and incautious judgments of his mind and motives have in these cases been withheld. But I have always approached as nearly as with brevity I was able to the inner soul and spirit, while also broadly indicating the historic importance, of each.

I am deeply indebted to Harper & Row for encouragement to prepare this edition, and for producing it in an attractive yet inexpensive form.

J. T. M.

East Middlebury, Vermont
9th May, 1964

PREFACE

In the congenial task of writing these sketches I have been faced continually by the problem of selection in respect both to persons and to facts. Critical readers will perhaps censure the omission of one, the inclusion of another, historical figure. Any selection of persons on the basis of their importance is, like an anthology of poems, subject to objections from various viewpoints. Here the choice turned not on the mere renown of the individual, but on a judgment of his creative force and influence in the development of Christianity. In the selection of facts I have sought to combine indispensable details of each life story with personality-revealing incidents and glimpses of the environing society. The aim has been to employ biography in the service of history, and to view the characters, as they lived, in vital relationship with the movements and persons of their environment. The book is designed for those unfamiliar with European history, as well as for students who have become acquainted with its main currents. It is not written for historical experts, and can only seek their approval as an aid to the inexpert.

It is no matter of surprise that a distinct moral elevation attaches to this chosen company of master-Christians drawn from ten centuries of European life. They exhibit much of the selfless devotion which has been the glory of the Christian tradition. But they are not faultlessly admirable, nor on every count heroic. If in the treatment of their struggles amid the favorable and thwarting forces of circumstance something of the intensity and poignancy of man's perpetual moral warfare has been conveyed to the reader, the book may serve in a modest way to quicken his understanding of life's true values. At least it offers him brief leave of absence from the distressing tensions of the contemporary scene, to share the company of some of the world's dynamic and history-shaping personalities, whose faith and purpose have been as a pillar of cloud by day and of fire by night to guide the march of humanity.

J. T. McN.

The Divinity School
The University of Chicago
June 14, 1935

CHAPTER I

LEADERS OUT OF CHAOS

"I know nothing of those ages which knew nothing," remarked an eighteenth-century scholar, dismissing from serious concern the period with which this chapter has to do. A century later a trained historian rose to inquire how the contemptuous sage, knowing nothing of those ages, knew that they knew nothing. Indeed the literary products of the "Dark Age" abundantly show that some men of that time knew a great deal. The darkness of the age consisted not so much in universal ignorance as in a universal derangement of politics and society.

The human scene has rarely exhibited more confusion than that which prevailed in Western Europe during the hundred years after Charlemagne.

The inner history of the Frankish Empire in the ninth century appears at first glance to consist of a meaningless series of political explosions and futile civil wars. Looked at more closely it is seen as the fresh assertion of local powers and interests which Charlemagne's efficient rule had temporarily held in check, and whose triumph was to produce the ever restless feudal society of a later time. It was of small advantage that the idea of the empire still withheld the Carolingian princes from extreme courses, that most of the campaigns were mere demonstrations of power attended by little bloodshed and much negotiation, and that among many warriors there was no conqueror. Had there been a conqueror there might have been a new unification. If the princes still had some regard for the imperial tradition, most of the vassals were utterly indifferent even to the welfare of that kingdom within the empire, to which they belonged. In time of crisis Charles the Bald could usually count on the base desertion of his sworn vassals. Even in so small a country as England political unity was not attained. The Northumbrian supremacy in the seventh century, and the Mercian in the eighth, scarcely even aimed at complete unification. In the ninth century leadership passed to Wessex, and under Alfred the inhabitants of England for the first time learned to think of England as a whole.

The enfeeblement of all political institutions in the ninth as in the fifth century afforded an invitation to a variety of invaders. Generations earlier the horns of the Moslem territorial crescent had been thrust against Christian Constantinople and Christian Aquitaine. But Christianity, in gaining ascendancy in the Roman Empire and in the "conversion" of the Franks, had been itself converted from a pacific into a military religion fit to cope successfully with Islam; and its warriors had flung back the swarthy hordes of the Prophet. The Emirate of Cordova showed no ambition to challenge the Frankish power north of the Pyrenean wall. But Saracen pirates and freebooters from North Africa and Spain harassed the coasts of Italy, plundered the Basilica of St. Peter and the venerable abbey of St. Benedict at Monte Cassino, gained control of the island of Sicily, and plagued with frequent incursions the southern states of the peninsula. In the closing years of the century, the Magyars, savage pagans from the Ural-Altaian plateau, pushed their way up the Danube valley and occupied the fertile plains of Hungary, whence they were soon to fling their troops of fierce, mobile, mounted bowmen upon Saxony and Thuringia, and even into Burgundy, laying Christian governments under tribute and threatening their overthrow. Still more devastating were the raids of the Northmen. Hungry and hardy savages from the Norse bays, experts only in navigation, war and plunder, scoured the coasts of England, Ireland and France, ascended the rivers and sacked the castles, churches and monasteries, mercilessly slaying clergy and laity and spreading desolation and a paralysis of fear. From 793 when, as the *Anglo-Saxon Chronicle* records, "the ravaging of the heathen men lamentably destroyed God's church at Lindisfarne," to 911 when the giant Norse chieftain Rollo set up the Duchy of Normandy, accepting Christian baptism and a French king's daughter's hand, the depredations of these ruthless invaders raged over widening areas of Western Europe.

We of the twentieth century can appreciate the soul-testing experiences of a time when the foundations of society rock and tremble beneath men's feet. In the ninth century it seemed to many that the foundations had already yielded, and that the whole structure was crashing to ruin. How men who were charged with responsibility behaved in such a time, by what faith they lived, for what ends they contended, cannot be other than matters of lively interest to those not wholly indifferent to the story of humanity.

The later life of Europe owes a vast debt to a few stalwarts of the Dark Age, who, each in his own way, combated the social chaos about them. Hinkmar (806-882), the stern Archbishop of Reims, and Anskar (801-865), missionary to the northern enemy's homelands, are of more real significance for history than any Frankish king after Charlemagne. Yet they are perhaps less the makers of the later age than the two figures to be sketched in this chapter: Alfred, the great king of a small kingdom, and Pope Nicholas who for a moment gained sway over the Christian West.

Alfred the Great

The Anglo-Saxon tribes who in the fifth century crossed the North Sea to Britain and in savage warfare wrested from its Celtic inhabitants the greater part of the island, in time proved themselves apt pupils in the school of civilization. Roman and Irish missionaries made them Christians, and introduced them to Latin culture. But decline was apparent before the Danish invasions, and now, amid desolation and disorder, it seemed that Englishmen might lapse into the state of their primitive ancestors. The learning and religion of the "golden age" of the early English church, the age of the Venerable Bede (d. 735), had passed away. Alfred wrote that at the time of his accession there were few south of the Humber and none south of the Thames who could translate from Latin into English. The monasteries had been largely secularized or destroyed; and on all sides men were reverting to savagery. Charlemagne inherited a strong kingdom with a rising culture; Alfred had to rebuild almost from the foundation. But inner contention and devastating invasions had now enfeebled the great Frank's empire. Charles Plummer writing of Alfred in 871, remarks: "The fate of England and of Western Europe hung, humanly speaking, on the heart and brain and arm of a young man of three-and-twenty years."

That the pagan Danes and Norwegians failed to do to the Christian English what the pagan English had done four centuries earlier to the Christian Britons, is due in some measure to Alfred's Wessex predecessors. His grandfather, Egbert, who had more power than any king before him in England, began the war of defense against the Vikings. Egbert in his youth had spent three years at the court of Charlemagne and probably learned there those ideas of government which appear in his reign and in the policies of his successors. He died in 839, leaving his realm to his son, Ethelwulf.

Alfred, Ethelwulf's fourth son, was born in 848. His mother, Osberga, died when he was five or six years old. In 853, and again in 855, the little prince was taken on journeys to Rome. On the first of these visits he was, in a ceremony of a nature obscure to historians, invested by Pope Leo IV with "the girdle, dignity and vestments of the consular rank;" for so the Pope wrote to King Ethelwulf. The second visit was made with Ethelwulf himself, who had long desired to see the apostolic city. Osberga was now dead; and on the way back the boy witnessed his father's second marriage. The bride was Judith, the thirteen-year-old daughter of Charles the Bald, grandson of Charlemagne and King of the West Franks. The marriage was solemnized at Verberie by Hinkmar, Archbishop of Reims, October 1, 856, and the ritual of the ceremony is preserved in Hinkmar's *Works*. It would be interesting to know what the little prince and the great prelate thought of each other.

The Anglo-Frank alliance was apparently designed as a combination against a common enemy, the Viking host. When Ethelwulf died in 858, Judith, perhaps in order to perpetuate the alliance, became the wife of his son and heir, Ethelbald, and when this prince died, 860, she returned to her father's court. Charles placed her under restraint at Senlis, whence she soon eloped with Baldwin of the Iron Arm, known to history as the first count of Flanders. Judith and her husband visited Pope Nicholas I to obtain his absolution for their marriage.

In the short reigns of Alfred's two remaining brothers, Ethelbert and Ethelred, the Danes were increasingly troublesome and destructive. Alfred had now grown to manhood. Having for some years coöperated with Ethelred as "Secondarius" or assistant king, on Ethelred's death, at Easter 871, he became sole ruler. He had married Elswitha, the daughter of a Mercian earl, Ethelred the Big.

Alfred had grown up in an age of disorder, and been trained in knightly exercises; but he had shown an extraordinary craving for books, and for the poetry of his race, which old men recited and minstrels sang at the rude court of Wessex. By choice he would have been a man of letters: by necessity he was a man of war. The year of his accession was called the year of battles. The Danes, fresh from a victorious campaign in Mercia, assailed Wessex. At Ashdown, one winter morning, the opposing forces met. Ethelred waited for mass to be ended, while Alfred, with his section of the army, charged up the slope "like a wild boar." Though the Danes were beaten with heavy losses, they soon resumed aggressive war. In that year of carnage Alfred fought nine pitched battles. It was in one of the earlier of these encounters that Ethelred received the wounds from which he died. At intervals thereafter the conflict was fiercely renewed, but the fate of England was not soon decided. The war-loving Vikings, who hoped, as one of them sang, that having fought with swords and died valiantly they would "drink mead in the hall of Odin from the skulls of their foes," were matched against Alfred's courageous men who fought to defend their homes and their religion. When it seemed that the Saxon resistance was at an end, Alfred, in a distressful winter spent at Athelney, organized a fresh campaign, and just after Easter 878 came forth from this "Valley Forge" experience to win the decisive victory of Ethandune (Edington, Wiltshire). Cold, hunger, and discouragement led the surviving Danes to make peace virtually on Alfred's terms. King Guthrum became his adopted son and received baptism. By a treaty of 886 the Danes were assigned a large territory, roughly fifteen modern shires, the northeastern half of England, in most of which area they were probably by that time in a majority. There followed a process of their Christianization and integration with the English stock, a process which was made possible by Alfred's fair and even generous treatment of his defeated foes. Alfred's later wars were with new Norse invaders from France and Ireland. In 892-894 occurred a fresh series of campaigns, the consequence of the landing of 330 shiploads of the enemy from France. In the course of his wars Alfred had built up a strong citizen army, and a navy surpassing that which his enemies could command. His son, Edward, and the King himself, repeatedly defeated and finally crushed these new invaders.

The wars of Alfred constituted a crusade against paganism. But paganism cannot be extinguished by war; and through all the heroic struggle Alfred well knew that war was not the major business of a king. That which gives to his reign its glory and distinction is his resolute purpose to build the institutions of government and to lay the foundations of a Christian civilization. While his sword flashed on the battle field he bore in his bosom, beneath his coat of mail, a copy of the Psalter. It was not his talisman, but his companion in every hour of relaxation,—a link to bind him to the world of mind and of spirit.

Alfred employed the intervals of peace in constant efforts to establish order and justice in his kingdom. His friend and biographer, Asser, says he was the only helper of the poor. In his *Dooms*—the revision of the laws of his predecessors—the rule is laid down: "Judge not one judgment for the rich and another for the poor." He was always ready to hear the pleas of his subjects: he sometimes intervened in cases where he thought the judges unjust; and he frequently rebuked these officials and urged them to read, or if they were illiterate to have others read to them, that they might acquire wisdom.

Though he was held in such admiration that he might have made himself almost an absolute ruler, it is evident that he was careful to consult his Witenagemot, or council of wise men, on important matters of policy, and so to preserve the constitutional character of the rising monarchy.

Asser tells us that the King "gathered craftsmen from all nations . . . men skilled in every earthly work." This is heightened language; but it probably has some relation to the facts. Specific evidence indicates that he designed patterns for his goldsmiths and instructed artificers and huntsmen, and apparently he carefully supervised a variety of arts and activities. His ingenious invention of a lantern, made of wood and planed sheets of ox-horn, as a means of regulating his time-measuring candles, reveals an interesting aspect of his versatile talent. He employed Flemish seamen to construct and navigate his ships, and encouraged Norwegian whalers and explorers; but it does not appear that he did much for the promotion of trade or agriculture. Patriot that he was, he was eager to use the service of foreigners where these might benefit his own kingdom.

Alfred's interests lay primarily in the restoration of learning and religion. He had seen the greatness of the church at Rome and in Frankland, and longed to revive its fallen glory in England. For this task "he sought from abroad that which he had not at home," capable scholars and teachers. A few of these were available in other English kingdoms. Werferth, Bishop of Worcester, who translated for him the *Dialogues* of Gregory the Great, was a Mercian by birth and training. So was Plegmund, whom he made Archbishop of Canterbury. These scholarly clerics represent a remnant of the learning that had flourished early in the previous century. At every opportunity Alfred had these and other scholars read with him and instruct him. But he needed more help than they could give, and he sought it in the Frankish empire. A century earlier English scholars had taken service in Charlemagne's educational reforms, and Franks were now to repay the debt.

We are free to call these continental teachers Franks only in a political, not in a racial sense. The two whom Alfred and his biographer name with special gratitude, Grimbald and John the Old Saxon, were probably nearly related to the men of Wessex in race and language. Apparently Grimbald came, on the King's invitation, about 885. He was a monk of St. Bertin's monastery in St. Omer near Calais. A native of that region could probably understand the West Saxon speech. John seems to have come from Corvey in Westphalia, the region which formed the original home of the Saxon tribes. After him followed, says Asser, "very many of the same Gallic nation," both learned priests and deacons, and children who were to be given a monastic training.

Like all reformers of the early Middle Ages Alfred relied on monasticism as the basis of religious and educational life. He founded a cloister for men at Athelney, probably as a memorial of his victory of 878, and appointed John to be its abbot. Conditions in the monastery partook of the turbulence of that age. On one occasion, John found himself attacked in his church by the hirelings of hostile clerics of his own race. He resisted valiantly, or desperately, and the ruffians fled; they were caught, tortured and put to death. Grimbald, too, in the end became the abbot of a monastery founded by Alfred, the "new minster" at Winchester. In addition to these foundations a cloister for women was built at Shaftesbury, of which the King's daughter, Elgiva, became abbess.

The work of the leaders from across the Channel cannot be estimated with certainty. Our sources on the subject are both scanty and inconsistent. In the case of Grimbald, a legendary story was invented which made him an unsuccessful disputant against certain doctors of Oxford—obviously an attempt to give a fictitious antiquity to the university. Another tale relates that the brilliant and scholarly Irishman, John Scotus Erigena, came to Alfred's kingdom and became a teacher at Malmesbury where he met a sad end at the hands of his exasperated students. (See below, p. 105.) All sensational tales of violence to the contrary notwithstanding, the finely illumined manuscripts that were produced in these Wessex monasteries shortly after Alfred's death testify to the peace, industry and learning that generally marked their existence.

The best known of Alfred's associates is the learned and gifted Welshman, Asser, whom he urged to join him in his educational work. Possibly Asser was the first of the foreign scholars to come, and he may have been Alfred's emissary in securing the others. He was a distinguished Welsh prelate, and it was with difficulty that he obtained freedom to go to Wessex. His agreement with Alfred was that he should divide his time equally between Wessex and St. David's. He regarded his function as of political significance; he was the link of unity between the long hostile Christian states of Wales and Wessex. His life of Alfred is evidently designed for his Welsh countrymen's instruction. The presentation of the ruler of the Saxon enemy as a most Christian king, and a flawless hero, was propaganda for peace. The work was also designed to restrain a certain political oppressor of Asser's in Wales by exhibiting the strength of his Saxon patron. What faults in Alfred are consigned to oblivion by Asser, we do not know. But Asser is a writer of unusual intelligence and enlightenment, and while the portrait of the King is doubtless in some degree idealized, it is nevertheless drawn from the living model, and marked by essential veracity.

What Asser most admired in the King was his sincere devotion to learning. The bishop is exceedingly happy to have had a part in the education of the King. But Alfred was able to rival his own teachers, and was himself the leader of the educational work. He translated or caused to be translated a number of Christian Latin classics into the speech of Wessex. These works—the *Dialogues* of Gregory the Great, the same author's *Pastoral Care*, the *Universal History* of Orosius, Bede's *Ecclesiastical History*, the "*Blooms*" or selections from Augustine, and Boethius' *Consolations of Philosophy*—were all highly regarded by the ecclesiastical scholars of that age. Alfred wished all his people to learn to read in their mother tongue; but the works he translated were primarily for the use of those of the clergy who were unskilled in Latin.

Some of these translations are principally by his own hand. The renderings are free; and passages are omitted and inserted without explanation. He added to the geographical section of the Orosius a discussion of the contemporary geography of the Continent, and the Norwegian Othere's account of his voyage to the White Sea, one of the most interesting of medieval travel documents. Profoundly interested in geography himself, Alfred was evidently anxious to spread among his subjects a knowledge of the world and its races.

The date of his death has been set as early as 899, but 901 may be regarded as more probable. The real Alfred is unknown to the many who leave off their study of him with a few children's stories, for the popular tales of him are nearly all late and misleading fictions. The judgment of Von Ranke that he "is one of the greatest figures in the history of the world" has won the assent of many later historians. His achievements are glorious. but his true greatness lies in his personality and his ideals. Though he ruled but part of England, he probably contributed more than any other ruler to the better elements of English national life.

In one of his expansions of the *Boethius* Alfred thus explained the principles that dominated his career:

Power is never a good, unless he be good that has it. . . . From his virtues he becomes worthy of power. . . . If you be wise and good power will follow you though you should not wish it. The tools that a king needs to rule are these: to have his land fully peopled; to have priestmen, soldiermen and workmen. . . . This will I say: I resolved to live honorably as long as I lived, and after my time to leave to the men who should come after me my memorial in good works.

Nicholas the Great

The rise of the Roman See to the peak of its authority in the thirteenth century, was a slow process punctuated by long intermissions. The names of most of the popes between Gregory the Great (590-604) and Nicholas the Great (858-867) scarcely deserve to be recorded in the memory. The pontificates of the second and the third Gregory exhibited some promise of the later development, but little of definite achievement. Such pontiffs as Zachary, Adrian I, and Leo III emerge from the obscurity of the series, largely because of the assistance their policies lent to the rise of the Frankish power. The ninth century saw only two popes of outstanding character and energy, Leo IV and Nicholas I, and the greater of these was Nicholas.

The weakness of the Papacy in that age of discord may well be deplored as one of the factors contributing to the prevailing tumult. It is something that for fifteen years the central power of the church exerted itself forcibly. Six of these years only were Leo's, 847-853; and his energies were so largely occupied in organizing resistance to the Saracen pirates in Italy as to make it impossible for him to deal effectively with the situation as a whole. But Nicholas took the world for his province.

Of the early life of Nicholas little is recorded. The date of his birth is unknown. He was the son of a Roman official, a man of means and character. Young Nicholas displayed unusual gifts and was given a careful education. He came to manhood handsome, courteous, virtuous, learned and eloquent. He was favored by three popes in succession, and enjoyed popularity in Rome. Leo IV made him a deacon, and he became the most trusted companion of the amiable but unsuccessful Benedict III who followed Leo. There is, of course, no truth in the legend of the woman-pope, Joan of Mainz, who was said to have held the holy office between Leo and Benedict; though the lurid tale of her deception and misconduct was accepted as history, by all but a few incredulous persons like Pope Pius II, from the thirteenth to the seventeenth century, when it was finally disproved by a French Huguenot scholar.

In the spring of 858 the Emperor Louis II visited Rome. This Louis was the son of Lothar, and a grandson of Louis the Pious, the successor of Charlemagne. He had been crowned by Pope Sergius II, and was friendly to the Papacy. He was concerned for the peace of Italy, the suppression of the Saracens, and the repulse of the revived ambitions of the Byzantine Empire. The imperial party had left the city when messengers brought word of the sudden death of Pope Benedict. Having no doubt learned, during previous conferences, to admire the able deacon who was Benedict's chief secretary, Louis promptly returned to Rome to secure the election of Nicholas. Possibly Nicholas would have become pope without his help; but the emperor's presence and favor made his election certain. He was consecrated April 24, 858.

Like most of the abler popes, Nicholas accepted the Papacy only with the greatest reluctance, and the report that he was carried by force to his consecration may possibly be well founded. An exalted conception of the office might well induce hesitation in entering it, even on the part of a man who knew himself fitted for leadership.

It is often stated that Nicholas was the first pope to wear a crown; but it is probable that some kind of crown without gems had been earlier used in the ceremony of the papal consecration. A fresco of the period apparently represents Nicholas in a procession with a jeweled crown on his head. It is not of course the triple crown of the modern popes; this appeared only in the fourteenth century. It was perhaps natural that the origin of the papal crown should have been associated with this kingly pope whom historians have looked upon as the successor of Charlemagne in respect to the sway which he exercised over the world.

After his consecration Nicholas took farewell of Louis in ceremonial fashion, some miles out of the city. The emperor had taken up his station and when the pontiff rode forward to where he stood, Louis went on foot to receive him, and led his horse by the bridle "the distance of an arrow's flight." The forged Donation of Constantine, a century earlier, had represented Constantine as performing a similar service to Pope Sylvester I; and the precedent was not forgotten by popes of subsequent times, since Louis's act dramatized the claim of papal suzerainty over emperors.

The policy of Nicholas was to be developed in a series of controversies. The most famous of these was with Photius who, a few months before the accession of Nicholas, had been elevated to the See of Constantinople. The Byzantine Empire at this time was ruled nominally by Michael III, the Drunkard, and really by his unscrupulous uncle, Bardas. Photius was a man of prodigious learning and, in a not too exact sense of the phrase, of honorable life. But he was the appointee of Cæsar Bardas, who had deposed and banished his predecessor Ignatius because the latter had boldly rebuked his vices. Nicholas refused to recognize Photius, and disallowed his election on the ground that the Roman pontiff had not been consulted. A synod at Constantinople confirmed the election, the Pope's envoys who were present being cajoled into supporting this action. Nicholas, with rising indignation, reproached the Emperor and the Patriarch, and asserted the supremacy of the Roman church "by whose authority and sanction all synods and holy councils have their force." He held a synod at Rome which condemned the offending legates and declared Photius deposed and Ignatius reinstated.

A controversial correspondence ensued, in course of which Nicholas expanded the theme of the papal supremacy as resting on the sovereign power bestowed on St. Peter. Photius, on his part, charged the Western church with heresy for having introduced the "filioque" into the creed, and alleged numerous defects in matters of ritual. The Nicene creed described the Holy Ghost as "proceeding from the Father." The word "filioque" ("and the Son") in accordance with Western opinion from Augustine's time, had been added in Spain in the sixth century, and the addition had later been adopted in Francia. Though no Roman council had formally sanctioned it, it was now favored at Rome, and Nicholas became its advocate. He summoned the learning of the Latin West to defend Western doctrines and customs against the Greeks. His opponent Hinkmar was now enlisted in the cause, and induced a number of Frankish theologians to write treatises in vindication of "filioque."

Photius, however, remained in uneasy authority until the death of Michael, who (while drunk as usual) was murdered by Basil the Macedonian. When this assassin assumed the throne he dismissed Photius, restored Ignatius, and cultivated the favor of Rome. But death overtook Nicholas before he could profit by this revolution. On the death of Ignatius (877) Photius resumed the Patriarchate, and held office with the consent of Pope John VIII.

Another aspect of the quarrel with Photius was the attempt of Nicholas to detach the rising Christianity of Bulgaria from the Eastern Patriarchate and bring it under the sway of Rome. But Boris, the Khan of Bulgaria, demanded terms with which Nicholas and his successor Adrian II were not disposed to comply. After a promising effort on the part of Nicholas to organize a Bulgarian bishopric, a deadlock was reached under Adrian, with the result that Bulgaria came permanently to be incorporated in the domain of Eastern Orthodoxy.

The Eastern policy of Nicholas was bold, but in the end unfortunate. He was more successful in his treatment of rebellious prelates and turbulent princes in the West. He was able to bend to his will the proud Hinkmar, Archbishop of Reims, who claimed authority for metropolitans, or archbishops, over bishops who were disposed to appeal against them to the pope. In this controversy, important for the centralization of the church, Nicholas appears to have made use of the Forged Decretals which had come into existence a few years earlier. The most competent experts now believe that this collection of fabricated documents purporting to be the authoritative utterances of numerous popes of earlier times, took shape in an effort of Breton clerics to escape subjection to the Frankish Metropolitan of Tours, during the conflict by which the chiefs of Brittany threw off the claims of Charles the Bald to govern them. Since they asserted the authority of the popes as against that of the metropolitans, they proved of immense permanent value to the Papacy in establishing its medieval power. Nicholas was probably the first pope to employ them. It is not necessary to assume that he derived his principles from them. Nor is it apparent that he knew them to be falsifications; though his familiarity with the forgeries of Photius, and his known consultation of the Roman archives, ought to have made him incredulous of such surprising documents.

John, the cruel and unscrupulous Archbishop of Ravenna, was another prelate whom Nicholas subdued. John ruthlessly oppressed his people, performed episcopal acts beyond his own province, and in insolent hostility to the Roman See forbade all pilgrimages to the shrines of the Apostles at Rome. The disaffection of John's own subjects enabled Nicholas to bring him to terms of humiliating surrender, in which he solemnly promised to abandon these practices and to visit the pope annually to answer for his conduct.

Nicholas repeatedly demanded, in imperious language, the obedience of great princes to the pope. This principle pervades his correspondence with Charles the Bald and Louis the German as it does the letters of Hildebrand, two centuries later. Against Lothar II, their nephew, who ruled Lotharingia from Aix-la-Chapelle, he stoutly asserted, in association with Hinkmar, the church's claim with respect to marriage. This young prince, having been compelled by his father to marry Theutberga, the daughter of a powerful vassal, decided to put her away and to marry his former mistress, Waldrada. Important political interests were involved in the cause of each of these women. A charge of misconduct was trumped up against Theutberga. The archbishops of Cologne and Treves abetted Lothar's plans, and in two synods the bishops of the realm followed their lead. Hinkmar wrote a long and vigorous tract shattering the legal case for the divorce, and continued to demand the restoration of Theutberga. It may here be remarked that no one seems to have rebuked Charlemagne for his free and frequent violations of the laws of marriage, but from this time forward such conduct on the part of princes was usually challenged by the clergy. With his usual decision and energy, Nicholas took up Theutberga's cause. In the wearisome struggle that ensued the wronged queen herself became unwilling to return to her unfaithful husband, but this made no difference in the pope's demands. Lothar repeatedly made, and as frequently violated, promises to satisfy Nicholas in the matter, but the issue was still unsettled at the time of the King's death. Both women survived him, and each ended her days in a nunnery. Incidentally the archbishops involved on Lothar's side were made to feel the power of the pope's discipline. It was perhaps with salutary astonishment as well as bitter resentment that the time-serving Gunther of Cologne complained: "The lord Nicholas makes himself emperor of the whole world."

These struggles sapped the physical constitution of Nicholas, though his indomitable spirit kept him unceasingly active through years of bodily pain. He died November 13, 867. Although his immediate successors made but poor efforts to carry his policies to fruition, he had, in many acts and utterances, laid a foundation on which popes of after centuries were to build the structure of world dominion. A generation after him, when the Papacy had sunk into degradation, a monastic chronicler affirmed that no pope since Gregory the Great could be compared with him, and recalled that Nicholas "mastered kings and tyrants and set his authority over them, as if he were lord of the whole world."

Nicholas is a canonized saint. He had none of that reckless generosity which has made his Eastern namesake, St. Nicholas of Myra, known as Santa Claus; yet he excelled in ascetic piety, and abounded in charitable works. The chronicler just quoted adds that, while terrible and austere to the wicked, "he seemed lowly, gracious, pious and gentle to those who observed the commandments of God." No man, perhaps, better combined the medieval type of piety with the qualities of a high-minded and cultured gentleman than this protagonist of papal imperialism, Nicholas the Great.

CHAPTER II

APOSTLES OF MONASTIC PIETY

Monasticism was the mode in which religion chiefly expressed itself in the Middle Ages. The "religious" was the monk. What there was of uncloistered piety was colored by that asceticism which found its institutional embodiment in cloister life.

The spirit of renunciation by which early Christians accredited and defended their faith, after the close of the era of persecution found its outlet in a vast movement of ascetic devotion. Institutionalized under the leadership of the desert saints of Egypt and Basil of Cæsarea, the movement was firmly established in the West in the late fourth and early fifth century. A century later came St. Benedict of Nursia, the immortal codifier of Western monasticism, whose *Rule* is to be dated about 526-529.

The *Rule* of Benedict is hardly surpassed in importance by any medieval work, since it was not only the regulative foundation of almost the whole series of Western monastic revivals but also one of the principal texts from which contemplative mystics derived their inspiration. Its humane and moderate asceticism, its insistence on humility, obedience, industry and stability, as well as poverty and chastity, and its plan of daily acts of worship, are basic elements of the medieval monastic discipline.

Benedict was a reformer of the prolific but disorderly monasticism which he saw about him in Italy, and which he describes in caustic language. He had no knowledge of the high success of the contemporary monasticism of Ireland. Formed in units which were often connected with the tribal organization, and enjoying a large measure of protection, the Irish communities of ascetics teemed with life. Emigration from the country took the form of monastic pilgrimages or missions. Characteristic of the spirit of this migration is the story in the *Anglo-Saxon Chronicle* for 791, of three Irish monks, Dubslane, MacBeth and Maelinmain, who were received by Alfred: they had reached Cornwall from Ireland after seven days at sea in a little boat of hides without sail or oars. Though many of these sea-going saints set out knowing not whither they might drift, others planned the course and object of their journey. A large number became effective missionaries or eminent teachers in the lands to which, by chance or by intention, they took their way. The white-robed Irish monk with his staff and his leather bag for books became a familiar figure to the people of many parts of the Continent. The bag often contained not only liturgical texts but copies of the classics, works of the Christian fathers, and penitential books of Irish origin, written in a peculiar script which the monk would teach to Continental pupils. For these men were scholars as well as saints.

The Irish form of monasticism with its religious intensity and its intellectual fertility had to yield place to the Benedictine, because the latter had advantages in organization and permanent practicability, and obtained the support of popes and prelates. But some elements from the Irish customs found their way into the work of later reformers of Benedictinism.

Monasticism, like the Papacy, passed through numerous

depressions and revivals. Its difficulties lay partly in the social disorder and partly in a certain conflict of its own principles. In times of war and insecurity too many recruits to monasticism were motivated rather by fear than by devotion, with the result that the spiritual temperature ran low. On the other hand, war, especially in the case of the Norse and Saracen invasions, often brought ruin to the houses of religion.

Monasticism suffered from prosperity no less than from adversity. Monks were pledged to industry and also to poverty; but industry proved a dangerous foe to poverty, and to the piety associated with it. The very reputation for piety often brought a shower of gifts to the community, and cloisters enriched with property inevitably suffered a relaxation of asceticism. An analogous problem of the relation of wealth and character appears in modern secular society.

Many of the revivals of monasticism were reactions against this oft-recurring relaxation. Men's consciences came alive with the realization that they and their comrades were violating their solemn vows, and under an earnest leader a small devout group started anew, in strict poverty and asceticism and in fresh commitment to the *Rule* of Benedict with such additional regulations as they imagined would secure continuance in monastic purity. Such is the story of Benedict of Aniane and his revival in the reigns of Charlemagne and Louis the Pious; and it is duplicated in the origins of the Cistercian movement.

The Cluniac revival, however, took its rise in an attempt to recover the lost ground of an age in which monasticism had been wrecked more by adversity than by prosperity.

This may account for the fact that it was not so intensely ascetic as the other movements just mentioned.

Cluny lies in a hill-encircled plain in the uplands between the Saône and the Loire. At the opening of the tenth century it was a feudal villa under the lordship of Duke William IX of Aquitaine, who prized it as an establishment for hunting. William grew old, had no heir, remembered his sins, and wished to obtain merit by bestowing a gift of property upon religious men. Eastward from Cluny, in the Jura highlands, was the monastery of Baume, whose abbot, Berno, earnestly attempted to govern it in accordance with the *Concordia Regularum* of Benedict of Aniane. Berno's faithful labors at Baume were reported to William, who took counsel with him about the foundation of a monastery on one of his own estates. Berno persuaded him to remove his hunting hounds from Cluny and make the place a home of monks. He gave to Berno, September 11, 910, a deed of the property. In this, "desiring to make provision while he may for his salvation" he bestows the villa upon the Apostles Peter and Paul, for the establishment of a monastery under the *Rule* of Benedict, with Berno as its first abbot. The pope is made defender of the rights of the monks; and a solemn execration is pronounced upon any prince, count, bishop or Roman pontiff who may violate the property.

Cluny was only one of six struggling monasteries that Berno controlled at the time of his death in 927, and the monastery was then still weak and small. It was his great successor Odo who gave Cluny its character and began its remarkable expansion.

Odo of Cluny

Odo was born in 879 in Maine, and was the son of a pious and surprisingly learned layman, Abbo. Though vowed by his father to St. Martin in babyhood, he was given a military training and became a page at the court of Duke William. But the exercises of war and hunting were unendurable to him, and he was permitted to fulfil his father's vow by becoming a canon of the church of St. Martin at Tours. In this office he was in the companionship of worldly ecclesiastics. He revolted from the careless life which for a time he had practiced with them, and studied Vergil, till, warned by a dream of serpents in a jar, he abandoned the poets for the Prophets and Apostles. With Bible study he now mingled an exaggerated asceticism, keeping himself in a narrow and unfurnished cell. He also read the Benedictine *Rule*, and proposed to become a monk. But the life of the monks at Tours, like that of the canons, was shocking to the earnest young ascetic. Odo now spent a period at Paris in the study of logic and music, and then returned to Tours to teach and write. But he soon set forth in quest of a suitable monastic home; and we find him, in 909, entering with a companion Berno's monastery at Baume. Here he distinguished himself by his humility, and in recognition of his learning was appointed master of the cloister school. He bore with invincible patience the hostility of unfaithful monks, and gained the complete confidence of Berno. At Berno's command he was ordained a priest. When Berno died, early in 927, the monks of Cluny unanimously chose the saintly teacher of Baume as their abbot; and the better element of the Baume community followed him to Cluny.

With ripened gifts Odo devoted himself to the upbuilding of the young institution. In his first year of office he secured from Rudolph, the ruler of Burgundy, a charter which reaffirmed the terms of Duke William's donation, and strongly emphasized Cluny's immunity from all secular and ecclesiastical interference. The monks were exempted from tolls in the markets, and numerous valuable manors were added to the monastic property.

Secure in the control of the monastery, Odo proceeded to erect suitable buildings, first completing a church which was left unfinished by Berno. We know less of the buildings constructed by Odo than of the difficulties faced in the task. The institution was still distressingly poor and an empty treasury threatened to put an end to the building enterprise. But John of Salerno, Odo's biographer, in the authentic style of medieval hagiographers, tells how St. Martin appeared, with kindly, bearded face, to Odo, promising that help would be provided. Confidence was restored; the hired workmen were retained; and funds were presently supplied by a generous gift.

Gifts and privileges, the world's subversive reward to piety, now came to Cluny in a swelling stream. Numerous charters granted by kings and popes multiplied the guarantees of the monastery's immunity from interference. Grants of property,—villas with their serfs, churches with their revenues,—and other sources of income, were made by wealthy laymen and women for the good of their souls. Bishops handed over church properties on an arrangement of easy annual payments of dues. From King Rudolph and the pope, the privilege of coining money was granted to the abbey. And in 931 Pope John XI presented to Cluny the extraordinary privilege of receiving from any disorderly monastery any monk who wished to amend his life, and harboring him until such time as his own monastery should be reformed. John XI was the son of the infamous Marozia; and there is a striking paradox in this coöperation of the Papacy, debased and dishonored as it then was, in the restoration of monastic discipline. There is a paradox, too, in the violation of the letter of Benedict's rule of *stabilitas loci*—that a monk should remain in his own monastery—as a means of restoring the Benedictine spirit.

It is not possible to describe in detail the internal life of Cluny in Odo's time, since the *Customs* of the monastery which have been preserved belong to a later period. Probably Odo was chiefly indebted to the regulations of Benedict of Aniane. Some of the latter's principles are exhibited in his own writings, and in the *lives* of Odo and his early successors. He seems to have admitted Paul the Deacon's interpretation of the rule of labor,—that it might be fulfilled by some other employment than manual work. It is now held by good authorities that the monks of the first St. Benedict's own cloister had the more menial work done for them by servants. Odo had a leaning toward study, and he laid the foundations of the later considerable literary development of Cluny.

Odo's writings include a work called *Conferences* (*Collationes*, a title employed by John Cassian who expounded the principles of Egyptian monasticism for Western readers about 430), which contains, amid much complaint of the wickedness of the selfish rich and of the worldly clergy, vigorous denunciation of the possession of private property by monks. At Cluny he enforced private poverty to the letter. He also excluded the eating of meat; a flesh diet was thought to induce fleshly sin. Yet his *Life of Gerald of Aurillac* is a panegyric upon a saintly man who ate flesh and drank wine in moderation, and of whom no miracles were recorded, but who was rich in good deeds, modest in apparel, and chaste in mind and behavior. It may be noted that while Odo believed in miracles, and many were alleged of him, he objected to making them the test of sainthood.

John of Salerno notes the practice of certain hours of silence; but this was modified by the use of a language of signs, by which "grammarians of the fingers and eyes" might become articulate. When St. Benedict in his *Rule* admitted the use of signs, he probably did not foresee the expertness that would be attained in this art where extended silences were enforced. "If the monks were deprived of the use of the tongue," John thinks, "those signs would suffice for all that they need to convey." (Detailed codes of the sign language are contained in the sources of later monasticism; apparently some nunneries excelled in its use.) Great care was taken for the dignity of the services, and in accordance with the practice of Benedict of Aniane, the psalmody was extended beyond that of early Benedictinism.

Cluny was mounting to greatness. Pope John's suggestion that degenerate monasteries were to be reformed, was to be carried out in hundreds of instances through the influence of the Cluniacs. Odo saw the beginning of this widespread restoration, and he was the traveling organizer of the movement.

Romainmoutier near Lausanne, Aurillac in southern Auvergne, and Fleury near Orléans on the Loire, were the first houses to enjoy, or suffer, transformation at his hands. He then went farther afield, to Sarlot, Tulle, Sens and Tours. His visitations were made at the request of some earnest ruler or bishop, and sometimes with the goodwill of a reforming minority of the monks. Each revived monastery helped to spread the revival to others, and the circle of Odo's influence continued to widen. His work was sometimes violently resisted, however. At Fleury the monks took pride in their early history and in their possession of the relics of St. Benedict of Nursia; they also took offense at the supplies of fish which Odo brought to replace their stock of meat. They met him with weapons; he withdrew only to return meekly riding on an ass. Then they repented and received him with tears. Fleury became a powerful ally of Cluny in the advance of reform.

Odo carried the movement into Italy, where many abbeys had suffered from raiding Saracens and predatory nobles. Alberic, then in control in Rome, and Pope Leo VII, invited him. Alberic in so doing may have been chiefly concerned to take from the hands of his political opponents the monastic properties they had seized. In the winter of 936, Odo, in peril and great hardship, first crossed the terrifying Alps. He was accompanied by John of Salerno whose description of the journey shows high admiration for the humility and charity of his master. The fame of Odo had preceded him, and he was greeted by throngs of common people and beggars. He became intimate with the folk, and liked to get children to sing in payment for the alms he distributed. Once, to relieve poverty, he bought laurel berries at an excessive price; and when asked by his companions what he intended to do with the berries he uttered a torrent of amusing explanations, making them laugh till they could not restrain their tears.

A mood of hilarity sometimes seized this earnest saint; but it was not his prevailing mood. He habitually walked with back bent and eyes fixed on the ground, a posture so suggestive of a laborer with a spade that he was nick-named "the Digger." The bent shoulders carried heavy responsibilities.

Odo found Rome in a state of turmoil, and measures of pacification had to precede reform. Before he died he had made four protracted visits to Italy, and had achieved important successes. In Rome three monasteries were restored, and one, St. Mary's on the Aventine, was founded by Odo. The historic house of St. Benedict at Monte Cassino, which had been wrecked and deserted, was planted anew. The reform was extended to a number of houses in southern Italy.

Enfeebled by malaria and fatigue, and knowing that his work was ended, Odo set out from Rome to use all his remaining strength in a journey to the shrine of his patron, St. Martin of Tours; and there, November 18, 942, he died an edifying death.

It remained for Odo's great successors, Odilo (994-1048) and Hugh (1048-1109), to consolidate and extend the empire of Cluny. Odilo wrought the enlarging connection into a completely integrated order, monarchically controlled by the abbot of Cluny. Hugh built the vast and impressive abbey church, that celebrated monument of Romanesque architecture. The order grew till it included nearly a thousand houses; and as many others felt the stimulus of its example.

Whatever we may think of the desirability or undesirability in the abstract of monasticism, or of monarchy, we can feel only gratitude to the men who, on the impulse of religion, bore into the feudal chaos of the tenth century a conquering principle of organization and discipline, and thus made possible the direction of Western Europe into a course of cultural and social progress.

Bernard of Clairvaux

The monastic spirit reached its peak in the illustrious Bernard of Clairvaux, a nobleman by birth, a monk by choice, an ecclesiastical leader by obligation, and one of the most influential personalities of history. He was born in 1090 at Fontaines-les-Dijon, a feudal castle on a hill with a few cottages on the slopes below, two kilometers northwest of the town of Dijon, and died at Clairvaux, August 20, 1153. His father, Tescelin the Fair-haired, master of the château, was of high Burgundian nobility, and his mother, Aleth, traced her line back to the ancient dukes of Burgundy. If he had concerned himself in the matter, Bernard could have qualified as a true Nordic, and might have taken pride in his warrior ancestry.

Monastic piety had appealed to his maternal grandfather, and Aleth was educated for the cloister. This intention was interrupted by her marriage; but she imparted some Latin and much piety to her six sons and one daughter, and denied them sweets and pleasures. In Bernard her hopes chiefly rested. When he went to Chatillon for his schooling she went to reside there with him. But there were periods in the castle; and Aleth kept her family in touch with clerical life by giving to a company of priests an annual dinner. On the occasion of one of these entertainments, when Bernard was about sixteen, she fell fatally ill, and, with the priests about her intoning a litany, "yielded up her spirit in peace." Bernard was ardently devoted to his mother, and we know not how far his affection and grief for her may have determined his religious career. For years afterwards he said daily, in silence, for her soul, the seven penitential psalms. Visions of her kept alive his devotion. He had grown to manhood and become accustomed to the occupation of arms, when one day, while riding to aid his brothers in a siege, his mother's face, with a look of reproach and disappointment, came before his eyes. He then resolved to devote himself to religion.

The monastery was the jealous rival of the home, but its leadership was usually drawn not from among those nurtured from childhood in the cloister, but from homes of rare religious culture. Monasticism was also the chastener of feudalism; but its great inspirers and organizers were drawn from the feudal nobility.

By the end of the eleventh century the prosperous Cluniac order had ceased to attract the most devout. Cluny was wealthy, and its ritual and culture partook of a spirit which is the accompaniment of opulence. Those ambitious of ascetic hardship would find its novitiate too easy, its diet too liberal, and its life too soft. The abbot Hugh attempted, with limited success, to check the trend toward relaxation; but after him came Pontius (1109-1122), who stained the fair record of Cluny with many misdeeds.

Numerous fresh efforts in monasticism were made in the eleventh century. In Italy arose the Camaldulians and the Vallambrosians; in France the Grammontines, the order of Fontevrault, and the Carthusians. Valiantly ascetic were all these; but none of them attained the dimensions of a general movement.

A new revival was, however, now in its inception. Robert, a monk of noble birth, departed from a decadent Benedictine house to found the abbey of Molesme. But unruly recruits broke the discipline, and with six faithful adherents he went in 1098—while the banners of the First Crusade were advancing in the East—to the wooded wilderness of Cîteaux, a few miles southwest of Bernard's birthplace, and about thirty miles north of Cluny. Robert was commanded by the pope to return to Molesme; but the group remained with Alberic as their abbot. Under the latter's successor, Stephen Harding (abbot 1109-1133) of Sherborne, England, a Bible scholar and a man of exceptional organizing talent, Cîteaux became the rallying-point of the higher devotion.

Bernard was twenty-two when impelled by a vision of his dead mother he abandoned worldly pursuits, and made his life-commitment to the monastic way. Two patterns of monasticism were represented by Pontius at Cluny and Stephen at Cîteaux; his choice was obvious. One day in the spring of 1112 Stephen received into the lodge in the wilderness which was the cradle of Cistercianism, the handsome youth, with his graceful form and gracious manner, his blond hair and auburn beard. It is a revelation of Bernard's powers of leadership that he brought with him a band of thirty, including four of his five brothers, whom he had persuaded to seek salvation with him. The sixth brother was soon to follow, and years afterward the father whom they had, affectionately, deserted.

The heroic spirit of Bernard embraced with joy the austerities of Cistercianism. He exceeded the requirements of the rule in abstinence and silence, and labored in the fields beyond his strength. Recruits were pouring in to Cîteaux, and he was active in their training. Growing numbers made expansion necessary. The abbey of La Ferté was Cîteaux's first daughter (1113), Pontigny (1114) its second. Bernard soon became a proficient monk. In 1115 Stephen sent him, with twelve chosen men, to a spot in the Bar-sur-Aube, ninety miles northward, a haunt of beasts and robbers, formerly known as the Valley of Wormwood but now called the Fair Valley (Clara Vallis), to lay the foundation of the monastery which shares the fame of its founder, Clairvaux.

It was characteristic of the Cistercians to select for their cloisters situations remote, solitary and forbidding. At Clairvaux prodigious labors had to be expended in clearing away thorns, brambles, trees, and brushwood, to make the place habitable and reclaim a small area for tillage. The extreme and unavoidable poverty of the pioneer years in the wilderness encouraged Bernard's asceticism and prompted an abstinence almost suicidal. He was saved by William, Bishop of Champeaux, who obtained authority to compel Bernard for one year to accept rest and food and the advice of a certain boorish but helpful physician.

On a diet of barley bread and beech-leaf salad, the gaunt monks made war on the wilderness. A distinguished visitor found the hush of the wooded valley broken only by "the sound of labor and the praises of God." They were primarily motivated by devotion; but the rule stressed industry, and the forest challenged them to labor. As a community they had to win a subsistence from the soil. In humility, obedience, and a fine spirit of coöperation, they wielded ax and spade, mattock and rake and sickle. Soon gardens and barley fields stretched about their rude buildings; and prosperity came upon them as an armed man.

Bernard, and the fame of the community's piety, attracted hundreds of postulants, and Clairvaux became the most active recruiting center of Cistercianism. When he died in 1153 the daughter houses of Clairvaux numbered sixty-eight, spread far and near; and some of these had begun to send out colonies of their own. The entire order by that date had a total of almost five hundred wholly or partially organized monasteries.

These numerals indicate that we should be mistaken in ascribing the order's growth solely to Bernard. Though contemporaries acknowledged him its brightest light, he shares with Stephen Harding the credit for the achievement. This is the more evident when we realize that Stephen was the author of the *Charter of Charity*, the chief constitutional document of the Cistercians, framed, in anticipation of growth, when there were but nine convents (1119). Antedating as it did de Montfort's Parliament by a century and a half, and the Swiss Republic by a quarter century more, and anticipating a legion of modern systems of representative government, the Cistercian constitution entitles its author to perpetual renown. Just as Cîteaux confronted Cluny with a conscious superiority in asceticism, so also the Cistercians reversed the monarchical principle of Cluniac government, adopting a decentralized though no less coördinated system in which authority was vested in a representative assembly and the abbot of the Mother House had no special prerogatives. On Stephen's part this provision was perhaps an act of typically Cistercian renunciation.

While Cluny attached to itself far more existing monasteries than it founded new ones, the growth of the Cistercians consisted almost entirely in new foundations. Hundreds of desert places were made by them to blossom as the rose. Europe's extent of arable land was vastly increased by the labor born of their devotion. They were the pioneers of scientific agriculture. They drained swamps, diverted water-courses, and studied the breeding of cattle, horses, sheep and poultry. In England they developed the wool trade which was the foundation of the nation's commerce. The cattle upon a thousand hills were theirs. Gothic abbeys replaced their lowly churches of hewn lumber. Historians of economics applaud their amazing contribution to the growth of material civilization. Inevitably they became so occupied with these activities that the religious impulse behind it all receded into a secondary place; and within a century of Bernard's conversion Francis and Dominic were needed to revive the ascetic life. Bernard lived to witness much of the numerical growth of the Cistercians, but not the spiritual decline which was the strange nemesis of their ascetic industry.

Bernard gave himself to monasticism with pure abandon, To him its austerities were joys. Fasting was more pleasant than feasting; and he fasted to emaciation. Sleep he regarded as sheer waste of time that might more profitably be given to prayer and tears. His fullest happiness was found in contemplation and mystic raptures. His sorrows arose from reflecting on his sins, of which he had a most exaggerated consciousness, from the injustice and irreligion of the world, and from the defection of unstable monks. Generally his monks adored him, and he cherished them with ardent attachment. The desertion of a few of them cost him agonies.

"Extra ecclesiam nulla salus" ("no salvation outside the church") was a hoary conception in his time. Bernard came very near to substituting "monasterium" for "ecclesiam" and holding that there is no salvation outside the cloister. It might be a Cistercian or a Carthusian cloister, or a house of Canons Regular; but Cluny was not approved.

This attitude appears in letters of entreaty and stern warning written to those who had fled from the heroic Cistercian discipline, or who hesitated to break all ties with the secular world. The flight of his kinsman Robert from Clairvaux to Cluny left him bewailing the loss of one "for whom to die would be to live," yet able to address to him stinging reproaches and offer him the hard alternative of return or damnation. The case of Adam, lured from Cîteaux to Cluny, was similar. In an impassioned epistle Bernard begs him to return, since it is "at the awful peril of his soul" that he withholds himself from his Cistercian brethren. "They who return," he concludes, "shall live; they who refuse shall die." Fulk, a canon whose uncle had induced him to return to the world, was sharply rebuked and called back to duty. "What are you doing in the town, O delicate soldier? . . . Take arms, take strength anew, while yet the battle lasts. . . . Angels attend and defend you." These admonitory letters abound with the vocabulary of war, the profession of the saint's ancestors. The monks constitute a soldiery of Christ, and good Cistercians are the shock troops of the sacred army.

The counter-claims of the home receive no consideration. When the solicitous parents of a young monk sought his return to their fireside, Bernard relentlessly denied the plea, and repulsed them as savage enemies of their son's soul. Bernard's only sister, Humbelina, who was "married in the world and devoted to the world," once came "as a snare of the devil" in fine array to visit him; but he refused to see her, till it was reported to him that she was dissolved in tears and willing to do what he might ask. A course of fasts and vigils, such as their mother had followed, was imposed, and after two years of this, obedient to Bernard's importunity and receiving from her husband "her hoped-for liberty," she left her family and entered a nunnery.

This relentless severity is matched in Bernard by a fervid realization of divine love. If his asceticism sometimes appears a sublimation of militarism, his mysticism is a sublimation of sex. Bernard has left eighty-six sermons on the Song of Solomon; and these bring him only to the beginning of the third chapter. Elsewhere he frequently employs the passionate imagery of this book. But the sublimation is complete. No trace of grossness survives the furnace of his spiritual passion. Other mystical writings such as *The Steps of Humility and Pride* and the *Treatise on Loving God* exhibit the progressive stages of the mystical experience. The former of these is based on a section of the *Rule* of Benedict. In the latter he proclaims that God is to be loved "without measure," and differentiates four stages of love's ascent, from self-love to that oneness of spirit with God in which a man cannot love himself except for God's sake. These works were combed by a hundred later exponents of mysticism, and form one of the prime sources of medieval and modern piety. Many of Bernard's letters, too, flash with gems of mystical thought. He knew intimately not only the one short book of the Bible on which he chiefly wrote, but all its books; and he habitually employs in exalted allegory a fund of Scripture quotations.

Bernard had to pay in terms of responsibility, the price of his fame. He was in great demand wherever the cause of religion was at stake. He declined numerous bishoprics and archbishoprics in both France and Italy. He contended with proud princes and menacing nobles. He arbitrated grave quarrels, political and ecclesiastical. He counseled the founders of the Premonstratensians, the Gilbertines, and the Templars. The reformer of Irish monasticism, Malachy of Armagh, died in his arms. His aid placed Innocent II on the papal throne; and he gave paternal advice and criticism to Pope Eugenius III, his own monastic disciple. He hounded heretics like Henry of Lausanne and Arnold of Brescia, and set on their persecutors. Loathing the critical methods of Abailard, who, he charged, "reasoned of the things above reason," he compassed the ruin of that scholar's intellectual sway. He preached to spellbound throngs that covered acres. He courageously defended persecuted Jews. Though a friend of peace he recruited a crusading army, by his eloquence "emptying cities and castles" of their manhood, and persuaded the greatest princes of the West to lead the confident host on what proved a campaign of disastrous failure. To the authentic record of these activities his contemporaries add hundreds of astounding miracles.

No one who reviews the career of Bernard can fail to be impressed with the seemingly invincible power of his personality. Yet he played the superman unwillingly, almost unconsciously. Writing to his friend Guigues, Prior of the Grand Chartreuse, he impatiently complains of the uncongenial tasks that are continuously thrust upon him: "I am a man born to labor—an unfledged birdling almost constantly hopping out of its nest, exposed to wind and tempest." Bernard was first and last a monk. All extraneous duties were relatively unimportant to him; and like a homing pigeon he promptly sought Clairvaux after every enforced absence. Such in brief was the career of the religious genius, who, in the language of Gibbon, "by a vow of poverty and penance, by closing his eyes to the visible world, by the refusal of ecclesiastical dignities, became the oracle of Europe."

Norbert of Xanten

Between the monastic orders and the secular clergy of the Middle Ages stood the Canons Regular (canonici regulares), or cloistered clerics. The attempt to secure an ascetic community life for the clergy began in the fourth century, and was promoted by St. Augustine. St. Chrodegang of Metz in the eighth century revived the plan, and the *Rule* of Chrodegang was approved by nearly a dozen church councils after his time. The residence of rural priests in cloistered retreats was difficult to secure; but a considerable number of the town clergy came into some form of community life. Often the discipline of their organization was lax; and reformers sought to improve it. Ivo of Chartres, following up in the late eleventh century Pope Hildebrand's campaign for clerical celibacy, organized the Canons Regular of St. Augustine, under a rule which had as its basis a letter and two sermons of that saint. This reform had some success; but as the houses of Augustinian Canons became widespread they increasingly resembled monasteries and were little associated with clerical reform.

Where the canonical rule was imposed upon unwilling clerics it was difficult to maintain. The new canon movement of which Norbert of Xanten was the founder began not so much at the instance of episcopal reformers as out of the ascetic enthusiasm of the twelfth century. It, too, was ultimately largely assimilated to monasticism; but it also helped to bring nearer to realization the medieval ideal of clerical piety and efficiency.

Xanten, where Norbert was born about 1080, is situated on the left bank of the Rhine, below Wesel. Its name means "saints," and was bestowed because it was the alleged place of suffering of the martyrs of the fabled Theban legion under Diocletian. But when young Norbert became one of them, the canons of the collegiate church of St. Victor in Xanten showed little of the devotion of martyrs.

He was the son of parents of noble rank, Heribert and Hadwige, and was related to the Franconian kings of Germany. He was sent to some excellent school, we know not where, and acquired a good Latin education. Presented with a church living, he became a canon at Xanten, and was distinguished from his fellows by his unlimited worldly ambition. He soon departed to Cologne to seek a larger sphere for his talents. He continued to climb, by the favor of influential churchmen, until, while still a sub-deacon, and refusing to enter the priesthood, he became almoner to King Henry V (1106-1125). He was handsome, cheerful, liberal, and clever, but of loose morals, and indifferent to religion.

When Henry went with an army to Italy in 1111, Norbert accompanied his master. The Emperor placed Pope Paschal II under restraint and induced him to sign away claims made by his predecessors, involving the right to appoint bishops. Norbert witnessed the humiliation of the Pope, and protested to Paschal his innocence of complicity in Henry's acts. Possibly a revolt of feeling caused by this incident may have been the reason for his refusal of Henry's offer of the bishopric of Cambrai. But he remained in Henry's employ till 1115, at which time Henry was under excommunication and his cause was in decline.

The records of Norbert's conversion indicate that it came

about instantly as a result of his experience of a lightning storm. But it is not unlikely that the failure of his hopes of a career had led him to reëxamine his plan of life, and that the storm experience only brought his inward struggles to a sudden solution.

His friend and biographer, Hugh, who wrote the story, evidently had in mind the narrative of Paul's journey to Damascus. Norbert was riding, with costly attire and trappings, though with but one attendant, from Cologne toward Vreden, when suddenly a tempest broke about them. The terrified servant urged him to halt, but hoping to reach a nearby village he kept on until amid the crashing thunder a voice was heard: "Norbert, Norbert, why persecutest thou Me?", and at that moment a lightning bolt struck in front of his horse making an indentation in the earth "deeper than the stature of a man," and the place was filled with sulphurous fumes, "as if from hell!" Horse and rider fell to the ground. Norbert lay stunned for an hour; then arose in a trance-like state, saying: "Lord, what wilt thou have me to do?" He remounted, and, changing his course, proceeded to Xanten, reflecting on the mercy of God.

Norbert now, for three years, gave himself to prayer, contemplation, labor and harsh penances. He induced Archbishop Frederick of Cologne to ordain him to the priesthood. At the ordination ceremony he astonished the assembly by appearing in the garb of poverty, and then, "inflamed with divine fervor," preached repentance and preparation for the life to come.

Some censorious allusions to the habits of his fellow clerics, and his suggestion that they should follow the canonical rule of Chrodegang, were bitterly resented. They set on the basest of their number to insult him, and the ruffian spat in Norbert's face. Soon afterward Norbert withdrew, or was dismissed, from the company of the collegiate clergy, and taking as his spiritual guide the saintly abbot, Conon of Siegburg, practiced the religion of penitence at that abbey, and in an Augustinian house. He thus became familiar with both Benedictine and Augustinian piety. He learned also the joys of religious solitude from a hermit named Lindolph, and built for himself a rude hut at Furstenburg in which he lived for two years.

But Norbert's retirement was a preparation for an active apostolate, and he seems to have begun to preach at this time. His return to ecclesiastical activity was attended by renewed opposition. At the Synod of Fritzlar, 1118, he was accused of preaching without a license, and (since he wore a penitent's robe of sackcloth) without the proper vestments. He claimed that the right to preach was conveyed with the priestly office, and reminded his accusers of the simplicity of the garments of John the Baptist and of Adam.

The urge to preach now sent Norbert out on a mission to the common people. His manner of life at this time identifies him with the class of preaching itinerants (Wanderprediger) of whom Robert of Abrissel, Bernard of Thiron and the heretic Henry of Lausanne, are notable representatives. It may have been because the methods of these popular preachers were well known in many parts of France that he now turned his steps into that country.

Norbert devoted to alms all his remaining property and started out, without beast or money, and barefoot. With two companions he journeyed far southward to the Abbey of St. Giles in the neighborhood of Nîmes, to meet Pope Gelasius II who had come to France to seek aid against his foes. On hearing his general confession Gelasius, perhaps not loth to encourage a convert from the imperial camp, gave him authority to preach wherever he wished. Norbert went about proclaiming both in churches and out of doors, a gospel of repentance and charity, sometimes, like St. Patrick and other early medieval missionaries, using a cattle-bell to summon the folk. His ability to use the French language was regarded as miraculous.

What roads of France he traveled we do not know, but soon after the incident at Nîmes he was in the north again at Valenciennes, where he met an old associate, Burkhardt, who had become Bishop of Cambrai. Burkhardt had known Norbert as a sleek and fastidious clerk, and when he appeared one frosty day with shabby garments and bare feet, the bishop embraced him, exclaiming: "O Norbert, whoever would believe or imagine this of you?", and speaking to his companions, recalled the fact that he himself occupied the see which Norbert had declined. One of them was so edified by Norbert's devotion that he later became his intimate disciple, his successor, and his biographer.

Norbert's papal patron died the following January (1119) and the French prelate who succeeded him as Calixtus II held in October a great council at Reims. Norbert came to it to ask a renewal of the permission to preach. But Bartholomew, Bishop of Laon, induced the pope to command Norbert to aid him in reforming the canons of the Abbey of St. Martin, Laon. Hesitant but obedient, Norbert undertook the task.

His experience here was less bitter but not more successful than his reform effort at Xanten. But he would make another approach to the same problem of clerical reform. In conference with the bishop he now planned to found a new community for which Bartholomew was to supply the site. In search of a location the two one day came upon a glade in the forest of Coucy, with a ruined chapel in its midst. Instantly Norbert chose this spot, and believing it to have been divinely indicated, called it *Præmonstratus*, "the place foreshown" (Prémontré). Hence the order which had its inception here, was called the Premonstratensian. He remained alone in the chapel that night, and dreamt of processions of the white-robed canons he was soon to organize.

Bartholomew and Burkhardt coöperated with him in the new enterprise. Norbert traveled and preached, gaining select recruits. From the service of Burkhardt he drew the capable Hugh, whom he had so fascinated at Valenciennes. After much consideration of the plan of the community, Norbert saw a vision of St. Augustine, proffering his *Rule*, and at Christmas 1121 the Augustinian *Rule* was adopted, with additional statutes. Bernard of Clairvaux lent the aid of his advice, and some elements in the Premonstratensian constitution and customs were imitated from those of the Cistercians. But Norbert was anxious to keep a door open to activity in the work of the church. He had failed to reform existing bodies of clergy; he now hoped by beginning anew in the wilderness to bring into existence a body of faithful clergy who would replace the incorrigibles and transform clerical life. In contrast to the monastic ideal of contemplation the Premonstratensian statutes stress the *zelus animarum*, the urge to save souls, which is to be expressed through teaching, preaching and the parish ministry.

The Premonstratensians soon entered on a process of rapid expansion. They became an order, with the sanction of Calixtus II, in 1124. A Second Order of Norbertine sisters was founded under the leadership of Ricovera, the widow of a nobleman of Clastres, and a Third Order of lay brothers under Count Theobald of Champagne. Soon many busy Premonstratensian communities began to appear in Belgium, France and Germany. A little later Palestine, Portugal, Spain, Italy and England in turn received them. In 1230 they possessed 663 abbeys. By the fourteenth century they probably surpassed all other religious orders in the number of their cloisters and members. In no small degree they fulfilled Norbert's plan. They strengthened the ranks of the clergy and furnished some of the ablest bishops. But as in other cases prosperity and popularity at length slackened the nerve of devotion and they lapsed into a state of decay. Norbert himself soon yielded to Hugh the leadership of Prémontré. It is indicative of his attitude to ecclesiastical office that in 1126 he consented, under pressure, to become Archbishop of Magdeburg, a see far across Germany, on the Elbe. Bernard repeatedly declined such opportunities; but Norbert saw a duty in the difficult task.

He came to the archiepiscopal palace bare-footed and travel-stained, and in the throng that awaited him was mistaken by a porter for a beggar, and told to move on. On learning his mistake the porter fled, but the ragged Archbishop pursued, overtook and reassured the trembling servitor.

As Archbishop, Norbert proved a militant reformer. He never obtained Bernard's easy mastery of the wills of other men, and had to fight his way inch by inch. He brought the incomes of the see, some of which had been appropriated by lay lords, into an orderly state, and systematically disbursed them with special care for the poor. Having for a time coöperated with the Emperor in the effort to convert the savage Wends by force, he adopted the more commendable method of sending among them Premonstratensian missionaries. His most difficult problem was that presented by the lax and untrained clergy; and this cost him an exciting struggle. Three times his life was attempted, once by a dispossessed archdeacon. Riotous citizens menaced him in his cathedral; one struck and wounded his chamberlain, supposing him to be Norbert. When at last, with his miter on his head, he confronted the rabble, they drew back, and he went to the altar and said mass in an unfaltering voice. For the sake of peace he fled to Halle, but they urged him to return; and thereafter he gained security and control. His policy was greatly aided by the members of his order whom he brought in to replace disaffected and incapable priests. Numerous houses of the order were established in the province.

But Norbert's energy was employed in yet larger concerns. He lent his support to Innocent II against the antipope Anacletus, and persuaded the Emperor Lothar to adopt the cause of Innocent. In company with Bernard, the Pope and the Emperor, he went to Rome. With the aid of the Emperor's show of force they gained their object, and Innocent, placed on the papal throne, gratefully made Norbert Primate of Germany.

He returned in broken health, with Lothar, whom he continued to advise till his death approached. He ended his strenuous career at Magdeburg, June 6, 1134. It was a strange fulfilment of his early ambition that at the end of the years of renunciation, when we may suppose he cared nothing for such distinctions, the Pope should have made him Primate and the Emperor should have appointed him Chancellor of the Empire. Norbert's achievement was that of imparting a monastic seriousness to the feudal clergy. A Norbertine writer has said with some justification that in this matter he succeeded where Gregory VII failed.

CHAPTER III

PAPAL RULERS OF THE WEST

History offers many instances of the enduring and pathetic fascination for masses of men, of certain places that have gathered to themselves associations of holiness or power. The East has Jerusalem, Benares, Mecca. In the West Rome has had no rival to contest with her the reverence of humanity. Memories of her imperial rulers, and of her apostolic martyrs, sustained through centuries of degradation an attitude of deference to the city which seemed the mother of civilization.

But without the contribution of purposeful leaders this prevalent sentiment would never have brought about Rome's second mastery of the world, the sway of the medieval popes. Among the saints and sinners whom piety or intrigue brought to the chair of Peter, only a gifted and zealous few perceptibly advanced the banners of the papal empire. From Nicholas I (858-867) to Martin V (1417-1431) there were one hundred legitimate popes. Many of them were unqualified for any task of distinction. Some were admirable and capable prelates, who through adverse circumstances or short tenure of office accomplished little of note. Perhaps a score have written their names indelibly on the history of the age; and three or four are among the world's immortals.

A graph of the Papacy from Nicholas I to Hildebrand would look like a W. Shortly after the middle of the tenth century, with the aid of the Emperor Otto the Great and his successors, the Apostolic See rose from its long depression of feebleness and shame. Pope Gregory V, a grandson of Otto, showed character and energy, but died young, in 999. His friend and successor Gerbert of Aurillac—as Pope, Sylvester II (999-1003)—was a remarkable scholar and an able administrator who, despite suspicion and misunderstanding, brought the Papacy to a level not attained since the days of Nicholas. From this peak the line bends downward for nearly half a century to the licentious and inhuman Benedict IX. So perverse were the times that even a reformer had to resort to simony. John Gratian, the son of a converted Jew, and a respectable teacher in the Lateran school, purchased the holy office for a thousand silver pounds in order to redeem it from disgrace, and called himself Gregory VI (1045). From this transaction we may roughly date the beginning of a recovery which continued through the age of Hildebrand.

A claimant called Sylvester III had already been in conflict with Benedict, and he remained in the field. Benedict reversed his decision to retire, and sought to revive his claim. Thus the well-intentioned Gregory VI found himself but one of three contestants, with his own claim damaged by a simoniacal bargain.

The Empire now had an able ruler, Henry III (1039-1056), who took Charlemagne as his model. Henry wished to see the Papacy united and effective, but not independent,—strong enough to assist him but not strong enough to embarrass him. At the invitation, it is thought, of a Roman ecclesiastic, Henry intervened to end the papal schism. At his bidding all three of the claimants were set aside, and Suidger of Bamberg was elevated to the Holy See as Clement II.

Except for a brief return to power of the irrepressible Benedict IX, the next six popes were German nominees of Henry. The Roman climate shortened their lives and reigns. The most distinguished among them is the Alsatian, Leo IX (1049-1054), under whom Hildebrand becomes an influential figure in the church.

Hildebrand, Pope Gregory VII

Hildebrand's family tree has not been traced beyond his father and mother, Bonizo and Bertha, humble folk of Rome, apparently of Lombard stock. Variant legends made Bonizo a goatherd or a carpenter. It was during his parents' temporary residence at Rovaco, a village near Soana in southern Tuscany, that the child of destiny was born about 1025. His precocious intellect and forceful personality attracted attention in his childhood. With the medieval attribution of brilliant gifts to diabolical inspiration, his name was turned by some into the equivalent of "Hell-brand"; and some told of infernal flames issuing from his clothing.

Peter, Abbot of St. Mary's on the Aventine, Odo's Roman monastery, may have been Bertha's brother. There at any rate Hildebrand went to school; it is not probable that he took a monk's vows, at least until he reached mature years. He also studied in the Schola Cantorum in the Lateran palace, where he came in contact with John Gratian, Gregory VI. Gratian may have felt a special responsibility for the lad, from the fact that his brother was the husband of Bertha's sister. This pope's first efforts to secure peace and power amid the hopeless confusion of Italy were attended by an action on Hildebrand's part which showed his mettle. He organized an army, scattered the Pope's foes, and awed the anarchic feudal nobility.

After the deposition, or abdication, of the three would-be popes, December 1046, Gregory VI was taken by Henry to Cologne, then the seat of the imperial court, and was accompanied by his loyal young supporter. The northern climate ended Gratian's life early in 1048. Hildebrand was, we may be sure, a diplomatic but unsympathetic observer at close range of the policies of the Emperor. He had leisure too, in this period, to store his mind with the provisions of canon law, on which he later relied in his conflict against the imperial claims.

It was long confidently believed that Hildebrand, after Gregory's death, went into retirement in Cluny, and there imbibed the principles that made him great. It is certain that he left Cologne, but not that he went to Cluny. He may have gone to Liége; he is known to have been at Worms. His later correspondence with Hugh of Cluny does not indicate that he resided there at this period. Nor do we need to seek in Cluny those ideas which inspired him. Indeed, it is probable that we should connect them instead with Wazo (Wason), Bishop of Liége 1041-1048, a reforming prelate who derived his inspiration from another monastic movement, the revival led by Gerard, abbot of Brogne, a century before these events. This movement had furnished a pattern to the English reformer, Dunstan, and had exercised a large influence on the clergy in Flanders. Wazo in 1047 boldly rebuked Henry III for appointing a new pope and demanded the restoration of the captive Gregory VI, who had been, he said, "illegally deposed by incompetent judges." He then induced a cleric to write a book *On the Pontifical Elections* which denied the jurisdiction of temporal rulers in the election of bishops and especially of popes. This is the animating principle of Hildebrand's later struggle against Henry IV. Hildebrand must have been familiar with Wazo's ideas, and must have noted with satisfaction that they found considerable acceptance among the northern clergy.

When Bruno of Toul became Leo IX, February 1049, it was at the advice of Hildebrand, who accompanied him to Rome, that, though nominated by the Emperor, he obtained a Roman election and was consecrated without the Emperor's participation. Hildebrand now became Cardinal Sub-deacon, and stood among Leo's chief counselors and assistants. Leo's vigorous policy called forth resistance in Constantinople. The Eastern church under Michael Cerularius refused obedience to Leo; and by solemn mutual excommunications Eastern and Western Christianity were formally severed, July 1054. In the West Leo made his influence felt. His commands affected the policies of such kings as Edward the Confessor of England and Andrew of Hungary; while Macbeth of Scotland, immortalized and defamed by Shakespeare, paid him a pious visit. He went to war against the Normans in Italy, was defeated, recognized their conquests and received their fealty.

Leo demanded celibacy of the clergy and held a number of synods in various parts of Europe for the purpose of effecting this difficult reform. But the prevalence of the marriage of priests and their refusal to put away their wives largely rendered these efforts futile. Not only honest marriage but flagrant vice appeared in the clerical order. That fervent ascetic Peter Damian in his *Book of Gomorrah* (1051) and Cardinal Humbert in his treatise *Against the*

Simoniacs (1057) exposed to their contemporaries and left on record for posterity a state of clerical morals that, with all allowance for exaggeration, is revolting in the extreme. When Leo died in April 1054, the "Hildebrandine reform" was only begun.

The last of the succession of German popes, Victor II (1055-1057), was selected by Hildebrand, the Emperor merely requiring that the appointee should be a German. During his short pontificate Henry III died. Thereafter followed a series of Italian popes. Nicholas II (1058-1061) is remembered for the institution in his time (1059) of the College of Cardinals, a committee formed of the cardinal clergy of Rome to choose a successor in a vacancy of the Papal See. The system of elections thus inaugurated has substantially been retained, and has largely fulfilled its original purpose, which was to make the Papacy self-perpetuating and independent of emperors and princes. The cardinals are appointed by the pope and the pope is elected by the cardinals. Hildebrand has been credited with the plan; but its chief author seems to have been Cardinal Humbert. Humbert was a scholar from either Lorraine or Burgundy, who had served Leo IX with distinction, attacked simony, and advocated drastic reforms. On his death (1061) Hildebrand was the one authoritative adviser of the Papacy.

Aided by a Norman army, Hildebrand set Alexander II on the papal throne in 1061, and thereafter fashioned the policies of the Holy See. Alexander's pontificate was disturbed by the hostility of Italian nobles who, with German aid, put forward an antipope. Seeking improved relations with the unreliable Normans of Italy, Hildebrand favored William of Normandy in his conquest of England, and papal legates attended his coronation at Winchester (1070). Henry IV had, in 1068, at the age of eighteen, come to personal rule in Germany, and his emerging policy boded ill to the papal cause. Such was the situation at Alexander's death in 1073.

Hildebrand was now Cardinal Archdeacon. He was a man of about fifty, of dwarfish stature, grown somewhat stout, with grizzled beard; and his flashing eyes and impatient manner revealed the fierce zeal that led his friend Damian to call him "Holy Satan." On April 22, 1073, as Alexander's body was borne to sepulture, the populace, at the instance of a German cardinal who afterwards deserted and attacked the Pope, called aloud "Hildebrand bishop!", and (while the College of Cardinals hastily met to regularize the election) carried the breathless archdeacon, willy-nilly, to St. Peter's and placed him on the throne. On June 29 he was consecrated as Gregory VII.

He immediately began to put new vigor into the papal policy. His war for reform was fought on two fronts, against clerical marriage and lay investiture. He aimed, as has been said, "to take their wives from the clergy and their investitures from the laity." But these are related aspects of his fundamental effort to check the process of secularization in the church. The "Hildebrandine" or "Gregorian" reforms were Hildebrand's radical answer to the problem of the relation of the church to the lay society. The clergy held properties in feudal tenure and had feudal duties to perform. Princes and dukes desired to see in church offices men who would support their policies. Therefore they intervened in clerical elections and fought for the right to control them—the right of investiture. The bishops they selected were often poorly equipped for spiritual duties, lacking in ascetic piety, and indifferent to irregularities in the lives of their clergy. This situation nullified the efforts to regiment the priesthood according to monastic standards. The reformers wished to elevate the clergy into a superior caste committed to a life of chastity. The dream of this reform was the more alluring when it was remembered that it would obviate the danger of the alienation of church property by its bestowal upon the sons of priests. Wazo, Humbert, Damian, Hildebrand and their supporters found in the Forged Decretals and in many genuine provisions of the Canon Law, reiterated and unqualified condemnation both of lay investiture and of clerical marriage. Hildebrand was able to wield the weapons provided by these documents more effectively than all his predecessors. He launched an attack in force on both fronts. In the bitter conflict that ensued he aimed not only to resist but to control the kings, and to assert for the Papacy a supreme and unquestioned authority.

In the struggle for celibacy his opponents were mainly in the ranks of the clergy. Many laymen favored for the clergy a continence which they themselves did not care to practice. Hildebrand suspended the non-celibate priests from saying mass, and forbade the faithful to attend their ministrations. Legates carried these pronouncements to provincial synods. They met with little official acceptance. German clergy responded to the demand with "cries of fury." French bishops pronounced it absurd; a mob of priests assaulted an abbot who defended it and pursued the Pope's legate with insults. In England a half-measure on the question was adopted, but not enforced. In some areas, however, with the support of bishops who had been trained in reformed monasteries, and with the coöperation of the people, the offending priests were obliged to send away their wives or concubines. In an age where asceticism was the norm of piety popular feeling could easily be aroused to reject the altar ministry of married priests. In a few instances, indeed, riotous crowds hustled the unfortunate women from the parishes. Some of them died of their hardships, and were buried in unconsecrated ground. But it was not until the Canons Regular were revived by Ivo and Norbert (see page 42 ff.) that any permanent advance was made toward the ideal of celibacy.

In the Investiture Controversy Hildebrand's chief antagonist was the Emperor, Henry IV, a young prince of loose morals, mediocre talents and strong ambitions. He freely appointed bishops in Germany. The Pope uttered fresh condemnations of simony, and excommunicated some of Henry's episcopal advisers for this offense. When Henry proceeded to place a number of his supporters in Italian sees, Gregory assailed him, calling him to obedience and penance. At Henry's bidding a synod at Worms pronounced the Pope's deposition, in solemn, scriptural language. At the same time leading German prelates wrote a vituperative letter to Hildebrand, charging him with base offenses. Hildebrand, whose popularity in Rome had risen on account of his courageous conduct when kidnapped by the aristocratic ruffian Cencius a few days earlier, had to protect from lynching the legate sent by Henry with this letter. He met the German attack promptly. In the name of St. Peter he hurled a decree of excommunication and deposition upon Henry's head, released his vassals from their oaths of fealty, and suspended, till they should repent, the bishops who had aided him.

The papal ban had its effect. The bishops began to withdraw their allegiance from the excommunicated King, and many of his restless vassals were glad of the sanction of rebellion. Henry was forced to negotiate. A diet was arranged to meet at Augsburg in February 1077 to take national action and restore peace. Gregory started out to attend it and complete the humiliation of the King. He crossed the Apennines but not the Alps; and rested at the castle of Canossa, in the territory of his ally, Matilda of Tuscany. Henry was determined to prevent the Pope's visit to Germany. He revoked the deposition pronounced against Gregory and started from Speyer for Italy, with his wife and a few servants. Near Geneva his mother-in-law joined the party. In an exceptionally cold January they came through the Mt. Cenis pass, and, descending by oxen and improvised toboggans, made their way to Reggio. On January 25, 1077, Henry climbed the ascent before the castle of Canossa and stood as a penitent in bare feet in the snow seeking admission to the presence of the Pope.

Matilda and Hugh of Cluny were with Hildebrand in the castle; and they urged upon him a policy of mercy. But he read the purpose of Henry, and realized that he had been robbed of a public triumph in Germany. It was three days before he could bring himself to admit the penitent. But in the Middle Ages an importunate penitent, even if suspected of insincerity, had to be taken seriously. Henry was admitted, promised amendment, and was restored to communion and to kingship. He had stooped to conquer.

Henry in his impenitent heart planned vengeance, and returned to Germany more than ever the Pope's implacable foe. With shrewdness learned in experience he built his power anew in Germany. His chief German opponent fell in battle, after receiving the papal blessing on his cause. Henry came to Italy and laid siege to Rome, captured part of the city and set up an antipope. All the while the Italian Normans under Robert Guiscard had stood in unstable loyalty to Hildebrand. Robert now brought to Rome an unruly army, thrust out the Germans, plundered the city, and carried the pontiff off to Salerno.

The struggle with Henry did not prevent Hildebrand from pursuing an active policy beyond the Empire. His legates and his letters went well-nigh everywhere, bearing the oft reiterated demand for subjection to the Pope. In Spain, Hungary, Poland, Bohemia, Sweden, Denmark, Burgundy, France and England he intervened in matters great and small. He attempted to have himself recognized as feudal suzerain, by divine right, over all temporal powers. William the Conqueror flatly refused to do fealty; elsewhere some measure of success was attained, but not such as could satisfy the Pope's impatient nature. Hildebrand felt, indeed, the oppressive strength of the world's opposition. His fantastic plan for a crusade, of which he was to be the military leader, was perhaps unconsciously due to the desire to escape from the hopeless battle in the West. He called for "justice" and "liberty," associating these principles constantly with the deliverance of the Papacy from the opposition of princes. Looking about him he saw not justice and liberty but treason, perjury, simony, lust and cruelty, and "the Bride of Christ enslaved." His later letters abound with complaints, mingled with passages that ring with a last-ditch courage like that of Sir Douglas Haig's "backs to the wall" proclamation of 1918.

At Salerno Hildebrand died, May 25, 1085. "I have loved justice," he said at the last, "and hated iniquity;

therefore I die in exile." The utterance shows that his fine courage had been touched by cynicism, perhaps because it had never been much tempered by kindliness.

It seemed that he had achieved little of his program. But his assertion of divine-right papal authority over the kings of the earth prepared the way for the consolidation of power under his successors. It is not only in terms of achievement in the objective world that his greatness is to be measured. There is greatness in his devotion to the cause with which he was identified. We do him an injustice if we judge him as a careerist, or an ambitious disturber of the world. He was not a charming saint, this "Sanctus Satanas," but a saint he was in the sense that, forgetting comfort and inclination, he lived and labored in unreserved commitment to that which he held to be of ultimate worth. This element of personal consecration does not excuse in our eyes the faults in Hildebrand's public ethics. But it largely explains the fact, which at once impresses itself upon the historical student, that the former frivolousness and irresponsibility have with him departed from the Papacy, and that henceforth for two centuries or more the conduct of the popes is stamped, almost without exception, by gravity and laborious devotion.

Lothario Conti, Pope Innocent III

Hildebrand, in the fanatical urgency of his demands, set objectives which his more patient and level-headed successors were able ultimately in large measure to attain. The Concordat of Worms, 1122 (preceded by a similar agreement for England 1107), allayed the investiture conflict. The emperor surrendered the right of investiture with ring and staff, the symbols of spiritual authority, while the touch of the scepter still symbolized the feudal tie to the secular ruler. But decisions on ceremonial, and even regulations about elections, could not solve the underlying problem, which was that the feudal bishop was obligated to serve two masters. If he must decide between them, which shall command his obedience? The pope deems the emperor his vassal; while the emperor claims to hold sway directly from God.

The *Dictatus Papæ*, a statement emanating from Hildebrand or his officials, declares that "all princes shall kiss the foot of the pope alone." Another symbol of vassalage was to hold the lord's stirrup while he dismounted and to lead his horse by the bridle. Nicholas I and Innocent II had obtained this honor from emperors. Adrian IV, the English pope, in 1155, after an embarrassing incident, had the proud Barbarossa do him this esquire service.

Certain factors in the social changes of the age notably affected the papal cause. The crusading movement, in its first phase, added to the eminence of the popes as the heads of Christendom. And the alliance of the Papacy with the Lombard League of cities gave the popes one of their proudest triumphs over the imperial power. The decision came at the momentous battle of Legnano, 1176, where town infantry routed armored knights, and the military importance of the bourgeoisie was first demonstrated in a major struggle. Both the crusades and the towns were in the end to prove unfavorable to the papal ascendancy, but in the time of Innocent the Great, this did not yet appear. Not unrelated to the expansion of bourgeois wealth was the rise of the university, an institution of incalculable significance. By Innocent's time a number of the earlier universities were active and becoming organized, and he himself attended two of them.

Yet the world of Innocent was still preponderatingly feudal. His father was a scion of the proud family of the Conti, so called because for centuries they had been counts of Segni in the Campagna. His mother came from the no less distinguished Scotti. Lothario, the future pope, was born at Anagni about 1160. He was educated at Rome and at the universities of Paris and Bologna. At Paris his studies were literary and theological; at Bologna, legal. Under Pope Clement III, his mother's uncle, he became a canon of St. Peter's, and at the age of twenty-eight, a cardinal. Pope Celestine III, who succeeded Clement in 1190, belonged to a family hostile to the Conti; and Lothario, having no position in the Curia, turned to writing books. His treatise *On Contempt of the World, or the Wretchedness of the Human Condition*, shows the aristocratic young scholar an austere and misanthropic ascetic. He discourses on the vileness of the human body and its functions in man and woman. We are born weeping, imbecile and naked, to experience a short life closing in pitiable senility. The miseries of the celibate are exceeded only by the cares of the married. Who can love an ugly wife, or keep a pretty one? The sins as well as the miseries of human life are treated at length, and wretched sinners are urged to flee to penance. It is all commonplace monastic moralizing, but unusually well expressed. He also wrote a symbolic work on marriage, and a treatise on the mass.

On the day of his predecessor's death, January 8, 1198, Lothario was elected by the cardinals, and on February 22, he was consecrated as Innocent III. On that occasion he preached a sermon that was at once a lowly confession of unworthiness, an act of dedication, and a manifesto of the divinely authorized papal world-state. He appropriates many passages of scripture, to the authorization of the papal dominion over the nations. "Who am I," he asks, "that I should sit in state above kings, and occupy the throne of glory?"

Thus began a great and eventful pontificate. Very different in temper was the high-born, scholarly and calculating Innocent from the wrathful and hasty Hildebrand. Yet their ideals and policies were fundamentally the same. Innocent made increased use of papal legates, and wrote more than five thousand letters. He labored to secure acceptance by the secular rulers of his theocratic supremacy. In Rome itself his problem was of special difficulty, for there republicanism had contended with papal monarchy for a century. He reduced the Prefect and the Senator, representatives of the emperor and the citizens respectively, to his complete control. He cleansed the papal court of much of its corruption, and cast laymen out of the Lateran household. Yet his favoritism to his brother, a propertied layman, caused revolt, and only after serious civil strife was he able to regain the mastery of the city.

The Emperor Henry VI had died in 1197, and Innocent secured the guardianship for the infant heir, Frederick, of the kingdom of Sicily. He used this office to the advantage of the Papacy; and drew all south and central Italy into subjection. Innocent bore a high reputation for legal justice; and the dispute over the imperial throne after Henry's death came before him for adjudication. In a learned decision he "decreed" that the Empire should go to the Guelf, Otto IV, on account of his ancestors' record of loyalty to the Papacy, rejecting the claims of the baby

Frederick and the Ghibelline, Philip. Otto, however, proved weak and unreliable, and the Pope kept up negotiations with Philip till the latter's murder, 1208. Finally Otto was excommunicated and Frederick, in his middle teens, allying himself with Philip Augustus of France, came to power. He was crowned Emperor in 1215, having previously promised to allow freedom of appeal to Rome, and to offer "greater obedience, honor and reverence" than his ancestors to the Roman See. In later pontificates he became a byword for indifference to religion and to Rome, but with Innocent he remained on the best of terms.

Innocent laid the Interdict upon France in 1200 in order to compel King Philip Augustus to receive back his divorced wife, Ingeborg of Denmark. Churches were closed, sacraments withdrawn, and the dead left unburied. The King dared not allow these conditions to continue, and the result was, temporarily, a papal success. Philip offended again, but later served the Pope's cause. His forces at the battle of Bouvines (1214) destroyed the power of the excommunicated Otto IV.

John Lackland, King of England, after numerous wicked acts which Innocent had protested or condoned, brought upon himself the papal Interdict in 1208 by his stubborn attempt to place John de Gray in the See of Canterbury against the Pope's nominee, Stephen Langton. The withdrawal of the rites of the church terrified the pious and the dying. John was blamed and hated by his subjects, lost control of the barons, and begged the Pope's mercy. Innocent had appointed Philip Augustus of France to enforce the ban on John and his adherents; and Philip was now enraged to find his warlike preparations wasted. John was obliged to do homage to the Pope through his legate

Pandulf, for England and Ireland, and to pay Peter's Pence and 1,000 marks a year. Pandulf's domineering attitude, and John's abasement of the kingdom, did not please the English. Langton himself was disposed to act independently of Innocent, and was out of favor with him. The ill-success of John's attempt to aid Otto IV at Bouvines so reduced his fortunes that the barons, under Langton's leadership, were able to extort from him the *Magna Charta*, 1215. This charter of English liberties ignores the claim of papal suzerainty, and Innocent denounced it in vehement terms.

We may not follow Innocent's numerous struggles to gain control in other lands from Sweden to Armenia. He collected Peter's Pence from the Scots (!), instructed a king of Hungary in the suppression of heretics, and taught a Bulgarian khan to call him "Master of the Whole World." He let loose a devastating crusade against the heretical townsmen and villagers of Toulouse, even affirming that "no faith is to be kept with those who keep no faith with God." He showed favor to the Jews. He aided the universities. He sent out preachers to enlist men in many lands for the Fourth Crusade. He condemned the crusaders who, drawn aside by the commercial imperialism of Venice, diverted their attack from the Palestine Moslems to the Byzantine Christians; but he reaped for the Western church the benefit of their conquest by establishing the Latin Patriarchate of Constantinople. He cautiously promoted the organization of the Franciscan and Dominican orders. He held in 1215 the Fourth Lateran Council to organize an overwhelming crusade against the Turks, to allay the discords of Europe, to extinguish heresy, and to reform the clergy and the monasteries. This imposing council, in which met 77 primates, 417 bishops, about 800 heads of monastic houses, and over 100 delegates of kings and rulers, was almost completely submissive to Innocent's iron will. The seventy capitula which at his bidding the council adopted, include prohibition of drunkenness, hunting, carelessness of apparel, fighting of duels, and numerous lesser or graver irregularities among the clergy. It was decreed that illiterates should not be ordained to the priesthood, that all adult Christians should come to confession at least once a year; that medical doctors should send for a priest before prescribing for their patients, and that Saracens and Jews should wear distinctive dress. Closing long disputation and uncertainty on the interpretation of the Eucharist, the Council affirmed in explicit terms the doctrine of transubstantiation.

It was also determined to undertake the crusade which was now Innocent's dearest dream. A papal legate was to be commander-in-chief; there was to be no more diversion of crusades, through trading interests, to make war on Christians. Innocent was active through the winter months, amid other cares, in a rather discouraging attempt to call into existence a mighty army. Overwork, it seems, brought on a stroke of paralysis, from which he died, at Perugia, July 16, 1216, in the midst of his labors, and at the height of his power.

That power has hardly been exceeded by the sway of any potentate in history. In area and population his dominions compared favorably with the empire of Trajan or the Antonines. The emperors of old Rome might claim divine authorization, but they could not hurl interdicts that bore with them everlasting penalties, nor cite from ancient and revered scriptures an explicit divine commission to rule the states of the world. Innocent often repeated from Jeremiah the words of Jehovah: "Constitui te super gentes et regna"—"I have set thee over the nations and the kingdoms." It seemed no absurdity for him to claim that the glory of secular princes was but a borrowed ray from the effulgence of the papal glory, and, compared with it, as moonlight unto sunlight. Innocent reigned as a king of kings, directing national policies and making war and peace. But holding by inheritance from Peter the Keys of the Kingdom, he ruled also, as only a medieval pontiff could, through the discipline of the church, an empire in the thoughts of believing men.

His character and policies partook of this duality of power. He was a man at once pious and worldly-wise, meek and bold; and his administration shows a nice balance between idealism and political expediency.

Innocent left a great heritage to competent successors. Honorius III and Gregory IX—both, as popes, very aged men—vigorously maintained the papal ascendancy. A time of distress but not of dishonor followed under Innocent IV. The death of the Emperor Frederick II (1250), enemy of the three popes just named, left Italy and Germany in a state of contention and anarchy. In 1261 the Western power yielded Constantinople to the Greeks. France was ruled in that period by Louis IX (1220-1270), a king who was a saint and a political idealist. His brother, Charles of Anjou, was drawn into Sicilian affairs by the French Pope, Urban IV (1261-1264), with tragic results for Italy. This pope induced Thomas Aquinas to write in defense of the Papacy against the Greeks; and Thomas affirmed, in language used with heightened emphasis by Boniface VIII forty years later: "It is necessary to salvation to be subject to the Roman pontiff."

Gregory X (1271-1276) was the last of the truly great thirteenth century popes. He restored the Empire under the new dynasty of the Hapsburgs, and died, like Innocent III, hopefully preparing for a super-crusade. Then followed eight popes in eighteen years. The last of these was the saintly but incompetent Celestine V, who abdicated after a pontificate of six months in 1294. His successor was the courageous but arrogant and misguided Boniface VIII, who in his famous bulls *Clericis laicos* and *Unam sanctam* asserted papal authority in the most absolute terms, but failed to curb the secular nationalism of France under Philip the Fair. With the defeat of Boniface (1303) the Papacy went over a precipice of disaster, from which it only partially recovered in the fifteenth century. Not even the wisdom and courage of an Innocent III could have kept intact the papal empire amid the new forces in politics and culture that came into play a century after his time.

CHAPTER IV

BROTHERS AND SISTERS OF THE POOR

Poverty is a relative term; and while all degrees of it appear in the Middle Ages, there was then a vast amount of extreme destitution. The masses lived so close to the fringe of subsistence that the accidents of war or weather often brought thousands suddenly face to face with starvation. As in our own times inequalities in the distribution of wealth prevailed. But more fundamental was the inadequacy of production, which is no longer the prime problem in economic life. The rise of a class of propertied townsmen probably did not diminish the insecurity of the non-possessors. Instead it would appear that the number of dependent paupers increased proportionally to the growth of wealth.

The church regarded the relief of the destitute as a duty, but did not attempt the elimination of the chronic pauperism. The social fact of poverty was accepted as one aspect of the inevitable misery appointed to the generations of mankind in their transient and disciplinary sojourn here below. Scholastic philosophers, it is true, under the influence of Aristotle, charged the kings with the task of the economic betterment of their people. But no one dreamed of attempting "the abatement and prevention of poverty,"—to quote a relatively modest American church declaration. Nor would such a project have been thought legitimate by the pious who looked upon almsgiving as a needful work in the scheme of salvation, and the poor as the necessary object of alms. "If there were no poor," Chrysostom had preached, "the greater part of your sins would not be removed."

Medieval religion embraced poverty as an ally. All sincere monasticism utterly rejected private wealth. In the estimation of the devout, members of the profit-seeking classes were of very doubtful religious status. It was known to be hard for the rich to enter the kingdom of God. Riches were a peril to the soul until dispensed in alms, but put to that use were of value in the remission of sins. When men of wealth became religious they felt impelled to strip themselves of their possessions. The lives of Norbert of Xanten, Peter Waldo of Lyons, and Francis of Assisi furnish famous instances of this renunciation; but the same course was followed by innumerable obscurer persons.

Lambert the Stammerer

Monasticism rendered a service to many poor lay folk, by the distribution of alms, and in some instances by the teaching of children. But all close fraternal contact with lay people was excluded by the monk's vows. A more personal treatment of the poor was undertaken by some good bishops and priests, and here and there by leaders of religious groups outside the monastic orders. When the crusades had called many young men abroad, so that many women were left widows or doomed to spinsterhood, Lambert le Bègue (the Stammerer) of Liége organized a community of mature unmarried women under temporary vows. The house of St. Christopher which he established may have been in some sense the mother-house of the widely-spread connection of the Beguines of the Netherlands. Much uncertainty prevails, however, on the origin of the beguinages, and Lambert's part in them. The name Beguines came later to be applied to a variety of associations both of men and of women in France and Germany, which seem to have owed their origin to other movements than that of Lambert.

Unfortunately there exists only the most fragmentary information about the career of this man of social vision. He was born, probably at Liége, between 1120 and 1135, of lower-class parents, and was always in close sympathy with the working people. He seems to have become a canon of the Church of St. Paul, and was so active in pastoral work that he was given a small church which he remodeled and used independently for the cure of souls. He was later in charge of a church in the outskirts of the city. He was an ardent opponent of clerical marriage and a treatise by him on that subject has survived. Half a dozen of his letters are also extant. These writings show him a man of wide interests, but shed no direct light on his connection with St. Christopher's, which is indicated by other sources. One of his letters, however, states that he "translated into vernacular verse the life of St. Agnes for the virgins, and the Acts of the Apostles for the use of all." The context indicates that in the use of these expressions he had in mind religious women to whom he had ministered, and the general congregation attending his church.

It has been denied that Lambert was the founder of the Beguines. Instead some connect this name with a word meaning "to beg," others with "Albigenses," others with French "beige," referring to the color of a penitent's robe. Many scholars now hold that the Beguine communities were organized of earlier bands of homeless mendicant women. A rather animated discussion over Lambert has thus arisen. Probably we are justified in saying that if he did not give the movement full organization he at least presided over its inception, and that his disciples Marie d'Oignies and Jean de Nivelles merely built upon his work in bringing the Beguinages to a more regulated state. Some of the difficulty has arisen from the fact that the later use of the word Beguine or Beguin is often in a sense almost equivalent to "heretic." Yet it has been shown that its earliest use is not in that sense.

Lambert's rigorist views of the priesthood, however, brought upon him charges of heresy. The specific charges had to do with the Eucharist and penance, subjects which would naturally come into discussion in connection with criticisms of the lives of priests. He evidently found himself engaged in a bitter conflict, in which he carried his appeal to the pope, we know not with what result. His death is placed by some in 1177, by others in 1187.

It would appear that the early Beguines gave themselves to the service of the sick and the destitute. Similar associations of men actively engaged in charitable work appear at Louvain by 1220. Later generations were to see in the Netherlands numerous fraternities, some of which engaged in service to the plague-smitten, buried dead paupers, and performed a variety of philanthropic tasks. Others became chiefly notable for their fanaticism and spiritualist heresies. The brotherhood movement was crowned in the Brethren of the Common Life (1378), a fraternity of the greatest importance in the fifteenth century both for its philanthropic and for its educational efforts.

Francis of Assisi

The fame of all other "brothers of the poor" has been eclipsed by that of the Little Poor Man (Poverello) of Assisi. Francis is the most beloved of saints; he is held in reverence by Christians of all communions, and even by non-Christians. When we see Mussolini paying tribute to him we may assume that the influence of the Poverello will remain to temper the harsh ideologies of the New Europe of today.

Pietro Bernardone, Francis' father, was a prosperous, hard-headed business man of Assisi. His mother, Pica, was of southern French extraction; and we may imagine her singing to her baby boy fragments of the romantic French ditties that were always echoing in his brain as a man. Pietro had high hopes for his engaging son as a future cloth-merchant like himself, perpetuating a dynasty of Assisi cloth-merchants, the honorable house of Bernardone. Francis early revolted against this prosaic program. In his teens he sowed his wild oats. "A zealot in folly," he was not gross in his quest of pleasure, but full of "witty jests, vanity, wantonness and buffoonery," fond of show and addicted to gay feasts. Between these gaieties he indeed sold cloth for his father; but from the dull realities of the bales of cloth he turned in fancy to behold a vision of a splendid hall hung with burnished armor. In medieval society the knight was the foe of the merchant, and it was knighthood that commanded the youth's dreams.

The quest of pleasure was followed by the quest of military glory. The bitter rivalry of Assisi and Perugia broke out in war. Francis, aged twenty, buckled on real armor, fought in a lost battle, and went with his war comrades to a Perugian prison. "Stone walls do not a prison make" for such spirits as his. He amused his companions with mirth and banter, and annoyed them with his egotistic assurance that he would yet "become a great prince." Freedom came after a year of this, and back in Assisi he was ill, and felt a revolt against the frivolities of his life. A new exploit attracted him and he was off for southern Italy to fight the pope's battle under a famous captain. But something which he never revealed happened to him on the way. Perhaps tried soldiers resented his airs and his impulses. One author reports an alleged vision in which he was called to the service of God. But he returned to the stuffy realm of cloth, and sought relief among the thoughtless companions of the former days.

The military phase was ended. But Pietro could not harness the young Pegasus to his plow. A strong tension had arisen between father and son. Probably the young man was often made aware that he was a very discouraging son and that his wasteful habits would bring down in ruin the house of Bernardone. Evidently Francis came to a mood of fixed hostility to the tasks of salesmanship, the mercantile occupation, and the whole wealth-getting way of life. The quest of glory was to be succeeded by the pursuit of holy poverty.

One night when his companions had made him master of the revels, suddenly amid the mirth they saw him in deep abstraction, and one said in jest, "Francis is thinking of taking a wife." "Yes," he replied, roused from his reverie, "a wife more beautiful, richer and purer than you can imagine." The chosen bride of Francis was Lady Poverty. Here was his own application of the romance of the knight and the lady made familiar to him in chivalric song and tale.

If the revels were interrupted by the incalcuable young man's new devotion, still more was the cloth business. Commissioned to take a consignment of Pietro's goods to Foligno, he disposed of it as arranged, received the money, sold also his horse, and went to the Church of St. Damian near Assisi where he disburdened himself of his wealth by leaving the bag of coins on a window ledge. Pietro, on learning of this, was exasperated beyond self-control. He rushed upon Francis in the public square "like a wolf on a sheep," hustled his twenty-five-year-old son home, and locked him in a narrow chamber. The most revealing fact we know about the mother of Francis is that when her husband was away she timidly and tenderly unlocked his prison.

The case came before Bishop Guido of Assisi for adjudication. The bishop admonished Francis kindly. But Francis eagerly took the opportunity to make, in a dramatic and symbolic act, a public renunciation of worldly goods. He stripped off his clothing, bundled it up and laid it before his father, while Guido drew the naked devotee under the folds of his own mantle. Provided by the bishop's gardener with a tattered tunic, he started barefoot up the wooded slopes of Mount Subasio, which overlooks Assisi, singing Provençal songs. He met robbers, and announced himself to them as "the herald of a great king." They flung him in a ditch full of snow; but he resumed his way, and his song.

He stayed for a while in a cloister, serving as a scullion, but, harshly treated by the monks, took up his residence in a colony of lepers, tending their sores and easing their distresses. He was a greatly changed young man, as all could see. He had never liked cloth, the commodity, but he had been exceptionally fond of fine clothes; and he was now clad in beggarly rags. He had loathed and shunned lepers; now he genuinely loved them. Once a warrior, he was now an ardent advocate of peace. A new piety drew him to the churches in and about Assisi, and he was distressed by their state of neglect and decay. Before a picture of the Crucifixion in St. Damian's he fell into a prolonged rapture. Perhaps it was then that the wounds of Christ became a constant element in his piety. As he gazed upon it, the figure on the cross seemed to move and speak, commanding him to repair the churches. He now went about urgently soliciting stones and labor for this work, and toiled at it with his own hands. One of the churches which he repaired was that of St. Mary of the Angels called the Little Portion (Porziuncula), at the foot of the hill of Assisi. Here Francis, when the work was completed, heard mass on February 24, 1209. It was St. Matthew's day, and the gospel lesson was from Matthew 10, the sending of the Twelve to preach the kingdom. As he listened to the passage: "As ye go, preach. . . . Provide neither gold nor silver nor brass in your purses . . . neither two coats nor shoes nor staves," he exultantly accepted the words as his own life commission. Forthwith he began to preach, and to gather a following.

A disciple, Celano, has left an intimate pen portrait of the saint at this period of early maturity:

He was charming in behavior, gentle in nature, affable in conversation, faithful to a trust, forward-looking in plans, firm of purpose. . . . He was ready to pardon, slow to wrath, quick-witted, of tenacious memory. . . . He was simple in word and deed, stern to himself, devoted to others. He was exceptionally eloquent, of cheerful aspect and benign countenance, and devoid of arrogance. He was of middle stature or less, with round head and somewhat long and prominent profile, a forehead smooth and narrow, dark, frank eyes, dark hair, straight eyebrows, and nose regular, slender and straight. . . . His speech was conciliatory or fiery and pointed; his voice urgent, sweet, clear and sonorous. His teeth were close-set, even and white; his lips delicate and shapely, his beard black and not plentiful. He had short arms and long fingers, unclipped nails, slender legs, small feet, and very little flesh on his frame.

The same writer tells us that from the beginning of his preaching his word was like a blazing fire piercing men's hearts and filling their minds with wonder.

The preaching mission of Francis and his companions wrought a great change in the lives of multitudes. Theirs was a message of great simplicity, yet of great variety. There were two or three things that Francis said and kept on saying with peculiar emphasis in his preaching.

One point of emphasis is the call to peace. It was his habit to begin an address with the greeting, "The Lord give you peace" and on entering a house to say, "Peace be to this house." These were not mere formal phrases; they expressed his earnest prayer and desire. Francis labored against discord and conflict in the homes and in the towns he visited, and exhorted contentious persons to seek peace and pursue it. The relation of voluntary poverty to peace was in his mind a very close and a very obvious one. He once explained to Bishop Guido his reason for refusing corporate property for the Franciscan order, in these words: "Signor, if the day comes when we have property we shall need arms to defend it. Then will follow disputes and lawsuits, and the hindrance of the love of God and our neighbor."

His preaching of peace was but part of a mission of pacification. In 1210 he used his influence to bring about an agreement between the *majores* and *minores* of Assisi. At the close of his life he brought together the bishop and the podestà of the city, who had been in bitter strife. He sent from his death-bed some friars to sing before the contestants his *Canticle of the Sun*, having added to it the line about "those who pardon for thy love." An affecting scene of mutual repentance and reconciliation followed the singing. Once near Perugia he met a former acquaintance who spoke in fierce anger of his lord who had taken from him his property. Francis implored him to forgive the wrong-doer, for his own soul's sake, and gave his cloak to the needy man. This proof that there was still some kindness in the world softened the man's anger to forgiveness. Such too is the parable underlying the story of the wolf of Gubbio, a wolf so big and so bad as to put the town in terror. Subdued by the saint's kindness "Friar Wolf" became a gentle and friendly companion of the townsfolk. Less improbable is the account of the conversion of the brigands of San Sepolcro by friars sent by Francis, bearing his gifts and words of persuasion, "Brother brigands, come to us, for we bring you good bread and good wine." We know that at Bologna Francis urged civic peace and unity and reconciled ferocious enemies to each other. He used a dramatic act of exorcism to cast the devils of discord out of Arezzo; and in many places by public sermon or personal appeal he turned his hearers from strife to peace. Under the spell of his earnest eloquence, says Celano, "Many, who were haters of peace and salvation, embraced peace with their whole heart."

This call to peace involved a call to repentance, and his followers were at first sometimes called penitents. Here he had much in common with the wandering preachers of the previous century. But the ideal of poverty was as closely integrated with repentance as with peace. Francis asked not merely a renunciation of material property but a conversion from the acquisitive and aggressive spirit of the wealth-seeker. Repentance in the Franciscan message meant primarily abandoning the acts and attitudes of hatred and strife, which in turn were associated with greed of wealth. Whatever of asceticism is involved in such teaching of penitence, it is basically a socially positive principle. Life is more than meat, and wealth must make way for love.

Again, the message of poverty led to the principle of simplicity. Francis preached and practiced a joyous affection for, and satisfaction with, simple things. Rejecting possessions over which men quarrel, he was attracted to those unpossessed things which all may share without quarreling. Birds and beasts, rocks and streams, flowers and trees, inspired in him a holy glee, and he loved them as few before or since have loved them. He preached to his sisters, the cowled larks; and he preached about them, praising the lowliness of their walk and the loftiness of their flight and song. He suggested that the emperor should command that they be given a feast of wheat each Christmas Day. His so-called *Canticle of the Sun* is a hymn of full-voiced praise for the goodness of God manifested in created things. The all-illumining sun; the moon, precious and fair; wind, water and fire, are his brothers and his sisters; his gratitude even embraces "Sister Death." One might think this the song of a poet on the open road, and in the bloom of health. It was poured forth when he lay infirm and almost blind, annoyed by an army of mice "running about over him day and night." Indeed it would seem that it was in order to rise above the malign influence of these vermin on his spirit that he began to sing his better thoughts and put the fragments together into the poem. The relation between the man and the mouse is reversed, but the sentiment is comparable, where in a less exalted mood Robert Burns compassionately calls a luckless mouse his "fellow-creature."

Meanwhile followers from all ranks of society, who variously understood or misunderstood Francis, had gathered to his side. He was in some places embarrassed by popularity; especially when admirers clipped fragments from his tunic for keepsakes, and to cure the sick, till there was no tunic left. Great men of the church instructed him in the founding of an order to which he contributed some measure of his spirit. He had no gift of organization, and before he died he left the command of the rising host to others. His physical stamina was taxed by asceticism and sapped by the labor of travel. He went on long journeys, chiefly on foot and always in scorn of comfort. Seized with a zeal to convert rather than to kill Brother Turk, he made four pathetic attempts to evangelize the Moslems. In 1219 at Old Cairo the guardians of the Sultan of Egypt whipped him and brought him before their master. He preached the Gospel, and had the courteous thanks of the potentate, but surprised him by refusing his proffered gifts.

Growing bodily weakness led to the intenser cultivation of mystical piety. The account of the stigmata, the marks of the wounds of Christ which Francis is alleged to have received on Mt. Alverna, is the most familiar and the most baffling element in his biography. The presence of the stigmata at the time of his death is so well attested that it is difficult to dismiss the story as allegory. If on more general evidence we can admit the possibility that the mind's absorption in the Crucifixion might in favorable cases induce such physical effects, we must recognize that in a nervous organism so hypersensitive as that of Francis the possibility is unusually heightened.

It is only half of Francis that is represented by the term *Jongleur de Dieu,* God's merrymaker. There was also in him not a little of the holy warrior who visits upon sin the wrath of God. There must be some core of fact behind the numerous tales of prayers of vengeance, worthy of the saints of the more barbarous age before him, which the admirers of Francis tell of him. When his principles were violated his anger blazed. In his absence a spacious building at Assisi was undertaken to house a convention of the friars. He came upon the scene uttering fierce invectives, climbed on the roof and began to rip the boards off. We are reminded of a certain incident in the Temple of Jerusalem.

There has been a tendency to debate the question as to the dominance of joy or sorrow in the piety of Francis. The question arises to any reader of the innumerable anecdotes told by Franciscan writers, which make him exhibit great variations of mood and utterance. Tendencies in the minds of the writers are often demonstrably reflected in these tales. But the careful reader will realize that there were times when like a young man in love, Francis did not know whether he was glad or sad. His life was lived under constant stress of emotion, which moved readily between joy and tears. In the height of feeling he craved music and song. Sometimes he would snatch up a stick and imitate the gestures of a violin player, while he "sang in French unto the Lord." "But," says brother Leo, "all this joy dissolved in compassion for the passion of Christ," and gave place to deep sighs and groans. Not insisting on rigorous asceticism in others, he practiced severe austerities himself. Yet his distaste for food was rather that of a lover than that of the calculating ascetic. He lived ardently, and was early spent. On October 4, 1226, having blessed his brothers and commanded them to lay him naked on the earth, he welcomed Sister Death.

The incalculable legacy which Francis left to the world does not include guidance on the problems of distribution in our present economic order. He was no economist; and such economic facts as came to his attention did not permit him to conceive of an economy of plenty for all. He touched the behavior of men in their problem of obtaining the necessities of life, only with the aim of alleviating the distresses of an economy of scarcity which was assumed to be normal. He chose mendicancy as a discipline in humility and a means of keeping his company of saints on a plane of contact with the poorest of the poor. He does not teach us how bread should be distributed, but that we should not try to live by bread alone. His religion made him not primarily a relief agent but a brother to poor men, teaching them their own mutual brotherhood and human dignity. His realm is not economics but religion; yet he can resolve tensions that arise in the economic realm by imparting a religious assurance of the irrelevance of economic good to the higher joys of human experience.

At a time when monasticism, with its aristocratic leadership, had lost its appeal and its vigor, Francis, the shopkeeper who would not keep shop, launched a revived Christianity, a religion of holy poverty, of social love and service, which challenged the middle classes with heroic demands for renunciation of the wealth they were engaged in accumulating and for fraternal treatment of the poor whom they were accustomed to oppress. For a countless number Francis has widened the frontiers of religion and enhanced the worthfulness of life.

Elizabeth of Thuringia

If this book were not to be confined to the treatment of persons remarkable for the originality of their work, it would be in order to review the fascinating life-stories of a few of Francis' disciples, such as the generous Bernard of Quintavalle, or the fearless and outspoken Giles. But this temptation must be dismissed, even in the case of Saint Clare, founder of the Order of Poor Ladies. Like the others she drew her inspiration so completely from Francis that her contribution to religion is largely merged in his.

We are more justified in the inclusion of the most celebrated woman-saint of central Europe, Elizabeth of Thuringia, who was the daughter of a king, and a sister of the poor. More than any other on German soil Elizabeth imported into the rough and harsh manners of the feudal age an element of Christian humanitarianism.

Hospitals for the sick were rare before the thirteenth century, although infirmaries were contained in all well-equipped monasteries. The monasteries also possessed *hospitia*, or guest-houses for pilgrims and travelers; and such hospices were being established in many places as the need for them arose. A few houses for the care of lepers were instituted in the twelfth century, some of them by princes and princesses. Matilda, the wife of Henry I of England, who was a daughter of the saintly Queen Margaret of Scotland, turned her own house into a leper hospital and tended the patients herself. St. Hedwig of Silesia

(1174-1243), the wife of a great duke and the sister of a queen of France, with her husband's coöperation founded and supervised hospitals in Breslau and Neumarkt. The mother of Elizabeth of Thuringia was Hedwig's sister, and her father was Andrew II, King of Hungary.

The medieval sources for Elizabeth's life are replete with miracles, obvious exaggerations, and romantic incidents amid which the seeker of facts must thread his way with caution. She was born in Pressburg in 1207, and was betrothed in childhood to Louis, the boy-heir of the Landgrave Hermann of Thuringia and Hesse. Admirers told afterwards how she was brought in a silver cradle, with an escort of Thuringian knights, from Pressburg to Eisenach, accompanied by a train of carriages with costly gifts, and how she was reared in the constant company of her future husband. But it is probable that she was past the cradle stage when she came; and certainly Louis was almost seven years her senior. She was brought up in the castle of Wartburg, a mile from Eisenach.

We may probably in some degree discount also the alleged hatred of her future mother-in-law—a familiar theme in fairy-tales. Yet she grew up in an unnatural and probably an unhappy situation. Her own mother was slain by an anti-German Hungarian faction in 1214. The story of her miraculous appearance to ask Elizabeth's prayers for her tortured soul may truly reflect the distress of the child's mind. Possibly it was the reversal of German interests in Hungary rather than any personal dislike that caused Sophia, Louis's mother, to seek the annulment of the betrothal.

The child was grave, quiet, religiously precocious, and disinclined to the festivities to which the dowager Landgravine was devoted. To the further annoyance of that ogre, Sophia, she resorted for companionship, we are told, to the homes of the poor and lowly. Young Louis was her faithful champion. On his father's death in 1216 he was called to rule the country. His chivalrous determination to fulfil the pledge of his betrothal increased as Elizabeth grew tall and attractive, and prevented her being sent back to Hungary or thrust into a nunnery. In 1221 they were married; he was in his twenty-first and she in her fourteenth year,—ages not remarkable in medieval marriages.

In her Wartburg home Elizabeth now devoted herself to the help of the poor. Louis fully approved her expenditures in their behalf. Though a pious prince he seems to have spent much of his time in war. Twice at the summons of the Emperor Frederick, he went to serve across the Alps. In 1227, persuaded by a bishop, he joined the frustrated crusade from which Frederick returned ill soon after sailing. Louis did not return. Stricken with fever he reached the Island of St. Andreas, only to die.

Elizabeth, now the mother of three children, had already mingled with her home duties an extraordinary amount of philanthropic work. At Neuburg, Eisenach and Gotha, Louis had assisted her in the foundation of hospitals. Whenever possible Elizabeth nursed the sick folk in person, often selecting the patients whose loathsome sores others feared to approach. While she and Louis resided at Neuburg he came home one day to find her nursing a dying leper who, after a bath, had been laid in the Landgrave's bed. Even this did not induce him to curb her measureless charity.

In 1225 Germany was visited by floods, plague and a

crop failure. The following winter and spring saw thousands in dire need. Louis was in Italy. Elizabeth disbursed alms from his treasury, and fed hundreds daily from a store of grain in the Wartburg. On his return Louis, against the complaints of his mother and brothers, approved her actions. During the famine she established an infirmary in a basement apartment of the Wartburg and there cared for twenty-eight patients.

The death of Louis was one of thousands of costly losses entailed by the crusades. All concerned would have fared better if he had remained at home organizing his government. When Sophia brought Elizabeth Louis's signet ring, the token of his death, her grief was insupportable. She had lost not only her life-companion but her sole protector.

According to the common account Elizabeth and her children were now thrust out of the Wartburg by Henry, the brother of Louis, and, since this villainous prince terrorized them, the people dared not entertain her, so that she was obliged to live as an outcast in an abandoned hut beside a noisy tavern. Various hardships followed, till the Bishop of Bamberg gave her a residence, and attempted to induce her to abandon her vow of perpetual widowhood and marry some baron. When her husband's knightly companions returned in 1228 bringing his body for burial, they boldly compelled Henry to make worthy provision for his sister-in-law. But there are some inconsistencies in this construction of the narrative, and it is possible that her poverty was of her own choosing.

The Franciscans had now come to Eisenach and Marburg. One of the friars, Rodeger, had been for a time her confessor. Later she had come under the spiritual direction of the celebrated inquisitor, Conrad of Marburg, an inhuman ascetic. After Louis's death, he was her only reliance. She submitted, as her maids afterwards testified, to his penances and floggings, and evidently feared him greatly. It is regrettable, but not surprising, that the young and devout Elizabeth yielded her nobler spirit to this dark fanatic. Her submission to him is the more understandable when it is remembered that Conrad had the confidence of Pope Gregory IX, and was an able recruiting officer for the crusades and very powerful in all Germany. On Good Friday, 1228, in the Franciscan chapel at Marburg, Elizabeth solemnly renounced the world and her kindred. This has been interpreted as joining the Franciscan Tertiaries, but the point is not clear. One of her two little daughters had already gone to a nunnery; the other two children were otherwise provided for, and taken from her care.

She received a substantial sum of money, and the castle of Marburg, from her brother-in-law, Henry. She soon left the castle for a wretched hut; but built a house and, adjacent to it, a spacious hospital, beside the town. She now resumed her care of the sick. The recorded incidents of her service reveal, through the ornament of miracle, the character of a medieval Florence Nightingale, who was as resourceful as she was self-sacrificing.

Medieval medicine as practiced generally was an elaborate science of error—utilizing weird concoctions brewed with magical rites—and only slightly redeemed by common sense. Medieval surgery was crude, inconsiderate and primitive. Poor St. Francis, for an affection of the eyes, allowed his forehead to be cruelly seared with hot irons. But medieval nursing was directly motivated by sympathy for the afflicted, used humane methods, and was often effective in bringing relief to pain and aiding recovery.

Elizabeth bathed the patients, made the beds, administered the medicines. In a crisis when all the towels were used she snatched curtains from the walls and cut them up for towels. When her protégés shivered in their beds she gave them her own blankets and slept between two mattresses. She went out with her servants to bring supplies to the poor of the district. She disposed of her jewels and silks, even her last precious keepsakes from Hungary, to provide alms. On occasion she even went fishing to add to the food supply. She was not easily fooled. To outwit deceivers who got into the bread line twice in the same day she abolished the line and had all sit on the grass till they were supplied. Once when she happily distributed coins to a throng of disabled old folk and poor children at the hospital court, she had a bonfire lighted and the crippled paupers sang around it far into the night.

The reader's sociological soul will rise to say that so far as the problem of poverty was concerned this was all a waste of effort. And it is a fact that Henry's wasteful expenditures were impoverishing his people more rapidly than Elizabeth could feed them. But what better could a woman in her circumstances do than to make the response of human sympathy to abject need? At least her philanthropy was not impersonal. She knew well many of the people she aided, heard their stories, talked with them, identified herself with them—a fact seemingly lost to Hans Holbein the Elder and other artists who depicted her in the Renaissance age. There is a story that St. Francis before he died sent to St. Elizabeth a worn cloak. The story conveys a suggestion of the truth that these two saints were kindred in their piety. But she was not like Francis, a preacher. Her teaching lay in the work of her hands; and her acts bore in medieval Germany eloquent testimony to the worth of human beings.

Her own excessive exertions and Conrad's sadistic demands for asceticism, wore out her young life. She was only twenty-four when she died, November 19, 1231. Dignitaries of church and state contended to do her honor. A church dedicated to her was built in Marburg. She was canonized by Gregory IX, in 1235. It was to her humanity rather than to her piety that Frederick II, the enemy of popes, paid tribute, when in 1236 he came to Marburg to have her body disinterred and laid away again in St. Elizabeth's Church, in an oaken coffin overlaid with gold.

Catherine of Siena

Through the first half of the fourteenth century Italy seemed to be sinking into more and more hopeless political confusion. The popes now resided at Avignon, in growing worldliness and ease but in declining power. Benedict XII indeed made a serious effort to recover the respect of the nations which John XXII had lost; but his successor Clement VI (1342-1352) brought the Holy See to shame. In Rome Cola di Rienzi, who had sought in vain to induce Clement to return to the city, attempted to establish a republic on the ancient Roman model and aimed at the unification of Italy; but his fanatical assumptions drew on an insurrection in which he perished (1354). Many of the Italian states passed through a bewildering series of revolutions, as the balance of power shifted between Ghibellines and Guelfs, between clan and clan, faction and faction. In 1348 the Black Death, entering at Genoa, smote the land. It was to sweep over all Europe in the following year.

Nowhere, it would seem, was the pestilence more destructive than in Siena, the center of a little republic which divided with Florence the former Tuscany. Three-quarters of the population perished; and from the ghastly scenes of death the survivors turned only to reckless sensuality. The lay-brothers and lay-sisters in the hospital that had served Siena since the late eleventh century mostly took flight. Nevertheless some of the hermits in the hills about the town left their retreats to minister to the plague-stricken; and a house of pious Dominican friars asserted the claims of religion.

The plague seems to have missed the house of the prosperous dyer, Jacopo Benincasa, and his wife Lapa, whose twenty-fourth child, Catherine, was born March 25, 1347. A twin-sister died soon after birth; a younger sister was later to complete this model Italian family. The house stood near the foot of the hill that was crowned by the church of the Dominicans. A short distance southward from it rose the Duomo, begun a century before Catherine, but still unfinished in her time. Neighbored by these monuments of religion the dyer's house was itself a center of piety; and if little Catherine's peculiar devotion was disapproved by her parents, it was only because it seemed dangerously excessive.

Her childhood was marked by a spirituality that is scarcely paralleled. Her joyousness in acts of devotion caught the attention of all. It was in a kind of spiritual dance that she would climb the stairs kneeling on each step with a prayer to the Virgin. One day when not yet six years old, while walking in the street, she saw Christ enthroned above the church of St. Dominic; her little brother had much trouble to bring her out of her ecstasy. At the age of seven she secretly vowed a life of virginity, and when a few years later she was induced to consider marriage, she soon with deep remorse for the very thought reverted to her early intention. As she gave herself continually to religious musings, her worried parents sought the advice of one of the friars; but he hesitated to restrain her piety. Her parents tried to cure the obsession by putting her to hard housework and denying her privacy. But she made, as she was accustomed to say, a cell for herself in the mind, shutting out the world. Identifying her exacting father with Christ, her mother with Mary, and her brothers with the Apostles, she yielded them scrupulous obedience "with great joy and diligence."

Her resources of imagination and will won the contest with her family, and she was given a room in which to practice penance and prayer. When about sixteen she took the white and black habit of the Dominican Tertiaries, and thereafter for three years spoke only to her confessor. At nineteen she experienced the mystic ceremony of her spiritual espousals with Jesus, at which the Virgin, St. John and St. Paul were witnesses, and David "played sweetly." Jesus gave her, she said, a ring which she, and she alone, could ever after see upon her finger. The stigmata, which she felt to have been inflicted during an ecstasy in 1375, remained also invisible.

She came from her seclusion conscious of a divinely imposed mission to her family, her city, Italy, and the world. She helped with the household work and insisted on subjecting herself even to the hired servants. She associated with other Tertiaries, who in Siena were all sober widows, some of whom resented her zeal till overcome by her affection. She engaged in ministrations to the sick and poor, and kept a lantern to take out in answering their night calls.

She gathered a few devoted disciples, men and women. In the last few years of her life acting in response to invitations or requests, she engaged in numerous missions in the interests of peace and of church reform. She lived in a state of sustained spiritual exhilaration which occasionally rose to rapture and never gave place to great depression. Yet she felt herself strangely elected to bear the burden of the sins of her generation. Her asceticism was so intense that food and drink always nauseated her, and her confessor, Raimondo, declared, obviously with exaggeration, that for long periods she took no nourishment except the communion wafer. For years she flogged herself thrice daily till the blood flowed. As she became more active in public affairs and better acquainted with social conditions she was more completely committed to the notion of expiating in the sufferings of her own body the wickedness that prevailed in the church and in society. Under this burden her nervous organism suffered agonies of pain. She used to say, "I die, yet cannot die."

Catherine had no formal education. She learned to read only when full-grown, and to write at the age of thirty. Her voluminous correspondence and her mystical books were dictated in rapid speech. She sometimes used three or even four secretaries at once, dictating as many letters to different people. Her letters vary from gracious guidance of weak souls to powerful exhortation and invective. Early editors thought it prudent to expurgate some frank phrases from the text. But even when most outspoken Catherine is pleading for love and holiness, or exhorting those at feud to reconciliation. Her *Dialogue,* a work in four sections, on Providence, Discretion, Prayer and Obedience, respectively, is a treasury of mystical theology. As

Francis exalted poverty, Catherine exalts obedience above all other virtues, as the antithesis of the pride, self-will and self-love by which men sin and suffer. This book is said to have been dictated in ecstasy; but it contains much thoughtful criticism and discerning appreciation of the religious forces of Catherine's age, in which her superior intellectual powers are manifest. The work of Francis and Dominic, "two columns of Holy Church," has never been more lucidly characterized than in the closing section of the *Dialogue*. It is noteworthy that Catherine's preference goes to Dominic, who by his attention to learning made his religion "a delightful garden, wide and joyous and fragrant."

In the *Dialogue* love of neighbor is stressed as a phase of love of God. The soul which has come from the "stormy ocean" to the "pacific sea" of divine love, "loves every rational creature," and endeavors to make response to God by service to others. "This love you cannot repay to Me, but you can pay it to my rational creature, loving your neighbor without being loved by him . . . because he has been loved by Me." Hatred and abuse of men is an affront to God. In full accord with this teaching Catherine so lived in the world of action that her years were filled with gracious ministries to her fellow-humans, and especially to those in greatest need.

She went to Florence to attend a chapter of the Dominicans in 1374, and returned to Siena at the end of June to find the town visited by a return of the plague. People walking the streets were seized by its malignant symptoms and the death-cart once more carried off the corpses to promiscuous burial. Catherine nursed and buried several of her own brothers and nephews. Leading a little band of women who were devoted to her, she labored with amazing energy in the infected houses, tended the sick, consoled the dying, decently buried the dead. Her confessor and disciple, the learned friar Raimondo of Capua, headed a band of devoted men in a like effort. Nothing so much endeared Catherine to the people as this sacrificial and uncalculating service. She escaped the pestilence, but fell ill of a fever and of exhaustion. On her recovery she stepped out upon the larger stage of church politics. From this time she was received everywhere as a saint and greeted with the profoundest reverence. A solicitous stranger thought it necessary to warn her against pride: she replied to him in a letter of singular courtesy, asking his prayers that she might be enabled to eat "like other creatures," as she longed to do.

Catherine was a forerunner of Elizabeth Fry in her concern for prisoners. Especially did she minister to those appointed to die. Nicolò di Toldo, a young nobleman who was in Siena on a visit from Perugia, made some adverse criticisms of the city government. He was arrested and sentenced to be beheaded. He had never taken communion; and now he raged against the priests who came to him. Catherine led him to repentance and aroused in him a mystical devotion that made him look upon death as martyrdom. She attended his execution, sustained his courage, and lovingly received his severed head from the block. She describes the incident in a rapturous letter to Raimondo.

Perhaps her supreme concern in social and political matters was the promotion of peace. In pity for souls and bodies ruined by war she constantly sought to bring an end to family feuds, and to the greater conflicts of her time. Seeking an agreement between two nobles of Montepulciano who disputed about a castle, she was led to engage in an evangel of pacification and repentance through the contado (county) of Siena, sometimes stirring with emotion large throngs of the villagers who came from far and near. In her absence the Sienese feared her disloyalty to them, but she wrote: "I love you more than you love yourselves," and assured them that she was plotting only against the devil. But Siena was to enjoy her presence rarely thereafter. She was called away to Pisa and to Lucca in 1375 on missions of pacification. A crisis now developed in the relations of Florence and the Papal States which drew her into world affairs. The tyranny of the pope's tax collectors had prepared the Papal States for revolt. The diplomacy of Florence used this situation to deprive Pope Gregory XI (1370-1378), a Frenchman unacquainted with Italy, of most of his territory; and his legate, seeking redress in Florence, was flayed alive. Gregory interdicted Florence, and his agents employed Sir John Hawkwood with his English mercenaries, and other condottieri, in a destructive and futile war.

Catherine had been writing to the Pope's legates, and to Gregory himself, urging fundamental reform. She mercilessly condemned the immorality, nepotism, greed and pride of the clergy, high and low; and she summoned the Pope to overcome his own defects and play the man. She insisted that he should bring back the Papacy from Avignon to Rome, and that the mercenary companies should be sent on crusade. She sent Raimondo to Hawkwood with a remarkable letter exhorting him to leave the service of the devil, and the butchery of Christians, and "to march against the infidel dogs."

It is interesting to compare Catherine's policy here with

that of the other woman prophet of her time in Italy, Birgitta of Sweden. Birgitta had urged and rejoiced in the return to Rome of Urban V (1367) and warned him against setting out again for Avignon (1370). She too lashed clerical sins and urged reforms. But in her pronounced disapproval of crusades she was less medieval than Catherine. After her death in 1373, and that of Petrarch in 1374, Catherine was the only great personality contending for moral idealism in Italy. She succeeded to the place of Birgitta in the public eye; and attained to greater esteem in Italy than the Swedish saint.

In June, 1376, Catherine was sent by a party seeking peace in Florence, to bear their proposals to Avignon. She made the journey, appeared before the Pope and cardinals, and made them wince with her fearless criticism. At Avignon, as Pastor paraphrasing Catherine's own words has said, "her nostrils were assailed by the odors of hell." Her denunciation of venal and loose-living clerics was not less caustic than that of her contemporary, John Wyclif. But unlike Wyclif she remained wholly loyal to the idea of the Papacy and the hierarchical organization. She accused Gregory of pusillanimity, but he was still for her "Christ on earth" and the fountain of authority. Gregory listened favorably to her plea. But Florentine ambassadors came later only to undo her peace efforts, and the war went on. Catherine remained to plead with Gregory to return to Rome. He had announced his intention to do so, but was irresolute and listened to contrary proposals. A forged letter of intimidation seems to have deterred him. It may have been through Catherine's exhortations that Gregory finally summoned the courage to set out for Rome. She met him at Genoa and revived his feeble resolution. He reached Rome in January 1377. But his health failed, and, disappointed in all his efforts, he died in March 1378. He had been too proud to accept possible terms of peace with Florence. There Catherine was now laboring and, in the hope of martyrdom, exposing her life to anti-papal factionists. She secured the peace at last after Gregory's death.

But for Catherine, who took to heart the woes of Christendom, disaster came upon disaster. The new pope, Urban VI, was soon deserted by the French cardinals who set up an antipope (August 1378) and so inaugurated the Great Schism of the West. Urban, whose intractable disposition alienated everybody else of influence, called Catherine to aid him; and loyally she labored till her strength failed, seeking to pacify the Romans, to amend the Pope's harsh temper, and, by letters and messengers to win for him the support of the potentates of the world; while also she went about doing good among the people of Rome. Bodily anguish brought her activity to an end; but her vivacious spirit was sustained until she died, April 30, 1380, at thirty-three.

There was no doubt a neurotic factor in Catherine's experience—in her visions and ecstasies, and in her sense of universal responsibility. But it was this neurosis that revealed her genius. If she had been "normal" humanity would have been the poorer. The tragedy of her life lay in the combination of boundless sympathy with profound intellectual realization of the evil conditions of her time. Her imaginative powers brought in upon her mind the ills, and upon her conscience the sins, of the age. In bearing them deep gladness mingled with the intensest pain. Indifference to human woe was impossible to her, and she found no relief in idealization. Though she saw people potentially good and great, she knew their actions to be mean, corrupt and cruel. She looked with unshrinking gaze and with keen appraisal, upon the horror of men's misdeeds. The cruelties inflicted on others were as swords in her bosom. In a sense the pangs she suffered were, as she supposed, redemptive. For no one could come in touch with her spirit—and no one today can even read her letters—without revolting from every suggestion of the baseness that would wound her sensitive soul.

The best lines of Swinburne's *Siena* are those in which he describes Catherine's ministry and influence:

Then in her sacred saving hands
She took the sorrows of the lands. . . .
And shields were lowered, and snapped were spears,
And sweeter-tuned the clamorous years.

CHAPTER V

THE GLORIOUS COMPANY OF THE TEACHERS

Melanchthon, during a visitation of the country parishes in Thuringia in 1527, wept with shame and despair at the soul-enslaving ignorance that he found to prevail. The state of intelligence among the masses had been still lower in former centuries. Before the rise of universities a very few had made through the church an entrance into the world of learning. Even those reputed to be scholars surveyed a restricted field of knowledge. They knew in part the Latin classics, but they had only a vague awareness of the Greek literature that inspired the Roman. With a few exceptions they were very little concerned with the task of recovering the older literature, or with the expansion of knowledge. The poverty of society and the political disorder, rendered hard the lot of the scholar. The feudal age offered too little security for the intellectual life and failed to provide in adequate measure the means of education. The educated class was childless; there was no hereditary caste of scholars. Generations passed with no marked rise in intelligence. The masses remained illiterate and largely uninstructed. In view of these general conditions a great debt is due to those few gifted men who gave themselves to a passionate quest for knowledge, and aroused in others the intellectual thirst.

John Scotus Erigena

The life story of the little Irishman of genius known as John Scotus Erigena is largely hidden from our knowledge. Since he was not a saint or an ecclesiastic, nobody thought it worth while to write his biography while the facts could have been recovered. His name doubly records the fact that he was born in Ireland, for "Scotus" in his time always meant "of Irish race," and "Erigena" (or Eriugena) means "Erin-born." He was one of an innumerable host of Irishmen of learning who, largely because of Danish invasions of Ireland, came in the ninth century to find a career on the Continent of Europe. We find him, a mature scholar, in the Palace School of Charles the Bald about 850. Pardulus, Bishop of Laon, then, probably at the suggestion of Hinkmar, induced him, as the Bishop himself writes, to undertake a refutation of Gottschalk's heretical teaching on predestination.

It has been thought that on coming from Ireland Erigena had joined the Irish residents of Laon, who probably constituted a colony of lay people. It is not certain that he was a monk or a priest; but he had most probably obtained his early training in some Irish monastery. The expression by which Pardulus describes him, "illum Scottum" ("that eminent Irishman"), indicates that he was a man of reputation, and he may have been already the chief master of the royal school. Thus far, however, he was apparently regarded as a "grammarian," that is, an expert in Latin, rather than a theologian. Whether the school was then situated at Laon or Reims or Paris, cannot be stated from the evidence. Erigena frequently dined with his royal patron, and reports of his table talk suggest that he was a humorist. Among these fragments is what is doubtless the most celebrated witticism of the Middle Ages. "Quid distat," asked the King over his wine, "inter Scottum et sottum?" ("What is the difference between, or lies between, an Irishman and a fool?") The Irishman retorted across the board, "Tabula tantum!" ("Only the table!") Jokes are improved by being connected with the immortals; this one can be shown to have been hoary in that age. It seems to have arisen from the failure of the Irish to sound the *c* in *Scottus* so as to satisfy Continental Latinists. Perhaps, however, Erigena, in the manner of many of our dinner orators, gave the *bon mot* a new popularity, as of recent vintage.

His work on predestination was promptly produced. It shocked his own friends and was condemned as heretical in councils of 855 and 859. In asserting predestination to good and not to evil, Erigena introduced a conception of the non-existence of evil which was derived from Neoplatonic Greek authors. The redoubtable Irishman was not taught by censure to abandon his alien studies and speculations. He accepted from the King a commission to translate from the Greek four treatises that went under the name of Dionysius the Areopagite, of which a fine uncial manuscript had been brought to Paris a quarter-century earlier. The translator probably believed these fifth century pseudonymous treatises to be the actual work of Paul's Athenian convert mentioned in Acts 17:34. On this supposition the Pseudo-Dionysius was read widely in Erigena's Latin throughout the Middle Ages; it was the chief source of the rise of Neoplatonic mysticism in the West. Anastasius, the papal librarian, who had been in Constantinople, criticized the translation as being too literal, but admitted his astonishment that "a barbarian from the ends of the earth" could have done it, and thought the Scot had been miraculously inspired. Greek experts seem to think it was the librarian who was the barbarian.

His astonishment has been shared by other medieval writers and by modern scholars, who have recognized the ample knowledge of Greek required to render the difficult thought of the original. A legend arose that Erigena had studied in Athens; but this is highly improbable. Recent scholarship favors the view that his mastery of Greek was acquired, not mainly in Ireland, but under Continental teachers. Ireland at least has the credit of having nurtured his superior brain. He certainly outclassed as a Grecian all known scholars with whom he may have come in contact.

His own thought was deeply affected by the writings of the Greek fathers and philosophers. The most notable of his original works, written about 867, is entitled *On the Division of the Universe*. Here, in an acute philosophical dialogue, he treats the four divisions of "nature" (that is, of all existing things): nature creating and not created; creating and created; created and not creating; and lastly, neither created nor creating,—God, the final cause to which all created things return. In treating of the return of all creatures to God he describes in lofty speculation an ascending series of existences resembling the emanations of Neoplatonic thought: the elements, light, life, sense, reason, intellect, the Word. The Word is identified with Christ, who incorporates all created things in himself and conveys them back to God. The influence of the Alexandrian fathers, Clement and Origen, is manifest here. The Neoplatonic drift to pantheism is also strongly apparent in the work. It further startled Western minds by a quite unorthodox emphasis on reason as prior to, and independent of, authority. The reference is primarily to the authority of the church fathers. There is no intention of questioning the authority of scripture; but by the full exercise of reason and imagination Erigena gave to scripture highly fantastic interpretations conceived in the interests of his mystical philosophy.

The circumstances of Erigena's later life, and of his own "return to nature uncreated and uncreating," are unknown to history. There is an inconclusive fragment of evidence that he was in the West Frank kingdom in 877, the year in which Charles the Bald died. The statement of William of Malmesbury that Erigena went to Wessex under Alfred and taught in Malmesbury ought not to be summarily dismissed. He had been tutor to the family of Charles, and hence to his daughter Judith, and he had probably met the boy Alfred at Judith's marriage in Verberie, 856. A few months after the death of Charles, Alfred crushed the Danes and won security. We know that he sought far and near for able teachers. Erigena had alienated the Frankish scholars by his writings, and, now that his patron was dead, may have welcomed a new opportunity in England. The story that he was finally stabbed to death by the pens of his infuriated students in Malmesbury is best treated with skepticism. It may take its origin in a figure of speech used by the nerve-wracked professor on reading exercises in elementary Latin. Or perhaps it is the literary sublimation of an impulse often felt, but rarely indulged, by students enduring the tyranny of the lecture room!

Erigena's was one of the most capable and fearless minds of all time. Like Roger Bacon four centuries later he was lonely from his very greatness. His influence upon contemporaries was far from being proportionate to his intellectual powers. But he achieved a two-fold contribution. By his translations he established the mystical tradition in the West. In his original works he explored the chief areas which the scholastics were to retread with less emancipated steps.

Anselm of Canterbury

The eleventh century opened with the scholar pope, Sylvester II, on the throne, who had been stimulated by the learning of the Spanish Arabs as had Erigena by the thought of the Greeks. But he wrote nothing of great importance, and he failed to make his scholarship fruitful in any educational movement. The century as a whole shows little general improvement on the ninth or tenth in educational conditions. But feudal units were beginning to congeal into national governments; and wherever governments were strong, monastery and cathedral schools were usually able to operate with a fair degree of security. Such was the fortunate situation of the rising abbey of Bec in Normandy when Anselm entered it in 1059.

Anselm was born in 1033 at Aosta in Savoy at the Italian end of the St. Bernard Pass. He was the son of a Lombard father and a Burgundian mother, both of noble rank. His father, Gundulf, could not be brought to consent to the early desire of his only son to become a monk; but he allowed the Benedictines of the town to teach the boy Latin. Anselm was out of sympathy with his father but continued to obey him till he was twenty-three. He grew up a clever learner, lonely, studious, and imaginative. Soon after the death of his mother in 1056, he left his home to become a wandering scholar. He crossed the Alps and for three years moved about the schools and cloisters of France. The fame of his fellow Lombard, Lanfranc, then abbot of Bec, drew him to the great Norman abbey.

He did not as yet purpose to become a monk, but to feast on the learning of Lanfranc. But when half a year later he was informed of his father's death (1060), he resolved to take the vows. At the advice of a prelate whom Lanfranc asked him to consult, he decided to neglect his inheritance in Aosta and to make his monastic home at Bec.

Three years later the fruitful association with Lanfranc was broken by the latter's removal to Caen. Herlwin, a pious ex-soldier, now became abbot, and Anselm prior, of the monastery. As prior he had a struggle with disturbers of the discipline, but he overcame his opponents by affection and generous behavior, and made a faithful friend of the most active of them, Osbern, whose early death was Anselm's greatest sorrow. Bec became a home of peace and good learning, and Anselm prayed, studied, taught and wrote. It was said that all the monks of Bec became philosophers under his instruction. In 1079 he succeeded Herlwin as abbot. Meanwhile England came under the rule of William of Normandy, and in 1070 Lanfranc was made Archbishop of Canterbury.

The abbot of Bec had widely separated daughter houses to visit, and fiefs to superintend on both sides of the channel; thus Anselm was obliged to engage in much administrative work and travel. He enjoyed the profound respect of the Conqueror, and the friendship and occasional society of Lanfranc; and he came to be favorably known in England. In 1087 William died, and William Rufus, his son and successor, in all things his father's inferior, became King. After Lanfranc's death, May 1089, the Red

King kept the See of Canterbury vacant for nearly five years, in order to enjoy the revenues. Then Anselm, having been induced to visit England to see a former friend, now ill, was put forward by admirers as a candidate for the archbishopric. The King would not have acted in the matter had he not fallen gravely ill. In expectation of death he confessed to Anselm his misdeeds and nominated him archbishop (1093).

When he hesitated from a sense of his monastic responsibilities and from the prospect of conflict with the impious and blustering Rufus, should he recover, Anselm was forcibly taken to his election by the bishops and clergy. The violent precipitancy of the bishops was due to their well-grounded fear that the King would change his mind; but Anselm wrote to Bec that their behavior seemed like that of lunatics. Later he told his brethren that in placing him beside Rufus they had yoked together a wild ox and a feeble ewe.

Thus at sixty years of age, and conscious of declining strength, Anselm entered on the most active phase of his career. The uncouth and violent-tempered King, who flung out insults freely to all, rarely spoke to him except discourteously. Anselm, on the other hand, was a completely self-disciplined gentleman, never failing in gracious dignity, but well aware of his rights and resolute of purpose. The controversy that followed was, however, not so one-sided as this personal comparison of the protagonists. It was due to the same conflict of principles that caused the clash of popes and emperors. Fundamentally it was a question of lordship, of the supremacy of the temporal or the spiritual ruler; and it involved numerous minor issues including the investiture of bishops, their recognition of the king's suzerainty, the king's exactions from church property, the authority of provincial synods, and the right of appeal to the pope. The fact that not only the ruffian Rufus, but the cultured and honorable Henry I, could not agree with Anselm, indicates that there was much to be said on the king's side.

We cannot here narrate the events of the dramatic struggle, which sent Anselm twice into prolonged exile (1097-1100 and 1103-1106). In 1107 a compromise was reached by which the king was to receive the homage of the bishops, but not the right of investiture with ring and staff. If we may not say that Anselm was always wholly right in his attitude in this strife, we cannot fail to admire the combination of firmness and good will which he maintained on all occasions. The world would be happier if its righteous controversialists would make Anselm their model. While not slack concerning practical and immediate issues, he was one of those "whose conversation is in heaven," and who, sustained by an inexhaustible fund of profound spiritual thought, can participate in the mutable and troublous affairs of church and state with a poise which is denied to superficial souls.

It is a satisfaction to note that Anselm's last years were spent in peace and honor. He died April 21, 1109, aged seventy-six.

Happily Anselm gave expression in writing to the wealth of his thought. While he was prior of Bec his lectures were so appreciated that he was asked by his pupils to edit them. As a result we have two books which show the basis of his religious philosophy, his *Monologion* and *Proslogion*. The theme of the former of these is "credo ut intelligam," "I believe in order that I may understand." Beginning with belief in God, Anselm brings rational support to that belief. Man's common desire of some particular real or supposed good implies the existence of an ultimate, universal good. He sees all nature in a chain or scale of beings ascending to one "highest nature" which is absolute being and has created all things of nothing. He calls this Absolute "supreme essence, life, reason, salvation, righteousness, wisdom, truth, goodness, greatness, beauty, immortality, incorruptibility, immutability, blessedness, eternity, power, unity, none other than the Supreme Being."

In the *Proslogion* Anselm attempts to set forth a ready and effective proof of that first fundamental of dogma, the existence of God. There is perhaps no more famous fragment of human thought than Anselm's "ontological argument" here presented and expounded. God is "that than which nothing greater is thinkable." Since the term "the highest thinkable" ("summum cogitabile") is intelligible, it exists in the understanding; but because it exists in the understanding it must exist in reality, else it is not the highest thinkable—since to exist in reality is higher than to exist in the understanding alone. Thus reason requires belief in God, and it is the fool, and not the man of reason, who "hath said in his heart: there is no God."

A monk named Gaunilon took up what he called "the Case for the Fool." He applied Anselm's logic to an imaginary island in the ocean, to show that the syllogism proves nothing, though it makes the head swim. Such will always be the answer of common sense to Anselm's sublime speculation. It is worthy of note that the argument first flashed upon his mind, after long cogitation, while he was in deep contemplation at mass. Only a mind withdrawn from the objective realities of life, and captured by the Platonic conception of the reality of universal ideas, can rest in such a proof of God. It is in the same book that Anselm furnishes a motto for piety in the words, "Take some leisure for God, and rest for a little in Him. Enter the chamber of thy mind; shut out all things except God and whatever will aid thee in seeking Him." This concentration upon God and things divine is the most valuable emphasis of the book. In this he is reviving Augustine's adaptation of the Platonic heritage to Christianity, though the language is partly indebted to Jesus.

Anselm's high Platonic realism is lucidly stated in his controversy with John Roscellin of Compiègne, over a question thrown out but not answered by the Neoplatonist Porphyry. Roscellin taught that genera and species have no reality in themselves, but are merely convenient ways of grouping the individual things in which there is reality. We might say that there is no reality represented by the expression "man," but there is reality in the men Tom, Dick, and Harry. General terms are mere *nomina*, names; hence Roscellin's thought came to be called *nominalism*. Anselm's contrary view was called *realism*, since it asserted the reality of universals and their priority to individuals ("universale ante rem"). Roscellin's theological application of the nominalistic philosophy naturally resolved the doctrine of the Trinity into a doctrine of three separate realities, and so destroyed the unity of the Godhead. For this assault on dogma he was disciplined in 1092 and compelled to make what was apparently an insincere recantation. Anselm, just before leaving Bec for Canterbury, wrote a treatise on the Trinity against Roscellin. He here defends the traditional doctrine in terms of realism, using the telling illustration of the source, the river and the lake of a watercourse which for convenience, and in ignorance of geography, he calls the Nile. His fountain is Nile, his lake is Nile, his river is Nile; any two, or all three of them, are Nile (Godhead).

Anselm's most influential book was finished during his first exile, the *Cur Deus Homo?*, which treats of the Atonement of Christ. Why, he asks, did God become man? It is characteristic that the fact of God's becoming man in Jesus' earthly life is not questioned but assumed. Anselm's faith must, however, "seek a reason." He uses the name of Boso, a former pupil in Bec, as a sort of devil's advocate in the dialogue of the book. No summary can give an adequate suggestion of the involved yet cumulative argument of this widely read work. As compared with earlier theologians Anselm may be said to lift the doctrine of the atonement to a new plane. He spurns the idea, which goes back to Origen of Alexandria, that Christ's sufferings were a ransom paid to the devil. He also rejects the view that the death of Christ involved God's condemnation of the guiltless. Instead the Son voluntarily took on himself humanity, in order that as man he might make atonement to the Father for the offense of man's sin. Sin for Anselm involves a quantitative debt which is incurred by violation of God's honor. And since he whose honor is violated is divine, the debt can only be paid by a divine satisfaction such as only the God-Man could give. It is evident that his thought is here affected by the customs of feudal society and its penal laws, by which offenders against persons were subject to penalties proportioned to the rank of the person injured and not to the injury alone. The whole treatment is to modern minds too artificial and juridical to have more than a historical interest. But at least it was the first exposition of the doctrine which showed adequate respect for ethical considerations.

We saw (pp. 18, 55) that the doctrine of the Holy Spirit had been a point of disagreement between the Latins and the Greeks since the ninth century, and that the two churches had been severed in 1054. An attempt at reunion was the principal business of the Council of Bari in southern Italy in 1098, shortly after the launching of the first crusade. Anselm, then in exile from England, was invited by the Pope, Urban II, to this council. Urban, in defending *filioque* made use of Anselm's metaphor of the fountain, the stream and the lake; and when the Greeks present were unconvinced he called out: "Father Anselm, Archbishop of the English, where art thou?" Anselm emerged from the throng of over 180 prelates, and presented the Latin position, to the great approval of the Westerns. He afterwards put together the ideas of this discourse in a book, *On the Procession of the Holy Spirit,* which is the classic of medieval Western thought on this subject. He gave a new direction to the discussion of the doctrine by resting his argument upon a fundamental philosophy of the Trinity rather than on the detailed utterances of the fathers.

Such in brief are the more celebrated works of the gifted Lombard who by his original and challenging ways of rationalizing the dogmas of the church, aroused the Western mind to philosophic interests and laid the basis of the scholastic movement. In contrast with that of Erigena, his thought is typically Latin: speculation is kept well within the bounds of orthodoxy.

Anselm was not only a philosophical theologian, but a personality of rare charm. His saintliness was unobtrusive, and his canonization, lacking popular demand, was postponed to the time of Alexander VI (1494). He was as gentle as he was resolute and as modest as he was learned. Some aspects of his character would have won the admiration of the stoic Marcus Aurelius. His calm in times of crisis almost suggests superciliousness, but it was due to his habit of absorption in great thoughts. After a tumultuous scene in which he was threatened by the Red King and his servile bishops, they noted that he slept soundly. Perhaps he might in some instances have appeared temporarily more successful if he had shown himself more aggressive. But without threat or boast, he adhered tenaciously to his ideals, and won from the sons of the Conqueror concessions which the angry hostility of a Hildebrand might not have secured.

Anselm was, moreover, one of the most humane men of that violent time. He once, near Windsor, protected an exhausted hare from both hounds and hunters, likening it to a poor dying soul pursued by demons. In his conception of the discipline of boys in school he was far in advance of his age. A perplexed abbot once came to him to explain that he had dutifully flogged his pupils "day and night," with the result, surprising to him, that they grew up brutal and dull. Anselm asked the abbot how a tree would grow if all its branches were so tied up that they could not wave. "How would you like it yourself?" he asked, and went on to condemn the inhuman severity of the method, and to urge the use of kindness, encouragement, and forbearance toward the young scholars. It is evident that in his own teaching he practiced the more enlightened procedure. In all this he was a force leading to a higher humanity. He was, in short, one of the most Christian and one of the most civilized men of the Middle Ages.

Peter Abailard

Peter Abailard was twenty-one when the twelfth century opened, a century eventful in intellectual history. The total area of available knowledge was in process of rapid extension. The Laws of Justinian had become at Bologna the basis of a new legal science which was to be a mighty force in the making of monarchical states. Constantius Africanus had brought from the Moslems of Sicily ancient texts on medicine, by which that science was to be remade. Contemporary with Abailard were such innovators as the Englishman Adelard of Bath, who visited Sicily and Syria and brought back Euclid and astronomical science; John Gratian, the codifier of canon law; and the Spanish prelate, Raimond of Toledo who employed a college of translators to make available to Latins the lore of Arabian philosophers. Trained scholars and eager students were multiplied in number. Some were learned and romantic hoboes in whose ears Lucan, Ovid, Horace, Vergil and Catullus had sung, and who echoed their classic masters in gay or plaintive lyrics of their loves and adventures. But most frequented the growing cloister and cathedral schools, or adhered to teachers who set up their chairs in response to the opportunity presented by assembled numbers. The rise of an economically prosperous class was making possible the release of many young men for pursuits of the mind. The passion for knowledge was to surpass the passion for holiness. Before the century's end it becomes apparent that the monastery will recede as the university advances. The emergence of the supreme institution of learning marks the beginning of a steady and cumulative progress in the culture of the West.

Abailard came from Brittany, whose people were of Celtic stock and of independent spirit. His father, Berengar, was a knight of Palet near Nantes, who had learned Latin in youth and who became a monk in old age. His wife Lucia, Abailard's mother, followed her son's career till he was past thirty, and in the end also entered a cloister. Peter, their first child, was born in 1079. He early acquired a fluent use of Latin and became an eager student of the Latin classics, and of dialectics. "Allured by the love of learning," he says, he "fled the court of Mars" (his father's calling and estate) "to be nurtured in the bosom of Minerva." He probably completed the Trivium under Roscellin, the nominalist, a fellow-Breton, and under Thierry of Chartres labored at the Quadrivium (arithmetic, geometry, astronomy, and music) but was disgraced in mathematics. He "wandered disputing through various provinces" like a knight-errant seeking a worthy foe, all the while acquiring the skill that was to bring him fame.

At Paris William of Champeaux, a high realist like Anselm of Canterbury, was teaching logic in the cathedral school. Abailard was thirty, William thirty-nine. Abailard entered his classes, offered criticisms, and obtained such a response that he resolved to become at once a professor himself. The step could then be simply taken. In the royal castle at Melun he opened a course of lectures, and drew some of William's students. He moved to Corbeil, nearer Paris, to William's greater embarrassment. But illness sent the upstart professor for a long visit to his home. When he came back to Paris, his rival had founded and entered a house of canons. Abailard, however, clashed with him again, winning the verdict of the students. He claims that William was forced to abandon his realism, and to move his school from the city. But he was able to prevent Abailard from entering the chair in the cathedral school. William soon afterwards became bishop of Châlons, in which office he died, 1117.

Determined to win Paris, Abailard now "pitched the tent of his school" on Mont Ste. Geneviève, a short mile south of the cathedral, and drew a large and increasing body of students, emptying the class-rooms of the cathedral where a new lecturer had been installed by William. From this success he was called by his mother to help arrange her affairs, as she was to enter a cloister. Whether on her advice, or for some other reason, he next went to Laon to study theology. Perhaps the motive, at least in part, was to tilt against another realist, the venerable Anselm, or Ansellus, of Laon, called by many admirers "doctor of doctors." This Anselm was a pupil of his namesake, Anselm of Canterbury.

Abailard describes his new teacher with sheer contempt. He was a tree with full foliage but no fruit, "the very figtree which our Lord cursed." When he ceased to attend Anselm's lectures he was himself challenged to lecture on a difficult passage in Ezekiel. The result was a course of lectures given with increased acclaim. Abailard, in his early thirties, had discredited the paladins of realism before the students; but he had made enemies of their more loyal adherents, who would have their revenge by ecclesiastical process.

Returning to Paris he became master of the cathedral school, and was the center of attraction for the student life not only of France but of Western Europe. He lectured now to thousands—clerics, monks, splendidly attired nobles and starveling scholars, a mixed multitude from the provinces of France, England, Germany, Scandinavia, Italy, Spain. Ladies of rank appeared among them; Abailard avoided their personal acquaintance. Others peered from their windows in admiration as he passed in early morning from his lodgings on Ste. Geneviève to Notre Dame. What academic teacher ever enjoyed such popular esteem?

His success, as friend and foe affirm, was due to his unique combination of intellectual gifts and personal charm; and it was probably the latter that gave him his public advantage over opponents, and his popularity with the average student. He was of fair complexion, we are told, in form slender and handsome, and his fine eyes, noble countenance and persuasive voice gave him an exceptionally pleasing public presence. His acute powers of argumentation were aided by a ready fund of literary knowledge and a mastery of the devices of rhetoric. But for a weakness of character he might have dominated his century as he dominated the Latin Quarter. But from this peak he fell.

Hitherto he had matched his gifts with men. He was now to use his personal charms upon a woman of personality almost as remarkable as his own, mingling her life with his in shame and piteous tragedy. Let Abailard make his own confession:

But since prosperity always puffs up fools, and earthly tranquillity relaxes the vigor of the mind and readily dissolves it by the allurements of the flesh, when I was already thinking myself the only philosopher left in the world, and not fearing any further occasion of disquiet, I, who had hitherto lived most continently, began to loose the rein to lust.

He was thirty-nine; Heloise, niece and ward of canon Fulbert of Notre Dame, was seventeen. He admired her beauty and her precocious learning. The trustful uncle welcomed the scholar to his house to be her tutor during his free time, giving him all the medieval tutor's complete control of her conduct. He had, says Abailard, entrusted a tender lamb to a ravenous wolf. She responded to his courtship. The renowned philosopher proved a matchless composer and singer of love-songs, while his lectures became lifeless repetitions of old material. With sorrow and rage Fulbert learned that his confidence had been betrayed. Heloise was taken to the house of Abailard's sister, where their son, Astrolabius, was born. They were later married; though she wished to avoid this, and even denied the fact to save her lover's career. Her devotion was complete and enduring. Nearly twenty years later she wrote that she would rather have been the mistress of Abailard than the empress of an Augustus.

She returned to Fulbert's house; but he was unforgiving and for her safety from his anger she was taken to reside, not beyond reach of her husband's visits, in the nunnery of Argenteuil, whose abbess may possibly have been her own mother. Fulbert plotted a savage revenge. Bribing Abailard's valet, he entered his bed-chamber with armed ruffians, and by an act of mutilation rendered him unfit both for marriage and for holy orders. Next morning the town was in an uproar. It was not a humane age; two of the perpetrators who were caught were similarly mutilated, and blinded. Fulbert escaped from the city.

Heloise took the veil at Argenteuil, and Abailard, overwhelmed with misery, entered the historic monastery of St. Denis, whose disorderly state he vainly attempted to correct. He opened a school in a dependent priory in Champagne, and again students assembled. A confused synod at Soissons, 1121, condemned and burned his book *On the Divine Unity and Trinity*, and placed him under restraint for heresy; but he was soon released to return to St. Denis. Frequenting the library, he unluckily found a passage in Bede which led him to think that St. Denis of Montmartre could not have been Dionysius the Areopagite. Abbot Adam was infuriated. Foul heresy, this retailing of English Bede's insult to France! Some friends among the monks spirited Abailard away to Champagne, and the irate Adam died suddenly while seeking his return, and was succeeded by the great Suger, trusted minister of Louis the Fat. Somebody intervened with the King in Abailard's behalf, and Suger generously released him from obedience.

At Nogent-sur-Seine in a wooded valley in Champagne, the outcast built for himself a hermitage (1122). But the student army learned of his freedom; they "left towns and castles" and sought out their idol in the wilderness. They constructed an oratory for him and a town of huts about it, and he called the place the Paraclete (Comforter). His foes might gnash their teeth. But soon he learned that new enemies were being enlisted against him, and he lived in deadly fear of the hostility of Bernard of Clairvaux and Norbert of Xanten.

Unexpectedly he was elected abbot of the ancient Celtic monastery of St. Gildas at Rhuys, on the Breton coast. Discipline in this abbey had completely broken down, and the monks violently resisted the new abbot's attempts to reform them. After four years in peril of death at their hands, he fled (1132?).

Meanwhile Heloise became prioress of Argenteuil, and

then the nunnery properties were taken over by Suger, and the occupants dispersed (1129). Abailard invited the prioress to form a community on the deserted site of the Paraclete, and with Pope Innocent II's assent the new nunnery was established. Heloise proved an exemplary abbess; but her letters to Abailard abundantly show that her emotions still centered in the singing and sinful philosopher of Paris days. The impersonal correctness of Abailard's replies may conceal a profound affection. Had he been indifferent to Heloise he would never have invited her to the Paraclete. He had cause to think that, should his letters fall into hostile hands, every syllable would be studied for evidence of new improprieties. These letters were called forth by his immortal *Story of My Calamities* (1133?) of which a copy came to the Paraclete. From this priceless fragment of medieval autobiography most of the quoted passages in this sketch have been taken. It is comparable to the *Confessions* of Augustine; but Abailard is less penitent and more aggrieved. Yet he brings himself to an acceptance of his fate: "The goodness of God humbled me, and won me to itself."

In 1136 Abailard resumed his old "camp" on Ste. Geneviève, and during most of the next five years was in or near Paris, writing and teaching. But the net of ecclesiastical power was closing about him, held in the firm hands of the holy man of Clairvaux. Bernard had been closely bound to the fallen rivals of Abailard, William and Anselm; the former indeed had ordained him a priest. Bernard's friend, William of St. Thierry, drew up proofs of Abailard's heresy. Abailard in his *Calamities* had complained of Bernard and Norbert as active enemies. The conduct of Arnold of Brescia, a pupil of Abailard and a stout radical, had aroused Bernard's anxiety and fury.

About 1140 Bernard, aged forty-nine, interviewed the sixty-one-year-old philosopher, and failed to convert him. He warned students against the "poison" of Abailard's books. The students sought a disputation between the antagonists; Bernard at first declined, but later decided to attend a meeting which was to be held at Sens, June 4, 1141. But on the eve of the appointed day he secured a gathering of bishops in which Abailard was condemned in absence. Whether the bishops were so bibulous and sleepy that Sunday night (as one reported at the time) that they could only say "'namus" ("we swim") for "damnamus" ("we condemn"), does not much matter in our judgment of the fairness of the procedure. Before the assembly next day, with Louis VII presiding, Abailard, seeing the faces of Bernard's admirers under many an episcopal miter, and knowing their intent, merely protested that he would not be "judged as a criminal," and appealed to the Pope. He did not appreciate the power of Bernard in Rome. Innocent II, who owed his throne to Bernard and Norbert, obeyed the wishes of the oracle of Clairvaux, and excommunicated the victim, July 16, 1141.

Abailard left Sens for Rome, but halted at Cluny, whose kindly abbot, Peter the Venerable, gave him all possible comfort during the months he had to live. The worn-out warrior of the mind gave himself to devotion, reading and writing. He addressed an *Admonition* to his son who lived obscurely as a monk. For his failing health the abbot sent Abailard to the abbey of St. Marcellus at Chalon-sur-Saône; he died there, April 21, 1142, aged sixty-three.

Why was Abailard, the idol of students, abhorred by the

responsible churchmen? Much that he taught was alarming to the guardians of the ecclesiastical institution; and he flung out his ideas unguardedly upon the "student mind." Although the aged Roscellin was among his enemies, his doctrine of universals approached so near to Roscellin's as to cause him to be, in his own century, designated a nominalist. This is, however, misleading. For him the universal has existence in the like or identical qualities by which the individual things are drawn together in the mind's experience of them. This view has been called conceptualism; a term which the historians of philosophy have left somewhat ambiguous. But it was his employment of dialectic upon the sources of Christianity that seemed most subversive. In *Sic et Non* (*For and Against*) he set over against each other irreconcilable passages of the fathers and scriptures. For instance, he cites the New Testament passages for and against the proposition "that all the apostles had wives except John." In the Preface he dared to infer from these contradictions that prophets, apostles, and the authoritative writers of the early church alike, had made mistakes. Such a view was still alarming in the nineteenth century, and is so in some quarters today. Abailard never said, as often stated, "Intelligo ut credam" ("I understand in order that I may believe"); but he did say "Inquirendo veritatem percipimus" ("by research we acquire truth"). The offense lay even more in the presuppositions and method of Abailard than in his actual revision of dogma. Not less than Erigena, he assumed the authority of reason and the value of criticism. This quality of mind is hostile to the Platonic-Augustinian mysticism of Anselm and his school, as Bernard fully realized.

On the Trinity his opponents selected his example of the

copper seal—its material, the stamped image upon it, and the image which it stamps when used—as destroying the equality of Father, Son and Spirit. This they miscalled Arianism; and they charged him with Sabellianism, or modalism, for his application of the terms "power," "wisdom," and "goodness" to the persons of the Trinity. Abailard repulses these charges in an *Apology* addressed to Bernard, written in Cluny, in which he shows that he has been misunderstood through lack of discernment by his cpponents of the meaning and use of words.

In his *Know Thyself* he develops his ethics of intention or consent. Not desire to sin, but the will to sin, brings guilt. Constitutional moral weakness, for instance a proneness to anger or lust, is morally neutral until the will consents. He uses the illustration of hungry men passing through an orchard of ripe fruit. This seemed a dangerous sophistication of morals, since it frankly rests guilt or innocence upon intention rather than action, and intention is difficult to deal with in the routine of discipline. Indeed, in the treatment of penance, Abailard denies that every priest can absolve from sin: the power to absolve was given to the Apostles alone. This amounted to an assault on the foundations of the medieval sacerdotal system, and shows the link of connection between the radicalism of Abailard and that of the anti-sacerdotal heretic, Arnold of Brescia. The point was not overlooked by his opponents.

Concerned with motive and intention as primary in ethics, Abailard treats the atonement as the incitement of love in human hearts by the tragic sorrow of the cross. The passion of Christ is exemplary. Men beholding it are given a new motivation in a love that binds the soul to Christ and frees it from the impulses of sin. This goes a long step beyond Anselm's quantitative theory of satisfaction; it virtually eliminates the notion of vicariousness in the sufferings of Christ and gives the doctrine a moral emphasis. The adoption of such a view would have meant an institutional as well as a theological revolution which, naturally enough, the mitered prelates at Sens did not crave. They, and Bernard in writing to the pope, fulminated against this construction of the doctrine, which seemed to them to undermine the Catholic faith.

Abailard was defeated, but from our modern point of vantage, it seems that in many respects he was a successful pioneer. The rise of the universities was aided by the popularity of his teaching. Scholasticism followed in modified form his method of inquiry, and this method is seen in its full development in modern critical thought. Only half aware of the significance of Aristotle, many of whose works he could not obtain, he was, nevertheless, a natural Aristotelian. He helped to prepare Europe for the thirteenth century reign of "the Philosopher," and in some measure anticipated the modern valuation of objective knowledge.

Thomas Aquinas

The age of mental sterility had been left behind; the Western mind was agitated and productive. Between the death of Abailard and the birth of Aquinas the earlier universities were organized; Aristotle's Physics, Metaphysics, and Ethics were introduced to Western readers; and the two orders of friars, Franciscan and Dominican, came on the scene. Through these three instrumentalities education was put on an entirely new basis.

While Robert Pullen at Oxford and Peter Lombard at Paris were supplying their students with safe and sane text-books in theology, called *Sentences*, a new assault on dogma was in preparation—not a revolt from within but an invasion from without. If crusaders assailed the military forces of Islam, Moslem learning menaced the fortresses of Christian thought. The twelfth century Spanish Moslem, Averroes, though ignorant of Greek, synthetized the Arabian studies of Aristotle. His conceptions of the eternity of matter and the unity of intellect were now to challenge the Christian doctrines of creation, the personality of God, and immortality. He was controverted in Spain by Maimonides, whose philosophic defense of Judaism anticipated the scholastic defense of Christianity. Frederick II sent a Scotsman in his service, Michael Scot, with other scholars, to Spain to gather the fruit of these Aristotelian studies. They, with Jewish help, obtained by about 1230 defective but invaluable translations of the higher works of Aristotle, the *Commentary* of Averroes, and Maimonides' *Guide to the Perplexed*. These treatises formed merely the core of a vast new translation literature of philosophy.

Alexander of Hales, an English Franciscan, was the first scholastic writer to face fully the new thought situation. Before he died in 1245 he had defended the faith in tomes so vast that Roger Bacon contemptuously described them as "more than a load for a horse." Others, too, labored industriously to make a way for dogma through the new knowledge. But their efforts did not prevent the rise of frank Averroism at Paris. The leader of this movement, Siger de Brabant, was a contemporary of Aquinas.

Thomas of Aquino was born in 1225 in the castle that stood on Rocca Sicca, a crag in the Apennines. He was the last of seven sons of the count and countess of Aquino, Landulph and Theodora. He was sent for schooling to the nearby abbey of St. Benedict, Monte Cassino, of which an uncle was abbot. Later at Naples Peter the Irishman taught him the Quadrivium; Peter, being a student of Aristotle, probably introduced the boy to the works of the Stagirite.

The sons of St. Dominic were now waxing great in the earth. To preach the faith and combat heresy they stressed the function of teaching, and their scholarship won them an entrance, much grudged by the organized guilds of the professors, into the tasks of university instruction. In 1244 young Thomas, a large, clumsy youth of nineteen, entered the Dominican order at Naples. The friars sent him to slake his thirst for knowledge at Paris. His family despised the mendicants and disapproved violently of this course of action; his brother waylaid him and confined him in a castle; but a year later he took his way, accompanied by the General of the Order, to the metropolis of learning.

At Paris in 1245 the Bavarian Dominican, Albert, called the Great, was the chief attraction to theological students. This genius who as a scholastic stands second only to his great pupil, was a little, bald-headed, eager man, twenty-two years the senior of Thomas. We may picture him sizing up the bulky young Neapolitan, noting the noble head above the ridiculously massive body, and gradually becoming aware of the unique powers so singularly housed. The shy reticence of the hulking youth led his fellow students to nick-name him "the Dumb Sicilian Ox." But Albert, on seeing some of his written work, called a halt to their ridicule. "The bellowing of the Dumb Ox," he told his class, "will resound through all the world." Thomas was indebted to Albert for much more than knowledge.

In marked contrast to the course followed by Abailard,

Thomas settled down to absorb gratefully all that Albert had to give him. He would make his own reservations and improvements of it; but he would get all there was of it. There was so much to get that even Abailard might have listened with approval. The patient genius sat for seven years at his master's feet, first at Paris and later at Cologne where a notable school was established (1248) in which Thomas was Albert's student assistant. Then in 1252, his novitiate ended and his thought mature, he entered at Paris on his independent teaching career.

In the convent of St. James on Mont Ste. Geneviève the Dominicans had challenged the ascendancy of the university doctors and secured teaching privileges from the pope. A hot contest was now arising, in which William of St. Amour, spokesman for the professors, flayed the friars and their mendicancy, while Thomas replied effectively for his brethren. The Dominicans obtained from Alexander IV a renewal of their teaching privileges. Thomas received the degree of master only in 1256, this step having been delayed by the controversy. He was now in the full tide of his career, winning the sober admiration of increasing numbers. He had become a good talker, a convincing lecturer, and a gracious and amiable gentleman.

He was sheltered from the world's distractions, not only by the religious environment provided by his order, but also by the strong fortress of his own mind. On occasions when he was drawn into affairs of the church or mingled in the society of great men, he sometimes retreated mentally to the happier and more orderly realm of his thought. Once having been induced to dine with Louis IX, the mighty Capetian King, he lapsed into a reverie amid the din of the table. Suddenly his face beamed with achievement, and he brought down his heavy fist with a bang, exclaiming: "That finishes the Manichæans!" The King, willing to have them finished, sent for writing materials that the useful argument might be recorded.

Thomas spent a long period in Italy, whether called by Urban IV in 1261, or by his predecessor. Urban had him deliver courses of lectures in various Italian centers. In 1263 he represented the Roman province in a chapter general of his order in London. He was sought for a number of episcopal sees, and in 1265 Clement IV appointed him to the archbishopric of Naples; but he steadfastly, if tearfully, declined. In 1267 he was appointed to the chair of theology in Bologna. Two years later he returned, at King Louis's request, to Paris; but he was back in Italy soon after the King's death, and settled in the familiar scene of Naples.

In his personal life, more than in his writings, Thomas was a mystic. His abstraction was not merely that of an absent-minded professor. He habitually engaged in protracted vigils and contemplative prayer. On December 6, 1273, while celebrating mass in St. Nicholas Church, Naples, he experienced an ecstasy which left him unwilling to write more. A friend urged him to complete his unfinished *Summa theologica*, but he replied that in the light of the revelation he had received, all that he had written seemed as chaff. Not long thereafter Gregory X summoned him to attend the great council that was to meet in Lyons for the settlement of the long dispute with the Greeks. Abscesses in his legs had impaired his health, but he started unhesitatingly on the journey. As he rode through Teano, he struck his head against the limb of a tree which a storm had left leaning over the road. At the castle of Magenza he became ill, and asked for a certain variety of herring which had been his favorite dish in France. The herring was procured; revived, he went on to a Cistercian house at Fossa Nuova. At the plea of the monks he began to dictate a commentary on the *Song of Songs,* a book which Bernard, as we saw, had taught the Cistercians specially to cherish. But his strength failed, and death claimed him, March 7, 1274. So innocent was his spirit that the priest who heard his last confession said it was the confession of a child of five.

When Thomas began his work of teaching, the fundamentals of theological instruction were the Bible and the *Sentences* of Peter Lombard. The Bible was sacrosanct; the *Sentences* useful and to a degree authoritative. Scholastic predecessors had begun the task of relating Aristotle to these fundamentals. Thomas had the advantage of standing on their shoulders, particularly on the shoulders of Albert the Great. But the field of actual knowledge to be absorbed was enormous and still expanding. He brought to the task a capacious memory and an almost unique orderliness of thought. He achieved an astonishing work of rethinking the old doctrines in terms of the new learning.

He secured fresh and adequate translations, and kept himself up-to-date in all the branches of knowledge. There was, however, one important interest of Albert to which he gave only minor attention, the realm of physical science. He was not opposed to such studies, but he had no vision of their importance for theology. Albert experimented to test the popular belief that horsehairs if left in water will turn into worms. Through some defect in the laboratory conditions he concluded that the belief was sound. The point is that he experimented. We do not find Thomas interesting himself directly in such matters. His absorption in ideas tended to lead scholasticism away from a field of investigation that has transformed the modern world; and the fact partly justified the bitter complaint of Roger Bacon (1214-1294) of the neglect of the experimental method. The great Franciscan scientist has had his way with us for the past century. Yet in the cycle of scientific thought we have been led back to the ultimate questions with which the scholastics were primarily concerned.

One who reads the lucid, dispassionate, balanced paragraphs of the Angelic Doctor, may receive such an impression of the author's composure and calm of mind as to forget that his whole labor was a warfare for the medieval church and her creed against a series of redoubtable foes. He seldom does his opponents the honor of naming them, and never resorts to the baseness of attacking them in a personal way. His real antagonists are ideas, not men. Yet he can be adequately understood only in the light of the forces he opposed in the great battle-ground of the Paris schools. He fought the battle of the Dominicans against the guild of Paris professors. He assailed and defeated the Averroists led by Siger of Brabant, at the same time claiming Aristotle against Siger's doctrine of the universal soul which the Arabian had professed to derive from the Greek master. He vindicated the Aristotelian studies, which Averroism had cast into disrepute among the orthodox, against an Englishman of his own order, Robert Kilwardby, and the English Franciscan, John Peckham. And he combated the Augustinian emphasis on predestination represented by his friend, Bonaventura, the distinguished general of the Franciscans. The echoes of these controversies may be discovered in much of his later writing. What he thought of Roger Bacon's objections we do not know. He was a man of exceptional humility; and it is not impossible that the "revelation" of the futility of his writings may have been in part a realization that his critics were not so far wrong as his admirers would have him believe.

Thomas was forty-nine when he died. He had been writing books for less than a quarter of a century. Yet the number and range of his books are very great. Dr. Martin Grabmann lists eighty titles. The most important are the apologetic work *Contra Gentiles* (*Against the Heathen*), written 1259-1264, and the systematic work, *Summa theologica*, of which Parts I and II were written between 1269 and 1272, and Part III was left incomplete. The former treatise was primarily intended for the instruction of Dominican missionaries among the Spanish Moslems and Jews. The *Summa theologica*, resuming the more important positions of the numerous early works, presents on an elaborate plan the whole system of theology. It was written, says the author, "for the instruction of beginners"; but the modern reader will hardly consider it elementary.

He was anxious, he says, to avoid "the multiplication of useless questions and arguments." Such futilities of his predecessors as "whether God can do more than everything" are eliminated. He does not escape the impression of massed detail, but the details do not run away with the plan. The items are bound together in an organic whole, as orderly as the structure of a cathedral. His method, an adaptation of the disputations of the classroom, is to propound a question, recite, usually from authorities, the leading objections to the answer he is to give; state the principal points that have been adduced on the favorable side, and finally draw his own conclusion in one or more statements or theses, usually supported by fresh arguments against the objections first presented. The pedagogic advantage of such a method is considerable. The teacher's thought is registered against contrasted opinions; and the possibility of vagueness or ambiguity in the reader's mind is reduced to a minimum. When once the vocabulary is acquired the argument can be followed with the intellectual satisfaction of a proposition of Euclid, or the delight of a well-ordered drama moving from scene to scene with cumulative power.

With Aristotle on his desk, Thomas could not rest satisfied with the logic of the Platonic realists. Nor is his position on universals either nominalism or conceptualism. It is best described as Aristotelian realism. The universal has reality, but its real existence is in the individual thing, not apart from it (*universale in re*). This position invalidates the ontological argument as stated by Anselm. For rational proof of the existence of God, Thomas relies mainly on the cosmological argument, which is based upon the metaphysics of Aristotle. All that exists has a cause, save the cause behind the series of causes. This first uncaused cause (primum movens quod a nullo movetur) is the eternal God. But if he finds the argument for God in Aristotle, the God he describes is the God of Augustine.

In the section of the *Summa* known as the *Ethics* (the first division of Part II), he sets forth the fundamental principles of the Christian practical life. For Thomas the chief end of man is the contemplation of truth. Here he quotes Augustine's phrase, "Happiness (beatitudo, blessedness) is joy in truth." The "last end" or supreme objective of humans cannot be in the active life which they share with the lower creatures, but only in the contemplative life which they share with God and the angels. For this Thomas has been called an "intellectualist" in contrast to Duns Scotus, who with his emphasis on the will has been described as a "voluntarist"; but to stress the contrast would be misleading. Thomas defines blessedness as "the final perfection of the rational or intellectual nature." Since God is "the highest intelligible good" our earthly bliss is in such partial contemplation of God as is here possible, and this is faith's anticipation of the perfect blessedness of the future life, "when we shall see God as he is." The moral virtues, with their attendant good works, are useful in preparing for, and disposing toward, the higher contemplation.

Thus is the whole practical phase of life subordinated to the celestial blessedness of the church triumphant. Men are so to live, eat, exercise, buy and sell, and rulers are so to govern, as to make preparation for that celestial life. All such matters are "means to attain that end." In the third book of the *Gentiles* he points out that bodily health, the exclusion of passion through the virtues, and the social peace of good government, are means toward the end of contemplation. On this Augustinian basis the ethics of Thomas is built up of materials largely derived from Aristotle, with fragments from Augustine and other fathers, and from medieval writers.

In the *Ethics*, and in his unfinished *Governance of Princes*, Thomas gives wise advice on politics. Though by no means a complete pacifist, he lays great emphasis upon peace as the chief good of society. The ruler is charged with the economic well-being of the citizens, which he must establish, maintain and promote. Political power, since it has to do with the temporal life, is subordinate to spiritual power, which ministers to man's eternal good. Since the spiritual power is for Thomas resident in the pope and the hierarchy, temporal rulers are subject to the Papacy. From Aristotle, from numerous medieval writers before him, perhaps from the constitution of the Dominican order, Thomas learned to appreciate deeply the principles of representative government; so that those who overlook his predecessors in this sometimes present him as the beginner of the strain of teaching that runs through Locke and Jefferson. There is no doubt of the fact that he gives countenance to this view of the political state. But for him the church is, by divine constitution, monarchical; and since he made political government finally subordinate to the divine right monarch of the church, even as the things of this life are secondary to those of the life to come, in last analysis it is doubtful whether his teaching promoted the development of government by the people.

The great Aristotelian was primarily a churchly theologian. In his treatment of the seven sacraments, in his view of the hierarchy and the Papacy, in his hymns and sermons, he is ever simply and reverently loyal to the traditions of medieval religion. His importance lies not so much in his originality as in the unrivaled clarity and persuasive force of the arguments with which he defended the medieval church in the thirteenth century intellectual crisis.

The modern church of Rome has expressed its gratitude to and admiration for Thomas Aquinas in superlative terms. But humanity at large also owes him a great debt, as it does to anyone who devotes superior powers of mind to the ultimate problems concerning God, and man's highest good. We profit by turning from the perplexing events among which we move, to the pages of a writer who saw all things in the light of the eternal. And when we imagine we are thinkers, it may be salutary to reëxamine, in the questions of Aquinas, the way in which some of the world's choicest thinking has been done.

Desiderius Erasmus

The Aristotelian renaissance of the twelfth and thirteenth centuries was followed by the Platonic renaissance of the fourteenth and fifteenth centuries. But there was a vast difference in the degree of assimilation of the ancient culture on which the two movements fed. With a few distinguished exceptions the older scholars were dependent on translations; the humanists were, or aimed to be, proficient in Greek and Hebrew. They were possessed, too, of avid zeal for the enlargement of knowledge, and surveyed a greatly extended area of the ancient literature. Some of them, led by Lorenzo Valla (d. 1457), learned to treat documents critically. Yet they were poles removed from mere pedantry. If they were fascinated by antiquity, or by remote regions of the globe, it was because they had an enthusiasm for humanity quite alien to the spirit of the previous age of asceticism, dogma, and syllogism. If we contrast Lothario Conti's views "on the wretchedness of the human condition" (p. 64) with Shakespeare's "What a piece of work is man! how noble in reason! how infinite in faculty!", we shall realize the nature of the humanist devotion to "humaner letters."

Both the earlier and the later revival of learning shook the structure of dogma. But as Albert and Aquinas christianized Aristotle, so Gemisthos Pletho (d. 1450), Marsiglio Ficino (d. 1499) and Pico della Mirandola (d. 1494) christianized Plato and the Neoplatonists. This Florentine school, while weak in critical discrimination, gave religion a positive standing in the Renaissance. In England John Colet and Thomas More felt the same impulse, and somewhat amended the weakness in criticism.

Erasmus felt strongly the influence of the English humanists; but his humanism was engendered in other circles. Behind him lay the "New Devotion" of the Brethren of the Common Life. Illustrious Christian humanists adorn the history of the Low Countries in the late fifteenth century, and give a lasting fame to Deventer, Zwolle, Groningen, and the cloisters of the northern Netherlands. The piety of Thomas à Kempis, the vigorous scholarship of Rudolph Agricola, and the fearless criticism of Wessel Gansfort, all helped to make the genius of Erasmus possible.

Gerard of Gouda and a widow named Margaret who was not his legal wife, were the parents of the great humanist. Apparently Gerard became a priest before the birth of Erasmus, their second son. His birthday was October 28, and the year probably 1469.

A poor school at Gouda, the famous academy of Hegius at Deventer, and a school of the Brethren at Hertogenbosch, gave him instruction to his middle teens. His parents being now dead, his unscrupulous uncles, in order to appropriate his inheritance, by threats and cajolery induced Erasmus and his elder brother to enter the Augustinian priory of Steyn (1486). He had been unhappy at school; and he soon became wretched in the cloister. Though his teachers had not discovered his genius, he had acquired solid Latinity and a passion for literature. It was now his ardent wish to go to the university of Paris. He obtained a papal dispensation to leave the monastery, and became secretary to Henry, Bishop of Cambrai, who soon released him to the university (1495).

Erasmus went to the College de Montaigu, where the Dutchman, Standonck, had set up an austere regime. His health suffered from the harsh discipline and the stale eggs, both of which he later alluded to with caustic humor. Among his teachers were the celebrated Noel Béda, and the Scot, John Major, bulwarks of the old regime in philosophy. At Paris Scotus and Ockham had long eclipsed Aquinas. Their followers had been called the "modern" school; but humanism was the new modernism. Erasmus revolted from his scholastic masters, and studied Greek. It is an interesting fact that the ponderous Major apparently lectured to Erasmus, Calvin, and Knox, and that all three rejected his theology.

Before taking the bachelor's degree (1498), Erasmus had gone to reside in the capacity of tutor, with a group of English students of rank. One of them, Lord Mountjoy, in June 1499 took him to England. In the English environment the spirit of Erasmus expanded. For the first time, at thirty years of age, he was happy. At Greenwich and Oxford he met More, Colet, Skelton, Grocyn, Linacre, Warham, men of "so much learning, deep, accurate, ancient," that he saw little need of visiting Italy. Later he praises with more moderation the libraries and scholars of Rome; but in Italy he made no great friendships. For More and Colet he had a genuine attachment. Of his numerous visits to England the longest was from 1509 to 1514, when, chiefly at Cambridge, he prepared his greatest work, the Greek version of the New Testament. Erasmus wrote a short, admiring life of Colet, which gives some color to the view that Colet's influence led him to critical study of the scriptures. Colet's earnest piety, too, seems to be reflected in the *Enchiridion* of Erasmus (1503), a book written in exposition of the simple undogmatic evangelicalism which was Erasmus' real religion. In a letter to Colet of 1504, he records his life-devotion to sacred letters. His *Praise of Folly* (1511) was written in More's house, and its title,—*Encomium Moriæ*,—contains a pun on More's name. Thus his most influential and characteristic works are connected with his English friends. But none of his English friends could have written any of them in a lifetime. Only one other work of Erasmus is comparable in distinction to these, the *Colloquies*, begun in 1497, pirated in 1518, and edited by himself in 1519. Among his numerous and varied writings of less note, his *Complaint of Peace*, 1521, is a remarkable pamphlet against war, and his *On Recovering Concord in the Church*, 1533, contains proposals for allaying the religious strife by means of a general council and the cultivation of a spirit of mutual tolerance.

In these works Erasmus is revealed as a man of shrewd wisdom rather than a great thinker or even a great scholar. He had little distinction in the class-room; it is his unique literary gifts that make him one of the most effective Christian teachers of all time. His felicity of style, fertility of conception, sparkle of wit, aptness of allusion, and sense of the reader's profit and delight make him the world's most distinguished man of letters. His subject-matter has more or less constant bearing on religion, and in that field his influence was more revolutionary than he intended.

Three things Erasmus did. In his *Folly* and *Colloquies* he set the Christian people laughing at innumerable forms of stupidity and credulity still current in religion. In his

New Testament he caused a new light to shine upon the Bible, which now became the fascination of scholars and the potent agency of reform. And in such writings as the *Enchiridion* he gave encouragement to a tolerant piety, centered in Christ, indifferent to dogmas and ceremonial, and freed from superstition and fear.

A stormy revolution was the thing he least desired; yet there was dynamite in his laughter as well as in his sober learning and enlightened religion, to wreck the structures of medievalism. He dissolves in satire the insincerities and the illusions of great and small in all ranks of life, and exposes with special familiarity the errors and deceptions that thrive in religion—superstitious and bargaining prayers and vows to saints, pilgrimages, indulgences, the petty sophistries of scholasticism, the ignorance and vices of monks and clergy. "I have discoursed of folly, but not altogether foolishly," he says. There is a wealth of subtle wisdom in his "folly."

Robert Grosseteste, Roger Bacon, and Nicholas de Lyra, had shown the need and importance of textual criticism of the New Testament, and Lorenzo Valla's vigorously critical *Notes on the New Testament* (1450), furnished a starting point for Erasmus. He had Valla's work printed, for the first time, 1504. In 1506 he published a Latin version based on critical studies. His Greek text was published at Basel by Froben in 1516. The great Spanish cardinal, Ximenes, had already finished his Greek text in 1514; but it was delayed in publication while Erasmus occupied the field. In 1517 he declined Ximenes' invitation to the university of Alcalá, and began a four years' residence at Louvain.

He was now at the peak of his fame and influence, and viewed his work with satisfaction. He was burdened, indeed, by the letters and attentions of innumerable friends and strangers, but optimistic about the results of the revival of letters, and forecasting the advent of an age of peace, piety, and learning. Then a giant strode across his path.

Erasmus welcomed Luther's early utterances, but saw in them an intemperate quality which made him cautious in confessing his approval. By 1519, at Louvain, he was in the midst of a commotion raised by Luther's books, and was being charged with responsibility for them. He told Luther that he would keep his neutrality for the sake of the revival of learning. The violence increased; his dream of peaceful reform was shattered, and his spirit embittered. Yet he long forbore to attack Luther: in 1522 he flatly refused the Dutch pope Adrian VI's request that he enter the arena for the Papacy. In 1524, on his own account, he moderately attacked Luther's doctrine of predestination as tending to undermine morality. The ensuing controversy left little humanism in the Lutheran movement. What there was of it remained chiefly among the disciples of Melanchthon, who never ceased to admire Erasmus.

The spirits of Erasmus and Luther have attended the development of modern religion, the former pleading for enlightenment and tolerance, the latter for decision and faith; the one for man, the other for God. Personally they failed to coöperate; but as their controversy recedes from us in time we see that historically they have wrought a great work of coöperation. Erasmus spent his late years largely at Basel, where, in close association with his printers, he edited some of the church fathers and wrote numerous treatises. Always sensitive, he grew suspicious and querulous. He had a few friends, but no body of supporters. Both parties had learned that he belonged to neither. The crisis of the reform at Basel sent him to Freiburg; the monks at

Freiburg made life intolerable for him. He was honorably welcomed back to Basel shortly before his death, which occurred July 12, 1536.

It is human but inconsiderate to demand that great men take sides on every contemporary issue. It takes character to be neutral when neutrality is unfashionable, but it is a kind of character which is rarely much esteemed. Erasmus was called a coward because he was "courageous enough to preach caution" amid the destructive strife. The Longford Castle portrait (1523) by Holbein the Younger well reveals the disciplined thought, wisdom, fastidiousness, mildness and disillusionment of the scholar, in that finely chiseled face, with the eyes weary yet alert, the wide mouth, close lips and faint, reluctant smile. The scholar sits in reflection, and the eyes are looking far away, as if over the heads of contemporary combatants into a problematic but inviting future. As we study the picture the thought comes that Erasmus is still looking over all our heads.

CHAPTER VI

THE NOBLE ARMY OF THE HERETICS

Jesus and Paul were heretics to the Jews, and Pope Leo IX was a heretic to the Greek Christians. A heretic is one who thinks otherwise than the accepted way of thinking. Where thought abounds, heresy is likely to abound. There was a rich variety of heresy in the early church. It was rendered easily recognizable by the creeds, and was somewhat checked by the force of authority. The official dogma of the ecumenical period was rarely challenged in the West during the early Middle Ages; but speculation on topics which the church had left undetermined, such as predestination and the Eucharist, led to the expression of opinions that came to be regarded as heretical. No medieval generation was without its heretical leaders; the later centuries counted them by hundreds, and their followers by tens of thousands. Thus, although there was one official religion, a full list of the sects, say for the fourteenth century, would probably be as long as the list of religious groups in the last census of the United States, a nation with no established religion.

It is difficult to invest the sectary of today with the badge of heroism. The situation was different in the days of the rack, the branding-iron, the gibbet and the stake. The troop of medieval heretics rightly recalls the great phrase of the Te Deum, "the noble army of the martyrs." With the martyrs of early Christianity they often shared that sublime courage which is based on the soul's downright conviction, on loyalty to reasoned principles. Whereas the martyrs were generally borne up by the corporate enthusiasm of the Christian group, the heretics more often met their hard fate alone. They were treated by the Gregories and the Innocents much as the Christians were treated by Decius and Diocletian.

Some of the heretics were ignorant, opinionated, or pathologically fanatical, and had no truth to speak. Others were men whose offense was that they outthought their contemporaries, and who take on significance from the force and value of their ideas as well as for the assertion of the rights of the mind and conscience. Many were people of puritanic morality, and a little self-righteous, who, taking offense at the callous worldliness of the priests, came to condemn broad aspects of the church system.

From Ratramnus, Gottschalk and Erigena in the ninth century to Berengarius in the eleventh, the roll of distinguished heretics is a short one. The first half of the twelfth century saw the emergence of a number besides Abailard. Outstanding among these are two scriptural evangelists of nearly Anabaptist principles, Peter of Bruys, who was burnt in 1126, and Henry of Lausanne who was hounded by Bernard to a fate not known, in 1148. The logician Gilbert de la Poirée (d. 1154) had trouble with the Trinity and still more trouble with St. Bernard, but escaped bodily penalties. The most renowned of Abailard's heretical contemporaries, however, was his pupil Arnold, the radical of Brescia, who, having asserted "apostolic poverty" as a basis for clerical reform at Rome, fell a victim to the pope and the emperor in 1155.

Peter Waldo

There are few personalities of the Middle Ages more fascinating and more baffling than the Lyons merchant who, having made a fortune by "sinful usury," became a saint but was pronounced a heretic, Peter Waldo. It has been suggested that the name Waldo, or Valdes, has reference to a place, probably the district of the Vaud, north of Lake Geneva, which was exposed to the influence of the heresies of Lombardy. But there is nothing to indicate that he drew from the region of his birth a tradition which determined his religious experience. In a center like Lyons a wide-awake citizen would have brought to his notice the emphasis on religious poverty, not only of monastics like the order of Fontevrault and the Cistercians, but of heretical Bible evangelists like Henry of Lausanne, and would probably be aware of the sect known as Apostolicals, fanatical devotees of poverty in Brittany and in Cologne. Medieval religion, orthodox and heretical, had little comfort for the conscience of a rich man.

The sudden death of a friend with whom he was in conversation is said to have aroused Waldo's anxiety about his own salvation; and apparently a trivial incident induced him to reverse the course of his life.

One Sunday in 1173 he stood with a crowd of townsfolk listening to a troubadour. The singer's theme was the legend of St. Alexis, a fourth century Roman saint who was said to have abandoned his property, gone to Odessa, and returned to live in direst poverty unrecognized in his father's mansion. Stricken in conscience, Waldo pondered the tale, and next day inquired of theologians what he must do to be saved. He was reminded of the Gospel words,

"Go sell what thou hast and give to the poor." He was resolved to obey, but first made provision for his wife and daughters. He asked his wife to choose whether she would have his money or his real estate, and she chose the latter, retaining their house. He sent his two daughters to Fontevrault. He systematically gave away his money and other personal property, partly as restitution to the victims of his former covetousness, and partly in alms to the poor. Once he scattered money to the needy in the streets, explaining to those who thought him mad that he did it in order that others might learn to trust in God and not in riches. He began to beg his bread; but his wife, feeling this to be scandalous, procured from the Archbishop of Lyons the sole right to provide him with food.

This story indicates that Waldo had begun his new life in obedience to a scripture command. Another account gives still more prominence to the scripture element. Waldo was very curious to know what was read in the lessons at mass, but could not follow the Latin. He engaged two priests to render the Bible into French; one translated while the other wrote. It was one of these priests who gave the account of this to an inquisitor who records it. Extensive portions of scripture were translated, and these Waldo learned by heart. It was then that he determined to follow apostolic poverty, sold his goods, and distributed alms to the poor. Thereafter he went about preaching and reciting the scriptures, and teaching portions to others who would memorize them.

Both accounts are so well authenticated that it seems justifiable to attempt a substantial harmonization of them rather than to cancel one by the other. Seemingly the best way to adjust to each other the two narratives is to assume that a considerable period of time, instead of one night only, elapsed between the incident of the Troubadour and the disposal of Waldo's property, and that in the interval the Bible translation was done.

We have here the rise of that striking phenomenon of Christian history, the uneducated Bible preacher of modern times. The earlier heretics had been either trained in Latin or ignorant of the Bible. By the hit-or-miss translation made by the priests for him, Waldo provided for medieval religion a new dynamic. Soon he attracted followers who multiplied the written vernacular scriptures and preached them widely. They wore a garb like that of the wandering preachers before them, and were in some villages familiarly called "the unshod." Becoming very expert in their ability to recite Bible passages, a talent much admired by the unlearned, Waldo and his preachers may have been a little elated by a sense of superiority to those with a Latin education who did not memorize but could better understand the sacred books. So at least their critics said. On the other hand, their ignorance of traditional interpretations at least served to liberate them from a mass of allegorical and tropological imaginings, and enabled them to give attention to the literal meaning.

To preach without a license was a violation of the law of the church. In 1178 Waldo was forbidden by Archbishop Guichard to teach publicly. He stood up and replied to the prelate by quoting, "Go ye into all the world and preach the Gospel," and added the words of St. Peter: "We ought to obey God rather than men." He was expelled from the province of Lyons. In the lent of the following year Pope Alexander III held the Third Lateran Council. To this great assembly came Waldo and a few disciples with an appeal to the Pope to permit them to resume their preaching. The learned Welshman, Walter Map, describes them as presenting to the pontiff an annotated French translation of the Psalms "and many other books of both testaments." Map regards their teaching of the scripture to the unlearned as "casting pearls before swine." He calls Waldo's followers (in the very language applied in the Vulgate to the apostles Peter and John) "unlearned and ignorant men." "They have," he says, "no permanent dwellings, but go about two by two, with bare feet, clothed in wool, possessing nothing, but like the apostles having all things in common, naked following the naked Christ." Map was appointed to examine two of their prominent men: it is not indicated that Waldo was one of these,—perhaps for the reason that he did not know Latin, as quite evidently those called to answer did. Map easily entrapped them by a question for which they were not prepared by theological training, and drew his reward in a broad laugh of derision from the assemblage. But their further answers and their manifest devotion so impressed Pope and council that they escaped complete suppression. They were forbidden to preach without the consent of the local clergy.

Waldo undoubtedly violated this injunction. Perhaps the laughter of the prelates rankled in his breast. In defiance of Guichard he filled the diocese with his propaganda. He was evidently resolved to disobey and take the consequences.

The consequences began to be evident in 1181 when John of the White Hands became Archbishop of Lyons. He took action at once against Waldo and his now numerous followers. They were scattered abroad through southern

France, Lombardy, and the Rhine country. But wherever they went they preached and circulated the scriptures. In 1183 at the Council of Verona the "Poor Men of Lyons" along with Cathari, Apostolicals, Arnoldists, Patarenes and other heretics, were condemned for preaching without license and for denial of the sacraments. That they had impugned the doctrine of the sacraments is possible but not evident. Their distinctly heretical phase was probably later. But they were already wilfully disobedient to the hierarchy and believed themselves justified in this by the commands of Christ and the example of the Apostles. Had not the church always insisted on the infallible authority of the Bible?

We cannot follow Waldo through his later years. If he survived the first dispersion there is a possibility that he went to Picardy. An official of the group, known as "the Picard" was in Bohemia about 1212; his identification with Waldo has been suggested. There is also a tradition of his organizing the movement in Lombardy. He was certainly dead by 1218 when Waldenses of Lyons and of Lombardy disputed as to whether he had gone to heaven immediately at death.

The Waldenses rapidly penetrated to almost all parts of Europe. Their spread was partly due to persecution which repeatedly dispersed their communities. In many cities their propaganda was associated with the industrial guilds. Women were active missionaries of Waldensianism, and this was one of the faults found with them by Innocent III. Waldensian peddlers and innkeepers industriously spread the vernacular Bible. It was their arsenal and the basis of their influence. They brought a biblical influence into numerous earlier and later sects with which they mingled

—Cathari, Humiliati, Arnoldists, Spiritual Franciscans. When the age of printing began their numerous printed versions of scripture became an increased embarrassment to the hierarchy.

A group called "the Catholic Poor" was organized from Waldenses who were reclaimed from heresy under Innocent III. But the majority grew more and more hostile to Roman dogma. They objected to the rites and sacraments of the church, the use of images, the doctrine of purgatory, and other elements of the church system, and set up churches of their own with a system of democratic rule and a coördinated work of charity. They anticipated many of the doctrines of the Reformation; but their refusal to take oaths, their rejection of the death penalty for crime and their opposition to war, illustrate a simple literalism which the educated and theologically minded Reformers do not share.

Waldo may not have been a man of great intellectual powers or organizing talent. We hardly know how far he was himself responsible for the movement to which his name is attached. But through his popularization of the Bible his influence is vastly wider than his sect. Luther's Bible met a demand which had been aroused by the Waldensian propaganda. Calvin's first religious publication was an introduction to the new French translation for the Waldenses by his cousin, Olivétan, in 1535. Waldo thus appears to have held a good deal of the future in his hand. His one simple original idea of giving the scriptures to the folk in their own tongue, and his devotion to this purpose in the face of power and of peril, entitle him to a place among the makers of historical Christianity.

Marsiglio of Padua

Padua at the opening of the fourteenth century was a vigorous and disorderly commune "indulging in a cycle of domestic revolutions and a wobbling foreign policy." A running fight was going on between the citizens and the clergy over the taxation of ecclesiastical property. A series of political convulsions attended by disastrous war ended with the loss of popular rights and the establishment of a virtual dictatorship in 1318. Nearly a century later the city was to come within the jurisdiction of its great neighbor, Venice.

The pride of Padua was the university founded by Frederick II, and now especially famed for its school of medicine. It happened that a notary of the university, and a worthy citizen, Bonmatheo de Mainardinis, had a brilliant young son named Marsiglio, born about 1278, who took the medical course and became a physician by 1311. Marsiglio had also a hankering after the profession of the law, but was advised by the celebrated Paduan poet and historian, Mussato, to continue in medical work. After an interlude of military service under Henry VII, the emperor who disappointed the high hopes of Dante, he went to the university of Paris. An able and aggressive young man, he was elected Rector of the university for the three months' term beginning in December 1312. His writings contain a reference to the university of Orléans, and he may have spent a period in the study of law there. But he was chiefly at Paris till 1316, and probably supported himself by the practice of medicine. During these years he was associated with the French scholar John of Jandun, and also, it is reasonably conjectured, with Michael de Cesena, general of the

Franciscans, and with the Invincible Doctor, William of Ockham, who was then boldly reviving nominalism and would soon with Cesena and Marsiglio enter the lists against the papal monarchy.

Marsiglio evidently began the study of theology in Paris. He was appointed by Pope John XXII to a canonry in Padua. In 1318 John refers to him as his "dear son"; and in condemning him, along with John of Jandun, in 1327, the Pope describes them as "unmindful of, and ungrateful for, benefits received." A recent writer on Marsiglio seeks to explain his recalcitrance toward his papal benefactor on the ground of his experience of parish life in Padua, and of his visit to the papal court at Avignon, where he became deeply aware of the corruptions at headquarters. The impression of this visit was evidently similar to that made upon Catherine of Siena half a century later. He describes the curia as "an abominable den of robbers," traders in simony, bustling lawyers, and intriguing priests who persecute the righteous—a scene of confusion, "horrible to contemplate."

But there are other facts to consider in accounting for his change of allegiance. The great public question in the church had now come to be that of the Spiritual Franciscans. Under the impulse of the strange apocalyptic prophecies of Joachim of Fiore, who had died before the conversion of St. Francis, but whose work was published afterwards, the Spirituals had become distinctly heretical. Their teaching that the Apostles possessed no property made them specially objectionable to the propertied clergy. They were, however, befriended by Cesena and Ockham, and by Bonagratia of Bergamo, another Franciscan leader. Pope John substituted for the compromise measures of

Clement V, a policy of severe repression of the "Fraticelli," as the extremists were now called. The panic caused by the anti-clerical rebels in France, the Pastoureaux, probably aroused the Pope's fear of the devotees of poverty. The years 1317 to 1323 are marked by a series of papal utterances against them, and by acts of relentless persecution in which numbers of the sectaries were burned. Marsiglio refers to their unjust treatment, and was probably largely aroused by it against the Pope.

In 1324 he was back in Paris, having given up his benefice. With some literary aid from John of Jandun, who may have known his Aristotle better than Marsiglio, he wrote at Paris, under the innocent title of *The Defender of Peace* (*Defensor Pacis*), a book which was a bomb hurled at the papal throne. Shortly after its composition the Emperor Louis IV, a patron of the Fraticelli, was excommunicated. Early in 1326, the authorship of the work having been discovered, Marsiglio and his literary colleague escaped, we are told, from Paris to the imperial court at Nürnberg. Marsiglio became the Emperor's physician and adviser, and was in great prominence in the service of Louis on his Italian expedition of 1327-1328. He assisted in the setting up of an antipope in Rome, and was the chief orator at the coronation of Louis. At Pisa the imperial party received three distinguished guests who had cleverly made their escape from the papal prison at Avignon: Ockham, Cesena and Bonagratia. Ockham joined the Emperor on the return journey to Munich. The two great heretics, the English philosopher and the Paduan publicist, seem to have lived out their lives at Munich. Marsiglio was court physician, but was occasionally employed, or permitted, to write. Ockham in this period wrote a great deal. On church reform they have much in common. Yet neither refers to the other by name.

In 1327 John XXII condemned those two "sons of Belial" and "pestiferous fellows," Marsiglio and Jandun, on the ground of opinions drawn from the *Defensor*, as "notorious heretics or rather heresiarchs." Frequent condemnations of the work followed. Clement VI, referring to Marsiglio as dead in 1343, calls him the worst heretic he has ever known. In the Reformation the book became an authority for some Protestant controversialists. Modern historians have held somewhat divergent views of the author's aim. Some regard him as a secularist, a protagonist of the secular state like Hobbes. Others look upon him as a religious reformer, a more academic Arnold of Brescia or a less evangelical Wyclif. In the present writer's judgment the latter view alone does justice to the *Defensor* as a whole.

The work is in three parts (dictiones). The first of these is a treatise on politics, based on Aristotle. It is to be noted that in presenting the six parts of the "civitas," or state, Marsiglio (or his collaborator) includes the "sacerdotium" (priesthood), along with the "pars principans," the governing part, as an essential element. The function of priesthood is "the discipline and instruction of men in those things which according to evangelical law [the New Testament] it is necessary to believe, to do or to leave undone, in order to obtain eternal salvation and escape misery." He does not say with Aristotle that the priests should be warriors grown too old to fight! Instead they are to be efficient men, trained for their office. All the discipline invented by human ingenuity may contribute to their task. If this language is sincere, and its sincerity is probably to be assumed, the book was not written in irreligious advocacy of secularism. There is much else in his work to confirm this view.

Marsiglio's view of the state is based upon the Aristotelian concept of the "lawgiver," the efficient source of the law, as "the whole body of citizens or the weightier (valentior) part of them." This expression, "pars valentior," which he frequently uses, seems to mean the numerical majority. He advocates the election of the prince, as opposed to hereditary succession. The entire conception is such as to lead the way to Locke, and indeed to Lincoln.

But the main drive of the book is against the Papacy, and church polity is the theme of the second section. The church is defined as the whole body of believers, the "universitas fidelium." Aquinas, we saw, advocated popular government in the state, but monarchy in the church. Marsiglio rests power in the whole body, equally in church and state. He denies to the pope all temporal jurisdiction and all coercive power. The clergy ought to be provided only with the necessaries of life. Any real property they have in use should be the property of the "lawgiver," the whole church. On the authority of the New Testament, which Marsiglio handles with historical skill, the primacy of the bishop of Rome is attacked. St. Peter's episcopate in Rome he calls a "saint's legend"; even if it is historically true, he asserts that Paul was bishop before him. The head of the church, and the "rock" on which it is built, is Christ; Peter and other apostles are members. The claim of supreme papal authority (plenitudo potestatis) in temporal matters is assailed as the cause of oppression and discord. "The beauty of the church, which is her unity," has been destroyed by the popes who in their ambition have "sowed tares and schisms." The title of the book is the serious claim of an advocate of peace.

Church government should be by means of a general council of representatives of all parts of the church, "pious men, priests, and laymen," of blameless life and skilled in the scriptures. He admits that early church councils were sometimes of priests only; but thinks the modern corruption of the clergy requires the corrective of lay representation. He apparently has in mind a permanent secretariat whose duty would be to arrange for meetings of the general council and act as its executive between meetings. Behind the authority of the council is the infallible scripture, in accordance with which the council must always act. In its decisions it will be guided by the Holy Spirit; but Marsiglio does not claim for it infallibility. The third *dictio* is an arrangement in propositions of the arguments of the other two. The *Defensor Minor*, written some years later, reiterates and expounds further the ideas of the former treatise.

Others before Marsiglio had urged a settlement of church questions by a council; for a quarter of a century the proposal had been repeatedly and frequently made. But no one had presented a reasoned and constructive argument for the conciliar principle of polity. The book was at once recognized as a staggering blow to the papal idea. Its circulation was greatly handicapped by repressive measures, since it was aimed against royal as well as papal absolutism. Yet its influence was probably great upon numerous writers who thought it unwise to name the heresiarch who had inspired them.

In Ockham, Henry of Langenstein, Conrad of Gelnhausen, Nicholas of Clemanges, John Gerson, Pierre d'Ailly, and a host of minor Paris teachers and other conciliarists; in Gregory Heimburg and other German anti-papalists before Luther; in the Councils of Pisa, Constance, and Basel, in Luther's demands, and those of the Lutheran princes, for a council, and in the conciliar polities of all the Protestant churches, we see how great the circle of Marsiglio's ecclesiastical influence became. His conciliarism is essential Protestantism. It involves the authority of scripture interpreted through the voice of the whole body of the faithful as expressed in a representative body. That, in effect, and not private judgment, has been the Protestant way.

John Wyclif

Within the decade in which Marsiglio's *Defensor Pacis* appeared was born England's arch-heretic, a man who was to be execrated by the medieval church, and described by an enemy as "the image of hypocrites, the idol of heretics," but admired by his friends as "the Evangelical Doctor" and by later Protestants as "the Morning Star of the Reformation." John Wyclif's birthplace was probably Wycliffe-on-Tees, in an area of Yorkshire sparsely populated and exposed to the repeated devastations of raiders from the Scottish shires. Probably enough, the ancestors of Duns Scotus, a son of Berwickshire, clashed with those of Wyclif across this much disputed frontier. His parents, Roger de Wyclif and his wife Katherine, belonged to the landed gentry. Katherine is known to have survived her husband; she was a widow in 1362, and in 1369 was associated with John as patron of the rectory of Wycliffe. She may not have lived to learn of her son's heterodoxy. There is evidence that his numerous kinsmen of the Wyclif name had no sympathy with his radical views. After the youth took the old Roman road to Oxford, about 1345, he had only occasional connection with his native village.

Oxford University already had a century of renown as the school of theology ranking second to Paris. Indeed through her alumni in Paris her Franciscan theology had leavened the Dominican tradition. After John of Salisbury the first great English intellect was Robert Grosseteste (1175-1253) who, says Roger Bacon, "was able to know all things." He spent some time as a Paris teacher, but made his great contribution at Oxford, where he was the first Chancellor of the university, and in his reforms as Bishop of Lincoln. As the friend and teacher of the early English Franciscans he founded a "school" at Oxford, in both senses of the word. The Oxford Franciscan school produced Adam Marsh, Roger Bacon, Richard Middleton, William Lemare, and John Peckham, first-rank thinkers of the thirteenth century. These men assailed Thomas Aquinas, before Duns Scotus (d. 1308), with greater power and subtilty, undertook to set him right. In Duns and William of Ockham, Oxford may be said to have conquered Paris. But even in Oxford Thomism was taken seriously, and had its advocates, in Wyclif's time.

Wyclif took to scholastic studies as a duck to water. But he did not attach himself to either of the friar orders, or feel greatly the force of tradition or party in his thought. Selecting and rejecting independently, he formulated his own opinions. He acknowledged a debt to Grosseteste and to Ockham. He seems ignorant of Roger Bacon, but was evidently quite familiar with Aquinas. Duns Scotus too had a part in the making of his mind; but even Wyclif found his thought difficult. Thomas Bradwardine, who came to a profound Augustinianism through a conversion experience at Oxford, and died of the plague as Archbishop of Canterbury in 1349, exercised a powerful influence on Wyclif in respect to the doctrine of grace. In other directions his thought was inspired by Richard Fitzralph of Armagh (d. 1360), an opponent of the now decadent friars and author of a treatise *On the Savior's Poverty*. Wyclif's reading was wide. It has been shown that he utilized the work of a rather obscure French theologian, William of Perault. Pope Gregory XI represented his views on church polity as a recrudescence of "the perverted opinion of Marsiglio of Padua, of damned memory." Although his learned biographer, H. B. Workman, thinks the similarity to Marsiglio accidental, the parallel passages are so numerous as to call this judgment in question.

Wyclif's career at Oxford has been in part reconstructed, not without some conjecture, by Dr. Workman. He was evidently Master of Balliol for some years before 1361. In that year, when in his thirties, he took the Master's degree. He received the B.D. in 1369, and the D.D. in 1372. He was connected with Queen's College for some time, and is thought to be the Wyclif who was Warden of Canterbury Hall for a period of sixteen months ending March 1367. He held a number of church benefices, and cannot be exculpated from pluralism. In absence he seems to have provided a vicar; and the incomes he received were moderate in amount. He lived unpretentiously and puritanically, and studied laboriously.

The attraction for Wyclif of Fitzralph and Bradwardine is sufficient indication that while he was at home amid the refinements of scholasticism the dominant interest for him lay in the practical concerns of religion. In matters of doctrine he is fundamentally not speculative. He does not seek abstract truth, but the way of salvation. He found the sure and satisfying way by following Bradwardine and Anselm back to Augustine and Paul, rather than by the paths of thirteenth or fourteenth century scholasticism. While he went to school to Ockham for some of the details of his theology, he repudiated Ockham's bold nominalism, which he regarded as destructive of the doctrine of divine grace and a solvent of all the generalizations that made up the creed. More tolerant of the Aristotelian realism of Thomas, he turned from this also, and consciously followed Anselm in the adoption of Platonic-Augustinian realism. On this basis he develops his thought of the church as the total society of the predestinate believers (universitas fidelium predestinatorum), a conception closely resembling the ruling idea of Augustine's *City of God*. The firm assertion of the reality of universal ideas governs also his treatment of the Incarnation. Christ entered humanity (humanitas communis), and was not an individual man merely, but, in a sense, the universal man (homo communis). If the universal has no reality incarnation would be in an individual only, and without significance for mankind. Wyclif's has the same horror of the Ockhamist logic as Anselm for Roscellin's, and for the same reason.

But this high realism led him at another point to heterodoxy. He could not tolerate the Ockhamist doctrine of the annihilation of the substance of the bread in the Eucharist; nor in the end rest satisfied with the Thomist definition, by which the accidents—shape, taste, etc.—are sustained by a vaguely conceived subsistence which is not the substance. He was largely moved here by other than logical considerations. He was convinced that the people, instructed to adore that which priests called Christ's body and which he thought bread, were being schooled in idolatry. He affirmed that the substance of material bread remains, and that "as Christ is at once God and man, so the sacrament is at once the body of Christ and bread." In some passages he went beyond this view of "consubstantiation," as when he states that the words "This is my body" mean "This effectively and sacramentally figures forth (figurat) my body." Thus Wyclif anticipates, in his never quite settled reasoning on the question, the doctrines both of Luther and of Zwingli.

Fourteenth century England in many ways asserted its growing nationalism and desire to fling off the influence of the popes in church and state. To prevent the pope "providing" or securing in advance for his appointees, benefices in England, the Statute of Provisors was passed in 1351; and to render illegal appeals to the pope over such appointments the Statute of Præmunire followed in 1353. Wyclif probably viewed this legislation hopefully at the time, but we have no evidence on the point apart from his later attitudes.

The payment to the pope of the tribute promised by King John, neglected since 1333, was definitely refused by Parliament in 1366. About 1372 Wyclif entered the service of King Edward III, and two years later received as a reward the rectory of Lutterworth. He went with a commission to Bruges in 1374 to confer with the pope's legates over the disputed payment of King John's tribute, and questions of church appointment. The conference accomplished nothing except to leave Wyclif definitely disaffected toward the Papacy. He now wrote treatises on *Divine Lordship* and *Civil Lordship,* in which he develops Fitzralph's argument of the lordship of the good and attacks the authority of the worldly clergy. He supported John of Gaunt, Duke of Lancaster, the King's intractable younger son, because he hoped that the duke's anti-clerical policy would aid church reform.

The bishops, out of hostility to Lancaster, called Wyclif to account before Convocation; but his patron strode upon the scene with armed retainers and prevented the trial (1377). Accusations were, however, carried to the pope, and Gregory XI, who had then just returned from Avignon to Rome, condemned Wyclif as a follower of Marsiglio. Wyclif in turn called Gregory the vicar of Satan.

He was now ardently preaching reform, and ruthlessly exposing the clergy, monks and friars, in the churches of London. He advocated the total cessation of payments to Rome, asserting that the pope ought to live in holy poverty, and called for the disendowment of the English clergy at the hands of the king. The death of Edward III (1377) and the succession of his grandson Richard II, removed the influence of John of Gaunt; but Wyclif showed as much courage as before, and was strong enough in the admiration of the people to maintain his freedom. He was hailed before the Bishop of London, William Courtenay, and Archbishop Sudbury, at Lambeth, and forbidden to carry on his propaganda. Far from being silenced, he published two treatises (*On the Church* and *On the Office of the King*) in which he clarified his ideas on reform.

All events now led to the deepening of his convictions. The opening of the Papal Schism (1378) fortified his antipapalism. The Peasant Revolt in England (1381) gave fresh evidence of the grievances of a section of the population against the clergy. Accused of instigating the revolt, Wyclif and his followers turned the accusation upon the Franciscans, whom the poet Langland accuses of preaching communism out of Plato. Richard now, prompted by the clergy, engaged in a disastrous crusade in Flanders on behalf of Urban VI, the Roman pope, against his adversary Clement VII of Avignon. Wyclif denounced the use of indulgences in connection with this campaign, and thenceforth finally cast off all recognition of the spiritual as well as the temporal authority of the pope.

A new council called by Courtenay, now Archbishop of Canterbury, in Blackfriars Church, Holborn, to deal with Wyclif's heresies in his personal absence, was disturbed by a terrifying earthquake (May 17, 1382); but the bishops condemned a series of errors taken, somewhat loosely, from his teachings. An able, radical and defiant work, the *Trialogus,* written in the months following this council, is the latest assertion of Wyclif's personal doctrines; though it was followed by numerous shorter tractates. Amid these activities of the late years of his life he found time to organize his adherents and institute a popular movement, and to coöperate with others in the translation of the Bible. Overtaxing his strength in prodigious labors, preaching, teaching, disputing, he was stricken with paralysis, first in 1382. A second stroke came while he was saying mass in Lutterworth, and he soon afterwards died, December 31, 1384. In 1428 his body was disinterred and burned, and the ashes cast into the Swift, a tributary of the Avon. "Thus," says the old historian Fuller, in his quaint style, "this brook hath conveyed his ashes into Avon, Avon into Severn, Severn into the narrow seas, they into the main ocean. And thus the ashes of Wyclif are the emblem of his doctrine, which now is dispersed the world over."

The biography of Wyclif is rendered difficult by his own lack of interest in it. He never takes the trouble to disclose his personal experiences, or to reveal the sources of the emotional drive that evidently lay behind his vigorous and courageous efforts. A passion for reform had somehow been engendered in his strong nature. While he drew inspiration from Augustine and Bradwardine, there is no specific evidence that he shared their conversion experiences. Though an academician, he felt deeply with the common people, and was concerned to give to them a new religious impulse. As he looked about upon the English scene, he saw what Chaucer saw, but made a different response. While Chaucer was amused, Wyclif was distressed by the secular temper of clerical life and the crude ignorance of the masses. Nor was his interest so largely social and economic as that of Langland, who in *Piers Plowman* pleads the cause of the rural classes against the greed of the prelates and the corruption of the monks and friars. Langland is the more medieval in his religious beliefs, yet Wyclif is more otherworldly.

Wyclif's spare frame, pale face, and ascetic habit of life, formed an index of his piety. He enjoyed a reputation for holiness which even his opponents recognized. In the spirit of evangelic poverty he revolted against the ambitious worldliness and religious indifference of the clergy, and the prevalence of the abuses of simony, pluralism, absenteeism, and favoritism in the affairs of the church. He saw no hope for the reform of the clergy by the clergy. Hence he turned for the inception of clerical reform to the king. Since wealth-seeking was the gravest aspect and chief cause of all the ecclesiastical evils, he would have the government impoverish the church in worldly goods that it might be spiritually enriched. The project is in essence the same as that of Arnold of Brescia and of Marsiglio of Padua.

Wyclif apparently did not realize the peril involved in inviting the crown to snatch the properties of the church. His teaching undoubtedly made the partial execution of this program easier for Henry VIII.

But further, he saw the influence of the Papacy in England as an element in the general corruption. Searching the scriptures and the fathers, he boldly concluded that the papal institution had no divine authority and no modern justification. It had usurped the place of Christ, and was antichrist. Through the mass on which the claim of sacerdotal power rested, the people were being betrayed into idolatry.

Like numerous opponents of the hierarchy before him, Wyclif relied on the authority of the Bible. He became devoted to the aim of giving the Bible to the masses as the book of true religion and the guide to salvation. His greatest positive contribution was the leadership he gave to the work of translation. The Lollard Bible depended upon the Vulgate, not the original languages of the scripture books. But, unlike the translations of the early Waldenses, it was a work of careful scholarship. In vocabulary it contributed not a little to the translation of Tyndale, who had mastered the Greek and Hebrew original. It was of the utmost importance in the rise of modern English speech. Had Wyclif had the aid of the printing press, and freedom to use it, he might have made England the Bible-reading nation it became two centuries later. As it was, the work was not printed until the middle of the nineteenth century; but the manuscript translation survived all attempts to suppress it, and was in increasing use at the beginning of the Tudor Reformation.

Because Wyclif "appealed from the Latin-reading classes

to the English-speaking public," his work was broadly based in the national life. He gave a kind of organization to his movement by the "poor priests" whom he trained to preach from the scriptures, and who went about, like the *Wanderprediger* of the eleventh century, in apostolic poverty, teaching the lay folk. At the beginning they were recruited from the ranks of the oppressed poorer class of the clergy. In time these were succeeded by lay preachers, with little schooling, who knew nothing of Wyclif's philosophical works, but could recite and expound the vernacular Bible. The adherents of Wyclif and his preachers were called Lollards, a word imported from the Netherlands where it had been applied to singers of popular religious songs. Despite much persecution the Lollard movement spread through half of England and entered southern Scotland.

Wyclif's Latin writings are voluminous; some of them have not yet been printed. His English works too are of considerable extent. Much of this vast literary output had almost no influence in England. But because Richard II's queen was a Bohemian princess and Bohemian scholars followed her to England, the ideas of his Latin works were revived, a decade after his death, in the university of Prague, where they were to aid in the inception of the vigorous anti-papal movement which is linked with the name of John Hus.

John Hus

Supreme among the innumerable martyred heretics of the Middle Ages, surpassing the great Savonarola in the clarity of his mind, the charity of his spirit, and the constancy of his soul, was the tall, lean, eloquent Bohemian, John Hus. "Hus" means "goose," a fact which was the subject of many puns; but it is really a shortened form of

Husinecz, the name of his native village in southwestern Bohemia. His father, also called John, died while the son was a baby; and his mother, though in poor circumstances, provided for his early education. If, as is now believed, he was born in 1371, he was about eighteen when he came to the university of Prague in 1389. Starving his way through the school with a diet of bread and peas, he received the B.A. degree in 1393, the B.D. in 1394, and the M.A. in 1396. In the early years in Prague street singing was his means of support. He later regretted spending his last coin on one occasion for an indulgence. In a letter he confessed the early sins of chess-playing and attending a travesty of the mass,—the common Feast of Asses.

The impecunious student became a professor of theology (1398) and lectured on the *Sentences*. In 1401 he took orders as a priest. In 1402 he was Rector of the university: the term of office was six months only. In this year also he was appointed preacher in the chapel of the Holy Innocents of Bethlehem, a sanctuary then recently built by two laymen for preaching in the Czech language. This large building in the heart of the city offered the young preacher the greatest opportunity for his talents. With powerful eloquence he held spellbound great congregations while he expounded the gospel, spicing his sermons with denunciation of the covetousness and deceit of unfaithful priests, freely condemning feigned miracles, indulgences and pilgrimages, and calling wrong-doers of all sorts to repentance.

Behind the message of Hus, and its popularity, lay three historic influences. First, there was the rising national feeling, of which the existence of the chapel for Czech preaching was in itself a demonstration. The university had a preponderance of Germans; the city itself was nearly half German-speaking. Racial antipathy had been in evidence for centuries. The Czechs resented the numbers and power of the German clergy in their country. Hus came from a frontier village where he may have fought with German boys. It is a mistake, in the light of his writings, to regard him as primarily a nationalist; but he relied on, and appealed for, the support of anti-German Czechs.

Another element in the background of Hus is the tradition of evangelical preaching in Bohemia. Waldenses were numerous in some parts of the country, and though he did not feel their influence himself, doubtless many of his followers had been inclined to his teaching by that of the Waldensian preachers. But for half a century before him semi-heretical evangelical priests had made a great impression in Prague. Conrad of Waldhaus (d. 1369) Milicz of Kremsier (d. 1374) and Mathias of Janow (d. 1394) had in turn criticized the clergy and the friars. Milicz had undertaken social reforms, and Mathias had assailed images and relics, and taught the scriptures with great fervor.

A third and a very important factor was the influence of John Wyclif. The queen-consort of Richard II of England was Anne of Bohemia, sister of King Wenzel the Lazy who now ruled in Prague. The royal marriage attracted numerous Czech students to England, who became admirers of Wyclif and carried his books to Bohemia. Hus himself copied five of Wyclif's tractates in 1398. By 1402 a number of Wyclif's greater Latin works were well known in Prague; others followed by 1407. It is impossible to say how far Wyclif's ideas formed, and how far they merely corroborated, the opinions of Hus. Certainly he freely repeats the very words of Wyclif on a variety of subjects; and his many quotations from Augustine are largely Wyclif's. Although not so radical as his English forerunner, he drew upon himself the odium of the orthodox by avowing his admiration for that "Catholic man and evangelical doctor." He wrote from prison at Constance: "Would that my soul were where John Wyclif's is."

Hus was now very active and prominent. He preached several times weekly; he exposed fraudulent relics; he was the Queen's confessor and enjoyed the favor of the King. He was appointed synodal preacher, and in this office denounced his erring clerical brethren in merciless terms. The Germans in the university generally opposed him, while leading Czechs applauded him. In Jerome of Prague he had an able ally, who, after a lapse in resolution, met the same fate as Hus with the same heroism.

Zbynek of Hasenberg, Archbishop of Prague, was in difficulties. Wyclif had been condemned in England and in Rome; and Rome did not care to have him honored in Bohemia, which in the Schism stood on the Roman side. Despite Hus and his friends, a commission of Prague theologians, chiefly Germans, condemned forty-five of Wyclif's alleged teachings. English admirers and opponents of Wyclif in Prague added to the liveliness of the controversy. Hus induced the "Bohemian nation" in the university to modify the condemnation of Wyclif (1408). Pope Gregory XII urged Zbynek to do his duty and extirpate heresy. Zbynek on "investigating," and after consultation with the King, wrote to the Pope that there was no heresy in the land! But this temporizing method could not long be followed.

The Council of Pisa in 1409, in an attempt to end the papal Schism, elected a new pope, Alexander V, but failed to secure the resignation of the other two. Hus favored the council, and declared for Alexander, while Zbynek for some months stood faithful to Gregory XII, and attempted to silence the preacher. Hus neglected his commands, and the King, who favored the Pisan Pope, made it impossible for the Archbishop to act effectively in the matter. Zbynek himself joined the side of Alexander, but remained hostile to Hus.

Meanwhile the King undertook a reorganization of the university, by which the Bohemians were given three votes to the Germans' one in its affairs. Hus had advocated some such policy. This was a reversal of its former constitution; and the Germans were so offended that they moved away in a body, to found soon afterward the university of Leipzig. The Czech minority which now formed the university made Hus once more Rector, October 1409.

But Wenzel was no longer prepared to support Hus in his radicalism. He may have feared German revenge, or the social revolutionary tendency which the circulation of Wyclif's works was likely to engender. Zbynek took courage to place Prague under an interdict, and not long after died, September 28, 1411, leaving a situation of dangerous contention. At Rome the enemies of Hus secured his excommunication, in terms that made him an outlaw, July 1412.

Hus replied by appealing to God and a church council, and continued his ministry for a month. Riotous scenes between Czechs and Germans led the King to ask him to withdraw, on the understanding that a national synod would be held to settle the dispute. He took shelter with friendly nobles in southern Bohemia. A synod met but failed of agreement. Hus preached in many places, and wrote books and letters which added force to his party throughout the nation.

The great Council of Constance was about to meet to heal the Schism and reform the church. Hus was invited to attend it on the safe-conduct of the Emperor, Sigismund. This guaranteed his safe return to Bohemia, whatever the council might decide. Hus afterwards told d'Ailly, Bishop of Cambrai, at Constance, that he might have remained in security where he was, since he had strong political friends; and the statement was at once corroborated by a Czech nobleman. Nor did his friends fail to warn him against trusting the Emperor's sealed promise. But he willingly accepted the invitation.

He felt confident that, if fairly heard, he could clear himself of the charge of heresy. But confidence of success does not fully explain his eagerness to go. He was willing, at any cost, to testify to the faith that was in him. His letters show hope for a favorable verdict, but therewith a steadfast resolution to give his life, if need should be, in testimony of what he deemed the truth. "It is better," he wrote, "to die well than to live ill. One must not sin through [fear of] the pains of death. He who fears death misses the joys of life. Truth is victor over all things. Victorious is he who is slain, since no adversity harms him if no iniquity has mastery over him." And again: "If my death serves His glory and your advantage, may He allow me to undergo it without base fear."

The Council of Constance has been regarded as the greatest international parliament of all time. The Emperor, numerous princes and magnates, and the ambassadors of others, the cardinals of Pope John XXIII, thirty-three archbishops, one hundred and fifty bishops, as many abbots, and perhaps three hundred professors were in attendance. A vast host of the curious or the covetous—including traders, actors and courtesans—swelled the population of the city. Hus came in November 1414, and was soon flung into prison, the Emperor too mildly protesting. He was taken from one loathsome prison to another. Chains were bound about his limbs. He suffered agonies from toothache and gall-stones, and once refers to his monotonous diet of porridge. His trial occupied a number of sessions of the Council from June 5 to July 6, 1415. His behavior was faultlessly heroic. Both in respect to the utterances of the accused and the insults of the accusers, the history of his trial and death is reminiscent of the closing chapters of the gospels.

The cause of Hus might be strong in Bohemia, but it was weak in Europe. He had offended the Germans. The French doctors led by d'Ailly and Gerson, were anxious to give proof of their own suspected orthodoxy, and fearful of a national schism. The English prelates in the council were embittered against Wyclifism, which despite persecution by fire was dangerous to their power. The Italians were not the friends of an opponent of the pope. Hus was often roughly silenced when he began to make his still powerful voice heard. He was accused of heresies alien to his thought, such as the absurdity that he had called himself the fourth person of the deity. Like Wyclif, Hus was a realist, while the council was dominated by nominalist disciples of Ockham. The name of Wyclif was raised at every point, and Hus was made to bear the burden of all Wyclif's views, some of which, such as the "remanence" (continuance of the substance of the bread) in the sacrament, he sincerely disclaimed. He was condemned, without objection from any. He made Sigismund blush with shame for the violation of his bond of honor; the Emperor in reality had hoped that he would recant and thereby escape the council's condemnation.

Exhorted to abjure his heresies, he refused "to lie in the face of God." The prelates degraded him from the priesthood, with a procedure which rather degrades them in our eyes. A tall paper hat, with figures of demons and the word "heresiarch" upon it was placed on his head. "My Savior," said Hus, "wore a crown of thorns." The Emperor ordered him to be taken to the stake. He went on foot, smiling as he passed a bonfire of his books in the courtyard of the cathedral. The stake was set in a meadow. Hus scarcely felt the flames; chanting portions of the creed, and commending his soul to God, he was choked into unconsciousness by a cloud of smoke. To prevent any treasuring of his relics, his ashes were shoveled into a wheelbarrow and dumped into the Rhine.

Hus did not say, as Luther supposed, that after the "goose" was burnt there would come a "swan" whom the papists would not burn. But he did say, in a letter of October 1412, that "other birds" such as, unlike the goose, could "soar into the heights" would "shatter their snares." He was thinking not of swans but perhaps of eagles.

There is little in Hus's doctrinal teaching that differentiates him from Wyclif. His books *On the Church* and *On Simony* are clearly much indebted to Wyclif's works of the same titles. He is scarcely so extreme in his denunciation of the pope, and he does not follow Wyclif all the way in the treatment of the Eucharist. But he goes beyond Wyclif at some points; chiefly in his demand for the giving of the wine to the laity. For three centuries the laity had partaken of communion by the wafer alone. "Communion in both kinds" was the demand of Hus and his followers, and was actually granted to the Bohemians by the Council of Basel in 1433. The significance of the demand lay largely in the fact that it represented the assertion of the importance of the laity in the church.

Hus like Wyclif insisted on the Augustinian ideal, eternal church of all the faithful, and taught that the true Catholic church on earth was "the whole body of Christ's faithful saints militant." His view may be illustrated from a letter of 1413, written to the Rector of the university of Prague:

As for the dictum of the doctor [an opponent in Prague] that the Catholic apostolic church and the Roman Church are the same: if "Roman Church" is taken here to mean the universal church of which the apostles are a part, then it is true. But if "Roman Church" means here "the pope with the cardinals," then it is not the same as the Catholic apostolic church just as no partial church is the universal holy apostolic church. . . . Even if it were possible that Rome, pope, cardinals and all, were cast down as Sodom, this holy church would still remain.

The humanist, Crotus Rubeanus, praising Luther in 1520, wrote: "John Hus has come to life again. . . . He will live as long as truth lives." Luther felt himself a kindred spirit with the brave Bohemian. "If such a man," he once said, "is to be regarded as a heretic, no person under the sun can be looked upon as a true Christian."

Yet to the supporters of the old order in the church a heretic indeed he was. His doctrines were revolutionary. He was the personification of a new Christian conscience.

CHAPTER VII

THE GOODLY FELLOWSHIP OF THE REFORMERS

The era of medievalism, in the life-stories of some of its creative personalities, has been rapidly scanned in the foregoing chapters, until we have become aware that, after 1300, what the creators were creating was no longer medievalism. The creative figures were those of the opposition party, and revolution loomed. *Respublica Christiana,* the Christian Commonwealth, to which all local governments were subordinate, was in disrepair. A rapidly growing and changing civilization made the old social controls inadequate. New interests in trade and commerce were commanding the energies of men. A natural acquisitiveness that had formerly often had as its object the prizes of eternity, was now directed to the things of time. The European had discovered the nature of this world, and mapped the farther shores of the Indian and the Atlantic oceans. He had opened books written by men for whom no dogmas had authority, and from these classics of Greece and Rome —the product of a privileged class in a world of slaves— had drunk draughts of liberty. The universities and the burgher schools had enabled many laymen to criticize the ignorance of three-quarters of the clergy and the greed and luxury of most of the others. The taxes needed to maintain the vast establishment of the church constituted a burden that was increasingly resented. National power in

France, England, Switzerland, Scotland, Spain, Bohemia, Denmark, and political and class discords in Italy and Germany, presented formidable problems to him who claimed the monarchy of the world. Leo X, for example, in the Concordat of Bologna, August 1516, accorded to Francis I (shades of Hildebrand!) the right to appoint the bishops in France. His reaffirmation, three months later, of Boniface VIII's *Unam sanctam* is simply pathetic.

The papal diplomacy had declined from the utterance of commandments to the negotiation of concordats. But no adequate concordat was possible with so incoherent a political mass as Germany then was. The peasant agitator, Hans Böhm, was not far wrong in calling the Emperor "a nonentity." He had reference to Frederick III, 1440-1493. After Frederick came Maximilian I, called "the dreamer" because he entertained vain hopes of power and glory. He left to Charles V, 1519-1556, a legacy of unresolved problems. Charles was greater as ruler of Spain than as emperor. In that office the interests of ambitious feudal princes prevented his rising above pretentious feebleness.

The most troublesome problem left by Maximilian to his grandson was the movement which arose about the electric personality of Martin Luther.

Martin Luther

Hans Luther, Martin's father, was born a free Thuringian peasant, married a burgher's daughter, Margarethe Ziegler, and while supporting a family of seven children, became, at Mansfeld, Saxony, the independent operator of a smelting plant and one of the four magistrates of the town. Of the two parents, whose work-hardened faces have been so unforgettably depicted by Cranach, the father made the greater impression upon Martin. Both were pious; both on occasion flogged their offspring, in sorrow and in anger.

It was at Eisleben that Martin, their first child, was born, November 10, 1483; he was brought to Mansfeld as a baby. Here he attended school, acquiring the subjects of the Trivium in no painless fashion. He was brutally punished at school. But this treatment was not exceptional; it was all a part of the school routine, and was probably not the cause, as some have held, of lasting personality-disorders in Luther. In these years, however, the superstitious beliefs prevalent in the district preyed upon his active mind, which was quite inadequately challenged by the school curriculum. In consequence, all his life the very air was for him full of devils.

But the gates into the intellectual life opened before him. His parents kept him in school; they hoped to make him a well-thriven lawyer. Through their sacrifices he was sent to schools at Magdeburg and at Eisenach. At eighteen he went to the university of Erfurt, where John of Wesel had attacked indulgences fifty years before, and where Mutianus Rufus now led a group of lively young humanists. He took his B.A. in 1502, his M.A. in 1505. He was a good student, whose only diversion was music. He betrays exceptional familiarity, for a theologian, with the Latin classics; but it is clear that he did not keep the company of the Erfurt humanists.

Hans Luther saw his hopes maturing. Martin would be a great lawyer, perhaps the adviser of princes. He presented the Master of Arts with a *Corpus Juris*, the lawyer's Bible. Then, after a visit to his home, Martin dashed his fond parents' hopes by entering the Erfurt cloister of the Augustinians. He wanted not to gain the world but to save his soul. But his father's disapproval, and contempt for monks, may have given him afterthoughts. In the cloister he did his utmost "to enter heaven by monkery." He taxed his strength by fasts, vigils, and prayers, seeking a sense of justification by establishing a standard of ascetic conduct. So he interpreted monastic duty, and scholastic theology, which he continually studied from Ockhamist teachers.

He had built up a conception of God as an exacting judge whose demands he found it impossible to fulfil. Sharing the eschatology of his time, the monk was in fear of hell-fire, not like moderns, of a nervous breakdown. But more than that, he craved the assurance of God's goodwill to him. He endured agonies in his assaults of temptation. Some of the symptoms were psychopathic. A major conflict surged in his mind. His temptations were not carnal; he was too wretched and anxious for that. "I thought not on woman, gold or goods, but my heart quaked and was convulsed [wondering] how God would be gracious to me." His real temptation was to reproach God for demanding the impossible.

But another concept of religion began to contend with the scholastic pattern. Eckhart and Tauler and the Friends of God, and John Gerson whom Luther called "Doctor Consolatorius," had testified to the mystical way of salvation. The anonymous *German Theology*, a gem of mysticism, came to his knowledge. Perhaps, after all, salvation depended not on what man did but on what God did for him. An old monk reminded him of the clause in the Creed, "I believe in the forgiveness of sins." Later, John Staupitz, vicar-general of the Augustinians, helpfully advised him. But the essential problem remained.

He was a rising figure in the monastery. In 1507 he took priests' orders; his father handsomely provided a banquet, and gave the priests some plain words across the table. The sturdy anti-clericalism of old Hans always impressed Martin, though it did not guide his actions. Staupitz drew him in 1508 to the new university which Frederick the Wise, Elector of Saxony, had set up in the little muddy town of Wittenberg. He moved to the Augustinian house there, and lectured on Aristotle's logic, not liking the task. In 1512 he became a Wittenberg doctor of theology, and now lectured in that subject in the university. Meanwhile he was sent on business of the order to Rome (1510-1511) where he learned what led him afterwards to quote the statement of Cardinal Bembo that Rome is the cesspool of humanity.

The lecture room required, and his whole being craved, a solution of his problem of God's justice. He wrestled with Paul's phrase "justitia Dei," "the righteousness, or justice, of God" (Rom. 1:17), until, when he coupled it with the clause following: "the just shall live by faith," a new light dawned. Henceforth for him the formerly terrifying expression meant, as he said, "not the justice by which God is just and punishes the unjust and sinful, but that by which a merciful God justifies us through faith." This clarification brought him peace, and power.

Justification by faith canceled the medieval doctrine of good works, undermined the structure of monasticism, and annulled the claims of sacerdotal religion. Gradually it appeared to Luther that he was no longer at one with either his mystical or his scholastic contemporaries. Incidentally he had become a constant and intelligent student of the Bible. Everything was now revised on a Pauline-Augustinian basis. He had, as he felt, drunk salvation from the scriptures, the Word of God. He was retreading the path of Wyclif and Hus, but with the difference that in asserting the authority of scripture he applied to it the organizing principle of justification. In lectures, sermons, and commentaries on the epistles and the psalms, he worked out his new theology.

The abuses connected with indulgences seemed the crowning expression of the doctrine of works which he had repudiated. The traffic in indulgences had often been resented, condemned and ridiculed. Wittenberg university had been founded on money confiscated by Frederick from an indulgence-seller. Tetzel, a Dominican with gifts of salesmanship, was now selling indulgences in a town on the border of Saxony, and some of his customers were known to Luther. Everyone knows how, on Hallowe'en 1517, the professor tacked on the door of the Castle Church (in which Frederick had piously assembled 5,000 relics), his ninety-five Theses assailing Tetzel's reckless claims and questioning the whole indulgence practice and principle. He expected a skirmish with Tetzel, and with his employer, Archbishop Albert of Mainz,—who was to obtain a large commission from the proceeds to pay his simoniacal debts. He did not foresee a life-long war with the Papacy, which would transform Europe.

But to challenge indulgences was in reality to impugn the Papacy. Indulgences were, in theory, gifts distributed out of the Treasury of Merit, which Alexander of Hales had expounded and the administration of which Thomas Aquinas had prudently reserved to the pope. Moreover, despite the protests of moralists like John of Wesel, and the immortal laughter of Erasmus, indulgences were a fruitful source of revenue.

As the Theses circulated, Tetzel's trade declined. He argued back, and Luther retorted. The indulgence issue gave place to that of obedience to the pope. Pope Leo X, with a poor sense of transalpine matters, at first thought the quarrel a mere expression of the rivalry of Augustinians and Dominicans, but learned to take it seriously before he died in 1521. Gradually the heavy artillery was brought into action. In debate with John Eck of Ingoldstadt Luther saw the issue more clearly than before. Eck stood on the ground of the "Roman obedience" and called Luther a follower of Hus. Luther, like Hus, thought the "Catholic Church" other and larger than the "Roman obedience," and denied the divine-right monarchy of the pope. Later, when he had read Hus, he admitted that he had been, albeit with Paul and Augustine, a Hussite without knowing it.

The Reformation would have been a relatively dull, undramatic movement, without the printing press; but the printing industry was likewise indebted to the Reformation. The demand for Luther's tracts, in Latin and in German, was heavy. Soon he had a following in every country in Europe, and Germany was almost at his feet. By 1520 his treatises show his reforming principles in virtual maturity. He appealed repeatedly for "a free general Christian council," and presented a long list of positive reforms which such a council should undertake. Side by side with justification he taught the priesthood of all Christians—a doctrine much misrepresented by careless interpreters of Luther. Believers' priesthood was that function of the church by which all its members religiously minister not to themselves but to one another. The special trained and ordained priesthood was not to be suppressed, but to be guarded with the highest qualifications, and to exercise its functions as representing the priesthood of all. But the common layman had an occupational calling, by which he too was to render service in the spirit of religion.

The young Charles V met his first diet of the Empire at Worms in 1521. Luther was summoned to appear, and a safe-conduct was provided. He remembered Hus, but resolved to face the danger, which he exaggerated, not realizing the strength of his political and popular support. Hus at Constance had no powerful friend. Luther was acclaimed by thousands on the way, and was welcomed at Worms by admiring throngs. A papal agent had written to Rome that nine out of ten Germans were shouting for Luther, and all were demanding a council in Germany. Yet Luther's courage was not born of public approval, but of simple conviction of truth. "Hus was burned, but not the truth with him," he said. Before the robed dignitaries of the Empire, the pale monk-professor, in an eloquent defense, sturdily refused to recant his teachings "unless convinced by scripture and right reasons." "I am bound to God's Word," he declared. "To act against conscience is neither safe nor honorable." Reason, conscience, and the Word: a trinity of authority. But there is another note in this daring utterance. "I owed this testimony of a loving heart to my native Germany." For the moment Luther was not only an incarnate conscience; he was an incarnate patriotism.

The distressed Emperor, wisely anxious to avoid the shame of Sigismund, and to secure Luther's safety, winked at his abduction by Frederick's knights to the Saxon Elector's castle of Wartburg. It was not the shade of St.

Elizabeth, but the shapes of demons, that haunted his apartment there. He fought the devil, if not as legend tells with an ink-well, at least with ink. Among much other writing he translated the New Testament from Erasmus's text, and by it shaped modern German speech as well as religion.

The next decade presented many a new crisis. Luther returned to Wittenberg and repelled the religious extremists who in his absence had engendered fanaticism. Always abhorring armed rebellion, he repudiated the attempt of the German knights to ride to power on the impulse of the Reformation by a violent revolution. He tried to bring justice to the aggrieved peasants, who, at the bottom of the social scale, were made to bear the burdens of the economic disturbance of that age of commercialization, monopolies, and economic agony. Yet when the peasants rose and became formidable, his horror of armed revolt overcame his sympathy and humanity. In the language of fury and panic he urged on the suppression of the "murdering and robbing bands of peasants." His savage words, "A prince can win heaven by shedding blood. . . . Stab, strike, strangle, whoever can," have never been forgiven him. Luther literally thought the rebels devils incarnate. It is sometimes forgotten that their behavior was fiendish enough.

Erasmus and other humanists had opened the way for Luther, and at first favored him in the controversy. But Erasmus advocated educational reform, not Luther's direct methods. Weary of being called either Luther's inspirer or his disciple, he assailed Luther's doctrine of predestination as relaxing to morals. In the ensuing controversy Luther alienated most of his humanist support (p. 141).

Thus by 1525 Luther had cast off many who had been

with him in 1521. He had broken alike with the revolutionary agitators and with the deliberate reformers, and had defined and delimited the movement he would lead.

The princes had won the peasant war, and they dominated the German scene; the Emperor had enough on his hands in Spain and Italy. The organization of Lutheran churches now proceeded, with the coöperation, and under the authority, of favorable princes and city governments. But Luther, and his brilliant assistant Melanchthon, supplied the leadership. The *German Mass*, 1526, which gave direction to the development of worship in the speech of the people; a collection of German hymns, enlarged in many succeeding editions; and a series of *Kirchenordnungen*, or plans of government for territorial churches, mark the rise of Lutheranism as an ecclesiastical fact. At the base of the structure was an organization of doctrine which reached authoritative utterance in the *Confession of Augsburg*, 1530. The Lutheran princes and magistrates promoted and protected the work of reform.

Without this record of leadership in constructive reform Luther would be significant and immortal. But in the long view it is the positive aspect of any movement that accredits it. Luther and his associates began a vast reconstruction of Christian institutions which gave permanence to Protestantism. Protestantism is at heart church-forming and unitive, not divisive; though some writers continue to repeat the contrary. The Lutheran congregations with their vernacular worship and hymnody, were given an experience of the communion of saints. Luther's view of the priesthood of all Christians was primarily a principle of mutual spiritual help, and tended to call forth the concern of the individual for the interests of others in all phases of social and economic life.

Luther inaugurated a religious revival which revitalized the German people and shed an incalculable influence throughout the West.

On June 13, 1525, while the court of Saxony was in mourning for Frederick the Wise, the peasant revolt was closing in butchery, and Luther was expecting his own death by violence, at forty-two years of age, and with an income ridiculously small, he married Katherine von Bora, aged twenty-six, daughter of a free farmer and now an escaped nun.

In 1523 a pious layman had brought a wagonload of nine nuns, who had seen the error of their vows, from Nimbschen to Wittenberg. Luther pitied their helpless state, and urged his prince's secretary to secure a relief fund for them. One by one they were married off; but Katherine was haughty, and let it come to Luther's ears that she would marry no less honorable a person than himself. Luther had declared for clerical marriage years earlier. He had vaguely intended to marry, "to spite the devil" and to strike another blow at the pope. His father, too, urged him to marry. Katherine proved a good homemaker, and Luther's home is one of the most famous and admirable in history. Happiness and affection triumphed over poverty and debt. They kept a kind of *pension* for students. Luther's dinner conversation was in part jotted down by some of these young men; and his *Table-talk* forms one of the most precious books of human interest of all time, mingling as it does frank humor, penetrating criticism, brilliant characterization, and warmth of evangelical religion. Luther at his ease is as distinguished as Luther in combat. Yet he remained the hard-working, hard-fighting leader of the Reformation.

In 1529 he and Zwingli, the Zurich reformer, conferred at Marburg but failed to agree on the doctrine of the Lord's Supper. Though Luther denied transubstantiation, he affirmed against Zwingli the presence of Christ's body in the bread. Luther, moreover, did not wish to compromise his loyalty to the Empire by an agreement with the Swiss who were traditional enemies of its rulers.

In his later years he resumed the controversy with the Swiss. He gave to the press an astonishing amount of work, and carried on a vast correspondence. He continued to oppose Rome, and in 1545 wrote an assault upon that pope whom he chose to call "His Hellishness St. Paul III." Probably the pains of growing illness increased his censoriousness. The sturdily built but thin and ascetic-looking young man who stood before the diet at Worms had now become fleshy, short of breath, and afflicted with painful ailments.

Though the veteran of long combat, Luther had often espoused the cause of peace. His last act was to arbitrate a quarrel between the two counts of Mansfeld, brothers whose father had been his father's lord. A midwinter journey to the place, attended by a great thaw and flood, which called from him the jest that "the great Anabaptist had almost re-baptized him," brought on a fatal illness. He died in the town of his birth, Eisleben, February 18, 1546.

Of all men of his century, Luther, the religious warrior, Germany's greatest son, is the man whose words and deeds have wrought themselves most effectively into the history of succeeding generations in Western Europe.

John Calvin

The Reformation was really not one movement but a series of similar upsurgings of religious forces, which took place in different territories and were largely independent in their inception, though later brought by their leaders into partial coöperation or unity. The reform led by Huldreich Zwingli (1484-1531), which protestantized the culturally more advanced sections of German Switzerland, owed little to Luther. Switzerland was a democratic confederacy, with an increasingly important class of intelligent townspeople. Zwingli was a humanist and a patriot before he became a reformer. He was actively concerned in politics, and it was in battle, though not as a combatant, that he came to his death. Zwingli rejected as idolatrous all non-scriptural forms of worship, while Luther retained such as the scriptures did not clearly reject. He admitted that in the Lord's Supper "the body of Christ is present by the contemplation of faith," but stressed the memorial rather than the mystical interpretation of the sacrament. From Zurich the Zwinglian movement soon passed to Basel, Bern, Schaffhausen and other parts of the republic, and began to affect the French-speaking areas extending southwest of Bern to Geneva, which were then in process of political attachment to Switzerland.

Under the stable monarchy of Louis XII, in the stately cathedral city of Noyon, was born, July 10, 1509, John Calvin, son of Gerard Cauvin and his wife Jeanne le Franc. Removed by generations from a peasant ancestry, John Calvin was nurtured with the advantages of bourgeois culture, and in close contact with clergy and nobility. For Gerard was the bishop's secretary; and he was able to secure for John the superior tuition provided by a local nobleman for his own sons, and to obtain for him, in infraction of the canon law, church incomes which served as scholarship money for his attendance at the university of Paris.

To this still not inglorious queen of universities the precocious boy came in August 1523. His teachers saw his talent and exploited his application. Under Maturin Cordier in the College de la Marche Calvin laid the foundation of his later mastery of Latin. As an old man Cordier was to teach by Calvin's side in Geneva. At the College de Montaigu, where Erasmus had found the eggs and the theology not strictly contemporary, Calvin spent three busy years. He swallowed, unfortunately for his health, some of the eggs, but rejected the theology. Montaigu, however, did him one service which a university course ought to do for talented youth. It taught him self-expression.

The curriculum ran much to disputations; and we may be sure that Calvin's voice, now passing from adolescent hoarseness to ringing clarity, was often heard delivering judgments on Aristotelian questions in ambitious Latin periods. Out of this, partly at least, came Calvin's unsurpassed ability to choose and use words. Doumergue calls him "l'homme de la parole,"—the man not merely "of the Word of God," but "of the word of man," who talked and wrote with mighty persuasion, confident in "the power of the Word put to the service of the truth."

Talent and training were to be vitalized by an infusion of religious and moral conviction. This may have been in process during the Montaigu period (1525-1528), for the student life was disturbed by the humanistic and Lutheran critique of scholasticism; and men were taking risks for their convictions. Louis de Berquin, who was to burn for

Lutheranism in 1529, was a student's hero. Though Calvin still thought himself a resolute papist, probably the new leaven had entered his mind.

Taking the arts degree in 1528 he expected to proceed to theology. But in Noyon Gerard had a quarrel with the cathedral chapter, and in a mood of anti-clericalism he commanded John to turn to the study of law. In such a situation Luther, at twenty-two, turned monk. Calvin, at eighteen, obeyed his father. He entered the famed law school of Orléans. But his joy was in humanistic letters, and it was Melchior Wolmar, a half-Lutheran German humanist, who held his admiration. Yet he took the law seriously, and aided a friend in writing a book in support of his French law master, Étoile, against the Italian, Alciati, under whom Calvin studied for a time at Bourges. Though he became a licentiate in law, he dropped the thought of that profession with his father's death, 1531, and studied at Paris Greek, Hebrew, and the Latin classics, under the Royal Lecturers then recently appointed by King Francis I.

Calvin was surrounded by a circle of young radicals who were humanist scholars and were inspired by Guillaume Lefèvre, the cautious evangelical humanist whom the Sorbonne theologians, led by Noel Béda, had condemned. As a humanist Calvin wrote a commentary on Seneca's *Treatise on Clemency* (1532) which has been regarded as a covert plea for lenient treatment of the Protestants. But there is no convincing evidence that such was its real purpose. What is clear enough is that the book implies a challenge to the absolutism of the French monarchy; the word "tyrant" is defined as "one who rules against his people's will." The author moves with the ease of familiarity among classical and early Christian writers, but his citations of Scripture are noticeably meager and incidental. He was not yet Calvin the Reformer.

Among his intimate associates was his cousin Pierre Robert Olivétan, who was now employed by the French-speaking Waldenses to prepare a translation of the New Testament. Calvin wrote the preface to this translation in the fall of 1534 when French prisons were being filled with Protestants and some were going to the stake. Before it appeared (1535) many others had suffered. Here Calvin identifies himself with the cause alike of French evangelicals and of Waldensians under persecution. "If we are banished from one country, the earth is the Lord's. If we are cast out of the earth we are not thereby cast out of God's Kingdom."

This decided stand had been reached some months earlier. Suspected of the authorship of a rectorial address delivered at the university by his friend Nickolas Cop, November 1, 1533, Calvin had fled from Paris. The address mingles Erasmian and Lutheran elements, and amounts to an assertion of biblical humanism against the Sorbonne, which had recently condemned a book written in that vein by Marguerite d'Angoulême, the King's talented sister. Calvin now passed through various parts of France, and visited the aged Lefèvre, who was protected at Nérac where Marguerite ruled and resided. By May 4, 1534, he had resigned his chaplaincy at Noyon. Calvin himself, mentioning no dates, says: "God, by a sudden conversion, subdued my heart—too stubborn for my age—to teachableness." We should probably place this sudden conversion between the two dates just mentioned. He probably now first despaired of reform on the mediating basis of Erasmus and Lefèvre. Men whom he loved were dying for a more resolute faith.

Calvin's simple words doubtless conceal a protracted mental struggle. Elsewhere he says that he had "passionately resisted" the inclination to join the Protestant cause, "out of reverence for the church." But he had become persuaded that true loyalty to the church involved "an effort to correct her faults."

"By nature shy and timid," Calvin still sought the part of a retired adherent rather than that of a leader of Protestantism. At Basel, where he was known to his landlady as "Martinus Lucanius," he prepared his *Institutes of the Christian Religion.* Francis I, to excuse his violence toward the Protestants, had charged them with the aim of political revolution; and the *Institutes* was designed "to vindicate my brethren whose death was precious in the sight of the Lord." It was a masterly rationalization of essential Protestantism, and was preceded by a letter to Francis I which stands among the priceless literary treasures of that age. In later editions the *Institutes* grew in bulk, and improved in orderliness, but changed little in fundamental emphases. Calvin in this work confronts the absolute monarchy of the Valois with the absolute sovereignty of God, as he confronts the corrupt and superstitious contemporary church with that church which is essentially timeless, invisible, and pure, and which he sees happily finding manifestation and visibility in the Reformation.

The *Institutio Christianae religionis* of 1536 is described in its sub-title as "*pietatis summa,*" a summary of piety; and it may be said that for Calvin theology is the exposition of Christian piety. The book exhibits in brief form the main elements of his entire theology. But later editions greatly expanded this outline, and for the whole range of his thought one must go beyond even the final edition of the

Institutes to his other writings, the commentaries, treatises, sermons, and letters. Although he was well versed in classical and Christian literature, his whole theology is oriented to the Scriptures, whose teaching he takes as fully authoritative. For him this teaching is centered in the Gospel message of redemption from sin in Christ. It is his frequent theme that the pious who died before Christ enjoyed Christ's fellowship, glimpsing in anticipation what Christ has fully revealed. Millions have learned from his pages an abiding realization of the majesty and omnipresent activity of God, of the splendour of His created works, and of His intimate dealing with human souls. His doctrine of predestination, derived from Scripture with the help of Augustine and other interpreters, is marked by a fresh emphasis on the aspect of reprobation. Although he warned against incautious preaching of this theme, what he called the "awful decree" (*decretum horribile*) has become for many the badge of Calvinism. But his doctrines concerning the Holy Catholic Church, and the duties of Christians in the spheres of economic and political life, are coming to be more clearly understood and more appreciatively explained by modern scholars. Few writers so distant from us in time exert so great an influence in our century.

Not despairing of the Valois house, Calvin now, under the name Charles d'Espeville, joined other French exiles at the court of Renée, Duchess of Ferrara, King Francis' cousin. But the Duke, under papal influence, was preparing to scatter the nest of literary Frenchmen whose presence had been encouraged by his wife's inclination to Protestantism. Calvin recrossed the Alps, planning to find leisure and protection in Strassburg. Owing to war conditions his way led through Geneva; and there sometime in July 1536 he took lodging for a night.

The adventurous Guillaume Farel, Lefèvre's most aggressive disciple, had been campaigning for Protestantism in French Switzerland, and had won insecure leadership of Geneva. This cosmopolitan city of 12,000 had just emerged from a struggle for liberation in which it had shaken off feudal and episcopal control. Farel had induced the assembled citizens to swear with uplifted hands to live according to the Bible and to establish a school for all children. But he realized that the constructive task was still to be done.

Learning that Calvin was in the city Farel made speed to his hotel, and with pleas and spiritual threats persuaded him to labor with him in Geneva. On the first of September a spare, animated Frenchman of twenty-seven, with black hair, high brow, thin, well-trimmed brown beard, dark, flashing eyes, shapely hands that eloquently gesticulated, and a clear-toned voice that under excitement might be shrill, lectured to the ministers and a few citizens and their wives in the cathedral of St. Pierre. The secretary of the council, not recalling his name, set it down that "that Frenchman" was placed on the pay-roll.

Such was the inception of a work which today all the world knows. Unable to bring the headstrong burghers to discipline, the reformers withdrew in March 1538. Farel made Neuchâtel the scene of his later ministry. Calvin went to Strassburg, where he gained church experience, made new friends, and married Idelette de Bure, a sickly but attractive widow. She died in 1549. Confusion in Geneva, repeated pleas from the magistrates, and "thundering letters" from Farel, led Calvin to resume the battle there, in September 1541. He drew up the *Ecclesiastical Ordinances*, a constitution for the Genevan church, which lays the foundations of the polity of the Reformed churches. The system gave large responsibilities to lay elders, and provided for a qualified ministry which included doctors or teachers. Persons of unworthy life, including idlers and spendthrifts, were to be "lovingly admonished" by the elders and ministers in the consistory, and if necessary excluded from communion.

The rigid discipline of Geneva is usually ascribed to a certain hard legalism in Calvin which had been fixed in his mind by the study of law. In fact the discipline begins from an entirely different source. Calvin was seeking to bring the invisible church to visibility, to establish in Geneva "the communion of saints" which he, with Luther, identified with "the Catholic church" of the Creed. Scandalous sinners and those who failed of their duties to the community, could not be admitted to the sacred society, or to the Eucharist which was the pledge of its fellowship. The discipline was devised to keep the sacrament inviolate. Geneva was to be a theocratic (God-ruled) state, in which the communion of saints would have its natural environment. Thus the discipline suitable to saints was applied, with the consent of their elected magistrates, to all citizens.

The same conception of the disciplined community gathered about the Christian communion, is the key to Calvin's teaching on economic questions, which contrary to the assertions of some, is the reverse of individualistic. The Christian in his calling honors God by productive industry for the well-being of the community. We are, says Calvin, "chiefly to study our neighbor's advantage." "No increase is advantageous unless it answers to the needs of the whole body. . . . Let no man be anything for himself, but let us all be whatever we are for each other."

The gay Genevese, "addicted to cabaret life," winced under the discipline which closed the taverns at night and excluded dancing, card parties, and showy apparel. Most of the regulations now employed had long lain idle on the statute books of the town. They were henceforth enforced with vigilance, on clear principles, by the Consistory and the Council. Numerous harsh and humiliating penances were inflicted. Till 1555 Calvin had an uphill fight. "Timid by nature" though he was, bold men tried in vain to intimidate him. More than once he expected failure. He passed through many perils, and laid low many an adversary. The most celebrated of his victims was burned at the stake in 1553.

The Spanish scientist and Anti-Trinitarian, Servetus, was a fugitive from the Inquisition whom Calvin had known in Paris and afterwards failed to convert by correspondence. Though warned, he came to Geneva, was arrested, tried, and burned. Calvin tried to have him beheaded, but afterwards defended his execution for heresy. The Calvinists who in 1903 set up an expiatory monument on the spot where Servetus suffered, charge Calvin with "an error which was that of his century." We had a right to expect that the author of the Letter to Francis I would rise above the error of his century. He harbored others who were far from Trinitarian orthodoxy. But toward Servetus he was relentless. This anomaly is partly explicable on the ground that Calvin viewed Servetus not merely as a heretic but as an aggressive enemy and a potential subverter of the Genevan church order.

Calvin, the academician, lacked the gifts by which Luther appealed to the average man. He might have failed in Geneva if the Genevese had not possessed a high intelligence-quotient. Yet more than Luther, by his recognition of lay authority in the church and of representative government in the state, he was the people's champion. He established in Geneva a theocracy which was also a democracy. He cleared out the old vice district of the city, and built a good hospital for the poor. He instituted a world-famous academy, whose alumni carried the energy of Calvinism through Europe, to make nations and to shatter thrones. He gave to Protestantism a body of theology comparable to the *Summa* of Thomas Aquinas. He strove zealously for Protestant unity, but succeeded only in forming a consensus with the German-Swiss leaders (1549). Protestantism has not yet caught up with his aim to weld it into one world-wide communion. In brilliant and vigorous tractates, and by richly suggestive scripture commentaries, he defended and advanced the Protestant cause when it was challenged and endangered by the revived strength of Rome.

Prodigious labors crushed his frail body. His voluminous works written with a mastery of style in Latin and French, were composed while others slept or in intervals between nerve-racking tasks. A number of malignant diseases crept upon him. Bed-ridden, he held his responsibilities to the end. When he died, May 27, 1564, the Little Council of Geneva declared: "God gave him a character of singular majesty."

The severity of Calvin's disposition has won him much dispraise. Having early acquired the most exacting habits of work, he had no free boyhood and later gave himself very little time for recreation. Though he theoretically opposed asceticism and approved of laughter, and would jest at dinner with his friends, he made an asceticism of his labor and his proud refusal of ease, and habitually bore with him an air of gravity. He eloquently extols the Creator's handiwork in the stars above and in the earth beneath, but shows little evidence of having paused to enjoy them. He praises the view from a house which he is providing for a friend, but does not mention the thrilling mountain scene from his own window. Those who blame him for all this are expecting a good deal of a sixteenth century man, and especially of an emaciated invalid with a continent's religious problems on his shoulders.

Thomas Cranmer

The Reformation in England arose primarily out of English conditions, not as a product of Continental influences. In the fifteenth century the efficiency of the clergy declined while the intelligence of the laity improved and the rise of the printing press offered the means of effective propaganda. The reign of Henry VII, the first Tudor, saw a remarkable expansion of English trade, and a revival of national unity and confidence. The introduction of the study of Greek, and the appearance of a group of Christian humanists at Oxford, marked a new cultural revival which, though inspired from Italy and the Netherlands, was nevertheless distinctly English. The most outstanding of these scholars was John Colet who in 1497 was delivering startling lectures on St. Paul's Epistles. It was at Cambridge, and within the reign of Henry VIII, that Erasmus performed his greatest labor for the Reformation. There, at Queen's College, 1511-1513, he prepared his text and translation of the New Testament; though he took it to Basel for publication. The young monarch seemed the model of a brilliant, learned and well-disposed prince. Crucial events impended, which would call unwillingly to leadership a certain plodding Cambridge scholar named Thomas Cranmer.

Cranmer was one of seven children of a Nottinghamshire

yeoman's family, and was born at Aslockton, July 2, 1489. His father, Thomas Cranmer, had him trained in the use of the crossbow, and in riding. In the latter he became so expert that afterwards "as a bishop he feared not to ride the roughest horses." In contrast to most other sixteenth century scholars, Cranmer was of robust constitution. Yet he was the victim of cruelty in his schooling. When his father died in 1501, his mother,—before her marriage Anne Hatfield,—took him away from the "marvelous harsh and cruel" village schoolmaster. In 1503 she sent him to Jesus College, Cambridge.

The poorly equipped university in the then swampy and scattered hamlet of Cambridge was entering upon a revival. But scholasticism still held its old footing on the curriculum, and Cranmer was fully initiated into the thought of "Duns and other subtle questionists." He became a fellow of Jesus College in 1511, about the time of Erasmus' arrival at Queen's. Erasmus does not mention Cranmer as one of his few and poor Cambridge students; but in 1535 he acknowledges receipt of the sum of "eighteen angels" from the Archbishop of Canterbury, and the context shows that Cranmer is classed among his younger English disciples. In 1511, at any rate, as his friend Ralph Morice tells, Cranmer turned from the old to the new learning. Erasmus, Lefèvre, and before 1520 Luther, fed his maturing mind. He read also in canon law and liturgics. In his laborious way he made careful notes of his readings. In 1523 he was ordained; he was now lecturing in his college.

It is stated, though on doubtful evidence, that Cardinal Wolsey, who was then establishing the "Cardinal's College" which became Christ Church, Oxford, offered Cranmer a post there. Anyway he remained at Cambridge, where Luther's books were officially condemned and privately read. The White Horse inn was called "Germany" because it was the haunt of a half-Lutheran coterie, several of whose members were later to perish at the stake. William Tyndale, the translator, who was at Cambridge about 1515-1520, and the ardent little Thomas Bilney, who won Latimer to Protestant opinions, are distinguished among the dozen or more known to have been connected with the White Horse group. Cranmer was no Lutheran, but he probably felt tolerant of the radicals, and may even, in a spirit of inquiry, have joined them on occasion.

Henry VIII had told Wolsey in 1515 that "the kings of England in times past had never any superior but God only." Although he engaged in a brisk controversy with Luther, perhaps fearing the political threat of religious novelty, he favored the humanists and was disinclined to take orders from Rome. When he decided to put away his Spanish wife, Katherine, for one who, he hoped, would bear him an heir, and the Pope hesitated to further the project, he found help in the advice of the rising fellow of Jesus.

The sweating sickness had visited Cambridge, and Cranmer with some pupils had fled to Waltham in Essex, when Edward Fox and Stephen Gardiner, Cambridge men both, came with Henry to the place. Cranmer suggested to them that the King refer the complicated case, which turned on the legitimacy of Henry's dispensed marriage with his brother's widow, to university canon lawyers. This very academic suggestion made Cranmer's career. Henry saw in it the happy solution of his troubles; and he took Cranmer into his service.

The English and Continental universities were now subjected to the King's propaganda. Cranmer was sent in a final effort to persuade the hard heart of Clement VII. At Rome he talked long and learnedly on canon law points to the Pope, who was far more concerned with the fact that the Emperor, Charles V, with whom he had made a firm peace after a disastrous war, was the nephew of Queen Katherine.

Cranmer brought back nothing from the Pope, but he had acquitted himself with credit, and he was now made, nominally, ambassador to the Emperor, and really to the Emperor's recalcitrant subjects, the Lutheran princes and theologians, and the university faculties of Germany. He was entertained by Andrew Osiander, the Nürnberg reformer, whose liturgical interests he shared, and whose niece, Margaret, he married (1532).

When a student, Cranmer had married "Black Joan," a maidservant of the Dolphin inn at Cambridge; she had died with her still-born child. His marriage to the young German woman might be expected to foil Henry's unrevealed but no doubt strongly suspected intention of making Cranmer Archbishop of Canterbury in succession to the dying Warham. He actually sent his new wife to England before him, and prolonged his stay in Germany after the King had ordered his return. In the end, with a heavy heart, he was consecrated Archbishop, March 30, 1533. He took the usual obligations to the Pope, though with a public affirmation which nullified them, and received the pallium from Clement.

Cranmer's blameworthy subservience to the King's will in connection with the annulment of Katherine's marriage and the marriage with Anne Boleyn is a fault mitigated by the fact that he religiously believed, with nearly all his English contemporaries, in the royal supremacy, and by his equally strong conviction formed from canon law studies, that the marriage with Katherine was illegal.

Henry had already subdued the English church in what was called the Submission of the Clergy, May 1532. Thomas Cromwell now replaced Thomas More as chief minister of Henry, and Cromwell's hand is to be seen in the series of laws of 1534 by which the papal jurisdiction in England was annulled. Convocation declared, Cranmer presiding, March 31, 1534, that "the pope has no greater jurisdiction given to him by God in this kingdom than any other foreign bishop." This declaration has been called the foundation of the English Reformation. But its real foundations lay on the one hand in the political and dynastic situation, and on the other in the religious influences that were associated with the circulation of the Bible in English.

Tyndale's New Testament had appeared in 1525. In 1535, with Cranmer's encouragement, Coverdale's Bible was issued. In 1537 came the "Matthew" Bible which Cranmer had induced the King to authorize; it was dependent on Tyndale and Coverdale. The Great Bible of 1539, which was ordered to be placed in all parish churches, was virtually a reissue of the Mathew Bible.

The authorization of the Bible was Cranmer's greatest stroke on behalf of the Reformation in Henry's reign. He engaged in negotiations with Lutheran theologians looking toward an alliance of England with the Schmalkald League of Lutheran powers; but the effort failed through Henry's opportunist policy. Yet Cranmer was not a Lutheran in his view of the Eucharist. Before Henry's death (1547) his slowly moving mind had come, through reading the old monk

Ratramnus of Corbie on the sacrament, to reject transubstantiation and adopt a position practically identical with that of Bucer of Strassburg.

In Edward VI's reign (1547-1553) Cranmer, now an out-and-out Protestant, invited Bucer and other Continental reformers to England, and advanced an ambitious design for the unification of Protestantism which was only abandoned at the young King's death. In this reign, too, he made his second great contribution to the reformed Church of England in the Book of Common Prayer of 1549 and its revised edition of 1552.

The doctrinal differences of these two liturgies are considerable, and there is no reason to doubt that the second and more Protestant book was more in accord with Cranmer's mature position. But the changes do not affect the general liturgical quality of the work. The superb gift of Cranmer for framing the language of public prayer is scarcely surpassed by any of the known or unknown authors of medieval liturgies, and probably not approached by any modern. The work could only have been done by a man whose mind was saturated with the Latin liturgies, and sensitive to the qualities of English speech as a medium of devotion. In addition to medieval sources Cranmer used the contemporary work of Cardinal Quignon and that of Melanchthon and Bucer in the *Consultatio* authorized by Hermann of Cologne.

The English Bible and the Anglican Prayer Book, each in its own sphere unique, have met the religious needs of millions as perhaps no other books have done. It was Cranmer who did most to establish the position of the one, and who chiefly compiled the other. The Bible is of course best known in a later (1611) version; the Prayer Book proved a more permanent monument to his genius. It is for these services that Cranmer is one of the makers of modern Christianity. The Forty-two Articles of Edward, made permanent as the Thirty-nine of Elizabeth, were also chiefly compiled by him. Among his other projects was the revision of church law: he framed, indeed, a remarkable compilation of laws for the church, which never came into force.

Cranmer has often been presented as a mere time-server, yielding to every wind that blew, and has often been defended from this accusation. He might on occasion exhibit a fine courage, but the heroic temperament was not his. He found decision difficult, and controversy distasteful. It was his nature to live, as far as possible, peaceably with all men, and especially to avoid conflict on matters that seemed secondary or open to reasonable doubt. His awe of kings was in sharp contrast to the attitude of men like Calvin and Knox, and was the chief reason for his compromises. It was also the cause of his weakness in dealing with Queen Mary (1553-1558), under whom he came to the fire.

At the opening of her reactionary reign he remained at his post while others fled. Imprisonment and continual subtle persuasion were at last effective in bringing him to recant his Protestantism. What could a man of his disposition, who had supported the monarchy against the pope, do now, when the monarch commanded and exemplified subjection to the pope? His conscience was entangled. But he came through the phase of surrender to one of triumphant testimony to evangelical Christianity. What his enemies hoped would be his final humiliation proved their own consternation, when in the hour of death (March 21, 1556), he recanted his recantation and in downright terms upheld a scriptural faith: "As for the pope, I refuse him as Christ's enemy and Antichrist."

They chained him to the stake, his long white beard "covering his face with marvelous gravity." He thrust forward his right hand that had signed his denial, and calling out repeatedly, "This hand hath offended," held it in the heart of the flames, and so stood, rigid and statuesque, until his form collapsed in death.

John Knox

Scotland in the late Middle Ages repulsed the English attempt to conquer her, and thereafter maintained resistance to England by an alliance with France which many Scots justly regarded as too humiliating and costly. The medieval church of Scotland, from Ninian to Knox, had a colorful history. With the rise of nationalism the clergy had often shown patriotism as against the papal obedience. They had supported William Wallace against Boniface VIII and Robert Bruce against John XXII. The church held national synods, which habitually but vainly called for reform; but it was really ruled by selfish nobles and venal ecclesiastics. The popes, by sale of church livings and other corrupt practices, aggravated instead of correcting the prevalent abuses. The country was poor, but the higher clergy, with few exceptions, were wealthy and worldly. A synod of 1549 charged the clergy as a body with "profane lewdness" and "crass ignorance." The monks and friars were decadent and unpopular. For a century, however, education had been steadily advancing. The universities of St. Andrews (founded 1413), Glasgow (1450) and Aberdeen (1494), and the influence of Scottish scholars returning from foreign schools, were leavening society with a new culture.

In 1545 John Knox was in southern Scotland, bearing a two-handed sword in defense of the scholarly young evangelist, George Wishart, whom he describes as a "man of such graces as were never before heard of within this realm." On the question of Knox's birth-date the evidence of early sources is inconclusive, but certain facts point strongly to 1513 or 1515 instead of 1505, the date formerly received and still used in library index cards. Among these facts is the difficulty of supposing that a man of Knox's qualities at the age of forty-one served as armed guard to a man who is known to have been about thirty-two or thirty-three, and felt for him such glowing admiration as the words just quoted reflect. The later date, too, would require his contact with the philosopher, John Major, at the university of St. Andrews instead of Glasgow; and this would conform to the evidence of his familiarity with and interest in St. Andrews, and his relative neglect of Glasgow.

We know that he was born in or near Haddington, a prosperous little town which had given Duns Scotus and John Major their early schooling. His father, William Knox, was probably a free farmer, and certainly, on occasion, a warrior. His mother, a Sinclair, may have had relatives of some rank; but Knox called himself "a man of base estate." He was "slightly under middle height, of well-knit and graceful figure" with broad shoulders, long fingers, deep-set gray eyes that flashed with animation, black hair, and a long, black beard; and there was, says one who knew him, "an air of command upon his brow."

He must have felt as a student the new currents of revolt and revival then passing over Scotland. A few had read Wyclif's Bible; many now read Tyndale's New Testament, at peril of freedom and life. Patrick Hamilton, a young priest who had learned Lutheranism abroad and was burned at St. Andrews, 1528, influenced many by his teaching and death. If Knox was in St. Andrews soon after this he would find St. Leonard's College there affected by the new leaven. He probably studied there under John Major, a now aging scholastic of high repute in Paris and Glasgow (see p. 138), who approved of Hamilton's burning. Knox was to leave Major's theology behind, but to accept the liberal political theory of his *History of Greater Britain* (1529). Somewhere in the diocese of St. Andrews Knox was a priest, and a papal notary, about 1540. Before joining Wishart he had been tutoring the sons of certain noblemen. When and how he became a Protestant we do not know; he connected his conversion with the reading of John 17. His Protestantism was essentially Zwinglian, this being the position of Wishart, who had translated the Swiss Confession of 1536. It is an error to call Knox without qualification a Calvinist. In the main he subscribed to Calvin's teachings; but it is doubtful whether his views were altered by Calvin's influence at any material point.

Cardinal David Beaton, Archbishop of St. Andrews, represented the French and the papal interest. He burned Wishart, and was murdered soon afterward, 1546. The assassins and their friends held the castle of St. Andrews till a French fleet forced their surrender. Knox came to the castle with his pupils; strong pressure by Protestants among the defenders led him to preach, which he did with startling effect. He was nineteen months a prisoner, defiant of the faith of his captors, in the French galleys. Then Edward VI's government gave him a task in England for five years. He preached widely, chiefly in the north of England. He agitated against kneeling in communion, as unscriptural and idolatrous worship of the elements, and induced Cranmer to insert in the Second Prayer Book an explanatory note on the question—the so-called Black Rubric. At Berwick he established a puritan worship. He found time to win the affections of Marjorie Bowes, whose mother, a religious hypochondriac, he counseled in edifying letters, and after his marriage accepted as a resident of his home.

Urged by friends, he fled from England (1554), after Mary became Queen. Among the exiles at Frankfort, he contended for a modification of the Prayer Book. An utterance in which he had called the Emperor "another Nero," gave his opponents occasion to have him sent away by the magistrates. He was called to the pastorate of the Marian exiles in Geneva, where he associated with Calvin and imparted puritan ideas to Englishmen. He returned to marry Marjorie, and to make a hasty and perilous trip to Scotland in order to strengthen the cause of the Protestants. Geneva gave him his most peaceful years: he humorously looked back upon it as " a den of ease;" while he praised Calvin's achievement in creating "a perfect school of Christ." In 1557 he wrote a violent tract *Against the Monstrous Regiment of Women* attacking the dowager Queen and Regent of Scotland, Mary of Guise, and Mary Tudor. The tract made Queen Elizabeth (1558-1603) his personal enemy; but her government coöperated with him and aided the Scottish resistance to the regent.

On May 2, 1559, he returned to Scotland. Certain nobles had formed in 1557 a "Covenant" to defend the "Congregation" of Protestants. They were now in full rebellion against the Queen-Regent. Knox exhorted their discouraged forces: "Yea, whatsoever shall become of us and of our mortal carcasses, I doubt not that this cause, in despite of Satan, shall prevail in the realm of Scotland." Hearing such words, "the minds of men began wondrously to be erected;" and the English ambassador wrote home: "The voice of one man is able in one hour to put more life into us than five hundred trumpets continually blustering in our ears." With English help the revolution was accomplished. The French defenders of the old system withdrew. England now stood by benevolently, while Scotland was inwardly transformed. In a great service of thanksgiving Knox prayed for the perpetual peace of the two nations (1560).

Six famous "Johns" now collaborated in framing the foundation documents of the reformed Church of Scotland. Knox was the least learned, and the most determined, of this committee. The *Confession of Faith* bears in parts the marks of his vigorous and denunciatory style, and is a militant manifesto of Protestantism. The *Book of Discipline* outlines a church polity with one order of ministers only, and lay representation, by elders and deacons annually elected, in the government, discipline, and finances of the church. It contains also a utopian scheme for the advancement of education by an appropriation of church revenues; but greedy nobles, calling this "fond imagination," seized most of the property which the plan required. Knox's own *Geneva Service Book*, based mainly upon Calvin's revision of a Strassburg form which was a radical modification of the Mass, became the *Book of Common Order* and was authorized by the Assembly of the church in 1564.

The reformed church took over and revived the parish

life, and drew a somewhat inadequate ministry from the old priesthood. But the lords snatched most of the revenues and kept the ministers and schoolmasters poor. Reaction set in with the coming of Mary, the young Queen who had been brought up in France, August 9, 1561. Knox thundered from the pulpit of St. Giles, Edinburgh, against the "idolatry" of the mass in Holyrood, as a thing "more fearful than 10,000 armed enemies." In several dramatic interviews with Mary, he defended the reformed church. To Maitland of Lethington, who questioned the right of the ministers to meet without call of the Queen, Knox said sharply: "Take from us the right of assemblies and you take from us the gospel." He here opened a struggle for the complete autonomy of the church in its relations with the state, a principle which was only finally and unequivocally acknowledged by a parliament of 1921. With the defense of the church he coupled the claim of subjects to advise and to resist their rulers. He told the Queen in plain language what he had learned from Major: "If princes exceed their bounds . . . there is no doubt that they may be resisted even with power." Mary, trained in a doctrine of absolute royal sovereignty, with "altered countenance . . . stood as it were amazed more than the quarter of an hour." Thus Knox, in the name of religion, and of that conciliar church government which is common to Protestantism, served notice on all political absolutisms.

Knox's wife died in 1560 leaving two little sons. Calvin, writing to comfort him, called her a "most delightful" woman. In 1564 he married Margaret Stewart, aged seventeen, daughter of Lord Ochiltree and a relative of the Queen, who, as the English ambassador reported, "stormed wonderfully" at the match. Mary's own affairs of the heart were less happy than those of Knox, and conduced to her tragic downfall. The year 1567 marks the secure triumph of the Reformation, and the close of Mary's reign. Moray, as Regent for the infant James VI, favored Protestantism; he was assassinated in 1570. Chivalrous supporters of Mary kept up a fight on her behalf till 1573. Knox had other hindrances to complete success. The Regent Morton authorized the appointment of bishops in order to milk episcopal revenues into the political pail. Knox, while not absolutely opposed to bishops, warned against this dishonest arrangement.

But his abundant energies were now spent. He was temporarily silenced by a stroke of paralysis, and after a period of renewed labor he died, November 24, 1572.

Knox's greatness was not of the intellect, but of conviction and will. His life for twenty-seven years was a rapid drama of countless vivid scenes. His writings are fairly extensive, but are concerned with the crises of the age more than with the fundamental principles of religion. Outstanding among them is his *History of the Reformation Within the Realm of Scotland* (to 1566), a book hardly surpassed in his century for mastery of English, or in any century for brilliant handling of character and incident, but judged by modern standards, quite defective as a historical work. He had in a high degree the uneasy conscience, the resolute mind, and the masterful will of the puritan. Harsh as Knox was to his enemies, he judged himself no less harshly. He confessed to all the deadly sins. He even deplored his lack of energy and courage, while others found him the personification of both qualities. Morton, perhaps still wincing from Knox's rebukes, said above his corpse: "Here lies a man who neither feared nor flattered any flesh." He was direct and often immoderate in speech, and some have professed to see in him only a baleful and destructive fanaticism. Yet an opponent, Lethington, complained that at Knox's behest "we must forget ourselves and bear the barrow to build the houses of God." The structure whose foundation he laid was the reformed Kirk of Scotland, through which that little nation was to become great. Not for love of contention but to make the Scottish Kirk "visible and beautiful in all her proper ornaments," as part of that true church which is both holy and catholic, Knox, according to his lights, contended to the uttermost.

CHAPTER VIII

PATHFINDERS OF LIBERAL CHRISTIANITY

Our ongoing human life deals relentlessly with formulas, systems, and confessions of faith. It is the wisdom of the historical mind to perceive that even the most revered formulations and institutions are not final, that the heresy of one generation is not seldom the orthodoxy of the next, and that no authority can annul the law of change.

In the sixteenth century few had learned this wisdom. The confessions of the Reformation were devised with a view to finality and permanence. The fiction that "the Bible alone is the religion of Protestants" is dissolved on consideration of these labored documents which proclaim, and yet largely supersede, the authority of the Bible.

These formulas had their uses. They gave a helpful solidarity to the groups adopting them. Yet some at least of the adherents of confessions looked upon them as steps toward a more inclusive grouping, and craved solidarity on a larger scale. Such is the attitude for instance of John Francis Salvard of Geneva and his associates who in 1581 put forth the *Harmony of the Confessions of Faith.* On the Roman side the faith was armor-plated by the decisions of the Council of Trent; and most Protestants were content to retire within their denominational and confessional block-houses and postpone the effort to build a common fortress.

Modern Christianity, including Roman Catholicism in a

less degree than the Protestant churches, has been profoundly affected, however, by personalities who felt the atmosphere of confessionalism too stuffy, and who either opened windows, or walked out, exposing themselves to the dangers, and breathing the free air, of private judgment. In this connection Liberalism is a convenient, if rather indefinite, term to include a variety of tendencies hostile to the rigor and fixity of the confessional definitions of religion.

From Hans Denck and Sebastian Franck to Peter Bayle and G. W. Leibnitz, there are about twenty-five of such liberals sufficiently famous to be readily recalled by anyone familiar with modern history. Most of these protesters exhibit the liberalizing influence of Erasmus, or, more broadly, the deposit of humanism in Protestantism. In Lutheranism, as we have seen, Melanchthon was the chief perpetuator of an Erasmian element; in the Reformed churches the tinge of humanism was deeper. Nor did it fail of expression in the Church of Rome. It would be difficult to prove the controlling influence of Erasmus in post-Reformation liberalism. Yet much of it that he cannot be shown to have inspired, he can be shown to have strangely anticipated.

Most of the liberals of the period were protesters on behalf of truth conceived intellectually. But a considerable number were offended by the confessions mainly for spiritual or emotional reasons. If it is objected that such men as John Arndt and Jacob Boehme were not liberals but spirituals, it may be replied that their aim as much as in the case of Herbert of Cherbury the deist or Peter Bayle the skeptic, was one of liberation from the confessional restrictions. Intellectualists and spirituals alike were humanists in that they asserted the claims of the human personality against literal formulations of faith. Such men as Michael Servetus, Giordano Bruno, and John Amos Comenius, were about equally intellectual and spiritual. A number of our liberals were fundamentally concerned with the problems of reconciliation and union in Christianity. This is probably true of Hugo Grotius, Comenius, George Calixtus, and G. W. Leibniz; and Christian union was the sole passion of John Dury.

Though we all recognize the immeasurable influence of the early liberals upon the Christianity of today, it is difficult indeed to appraise their relative importance, or to discern among them creative geniuses to whom the modern enlightenment is specially to be ascribed. The three here selected are respectively an Italian, a Dutchman, and a German. One could almost as well have defended the selection of a Frenchman, an Englishman and a Czech. But at least it will not be doubted that the exponents of liberalism here treated stood for principles which have been increasingly meaningful to the passing generations.

Faustus Socinus (Fausto Sozzini)

The parents of Faustus Socinus were members of distinguished families of Siena, where he was born December 5, 1539. His father, Alexander, a brilliant law scholar, died at thirty, and Faustus was personally educated by his devoted mother, Agnese Petrucci. His education was literary rather than philosophical; but he felt the influence of the Reformation together with that of the Renaissance, and could say in later life that he had never been an adherent of the Roman church. His father's younger brother, Lælius Socinus (1525-1562), was a figure of some importance in religious circles. He may be classed with Michael Servetus and Bernardino Ochino as an early Anti-Trinitarian. As Vicenza about 1546, Lælius was a member of a group of advanced thinkers whom the Inquisition presently scattered. During the years 1547-1552 he visited most countries north of the Alps, conferring with Protestant leaders. He was on good terms with Melanchthon and Calvin, and was particularly friendly with Bullinger. Fresh from these associations he returned for a visit to Siena, 1552. Young Faustus was stirred with admiration for his traveled and accomplished uncle. Lælius, however, was a cautious soul, who, as Faustus afterward explained, "would not reveal his mind to everyone . . . lest the weak should be offended." He did not, however, wholly conceal his opinions, and Calvin admonished him against "the itch of questioning," recognized his disapproval of the death of Servetus, and was relieved when Bullinger drew from him a satisfactory statement of his faith. Lælius died at Zurich in May 1562, and Faustus went from Lyons to that city to care for his personal property. The view that Faustus obtained his opinions from a perusal of papers left by his uncle is now discredited, but this does not preclude the recognition of the fact that Lælius had awakened his interest in theology, encouraged his inclination to free inquiry, and given him one or two vital suggestions toward a doctrine of the Godhead.

The Inquisition was astir in Siena in 1561, when Faustus went to France, and settled for some months at Lyons. His uncle's death, as we have seen, drew him to Zurich, and this was the beginning of a year of wandering and uncertainty. That he had given up traditional Trinitarianism is shown by his *Explanation of the First Chapter of John's*

Gospel, 1562, in which, following Old Testament parallels, he argues that "the Word was God" meant "the Word was divine," not "the Deity."

Having spent some time in Geneva he settled at Florence, where he lived from 1563 to 1574, in the employ of a sister of the Duke. During this period he conformed to the Church of Rome, and avoided writing anything hostile to the church's faith. In a book *On the Authority of Scripture* published anonymously in 1570, he succeeded in pleasing both Roman Catholics and Protestants, though the work bore suggestions of a critical approach. He grew weary of caged comfort, and betook himself in 1574 to Basel, to plunge into biblical and theological study. His heterodox views alarmed the stiffer generation of Zwinglians and Calvinists who were now on the scene. He circulated in manuscript a book on the work of Christ in Salvation (*De Jesu Christo Servatore*), 1578, which assembled the arguments against the traditional doctrine of propitiation, and set forth a conception of moral influence. The doctrine pivots not on the atonement made by Christ, but on man's acceptance of it.

Associated with this view of salvation is the idea of God as omnipotent will, unhampered by decrees or commitments, willing his own pleasure, which is always good. This conception of God resembles that of Duns Scotus; but Socinus was untrained in scholastic theology and may have acquired it from other sources. God, conceived as will, is almost necessarily one person; and the subordination of the son to the Father is a point of emphasis. Jesus became immortal at his resurrection, and received supreme authority over those who are saved. He held the Eucharist to be a memorial only, and thought Baptism unnecessary.

Lælius Socinus had gone, recommended by Calvin and Bullinger, to Poland in 1558-1559, and his visit had aroused interest in that country on the part of many in Western Europe.

George Blandrata, a Piedmontese physician, who had studied and disputed in Switzerland, was now in Poland propagating unitarianism. Francis David, a Polish Reformed bishop, carried the doctrine so far as to reject prayer to Christ, and Blandrata, fearing the hostility of Bathory, the dictator of Poland, invited Faustus Socinus from Basel to persuade David to moderation. After long effort he failed to accomplish this. David died in prison. Blandrata was strangled by his nephew; and Socinus remained in Poland.

The attempted Reformation in Poland had come to a stage of confusion, and Socinus sought to bring moderation and peace among the parties. A Polish noble, Christopher Morstyn, gave him protection, 1579-1582, and Morstyn's daughter, Elizabeth, became his wife. In his travels and discussions he was often in danger of his life. He was accused of Arianism and of sedition. He published a number of books, preserving his anonymity in order to retain the income from his Siena property. When this was cut off he confessed his authorship, and called forth a violent attack instigated by Jesuits. In Cracow, 1598, he was seized in a sick-bed by students and dragged through the streets, and his books and papers were burned. Threatened with sword and fire, his answer was: "I retract nothing. . . . Do you what God permits." But he had six years more to run the gauntlet of this violent hostility, and to build up a connection of Socinian churches. He died at Luslawice, March

3, 1604, eager for that immortality which he regarded as the portion of the righteous alone.

The radicalism of Socinus is as marked in ethics as in theology. He derived from the Sermon on the Mount an absolute pacifism, utterly rejecting all warfare as forbidden to Christians. His pacifism is thus more thoroughgoing than that of Erasmus. Tolerance, he regarded as one of "the marks of a true church,"—a novel and startling idea to his contemporaries.

There were marked limits to his liberalism, particularly in his treatment of scripture. But he dared to take wide departures from the standard views, and advocated his heresies with such ability as to compel attention. The role he played required a fine moral courage. The assault on the doctrine of the Trinity which Servetus and others had begun, was extremely alarming to most Christians and had already called forth persecution and insult. About the time of Servetus' death an English archdeacon, John Philpots, wrote a book to justify his act of spitting on an "Arian." Socinus came from a soft nest in Florence to publish opinions that were calculated to bring upon him insult and abuse, wherever he might live; and through his later years he exhibited a courage consistent with his message. Repression was to eclipse his work in Poland. But when his following in seventeenth century Holland and England is considered, it becomes plain that Socinus was in the first rank of those who opened the way to a modification of the intolerant confessionalism of early Protestantism.

Jacob Arminius

Jacob Arminius was born at Oudewater, between Utrecht and Leiden, October 10, 1560. He was the son of a cutler named Hermand Jacobszoon, who died in Jacob's early childhood. The boy's uncle, the strongly Protestant parish priest of Oudewater, cared for his education. The Dutch war of liberation from Spain was in progress during his school days at Utrecht. In 1575, his uncle having died, he took his way with a professorial friend to Marburg, to learn on arrival there that Oudewater had been sacked by the Spaniards and his mother slain. He returned to the Netherlands, and after a period at Rotterdam, attended the newly formed university of Leiden.

At Leiden he became acquainted with theology and with the theological controversies then being waged. Arminius was an outstanding student, and in 1581 the officials of the Guild Merchant of Amsterdam, in accordance with a custom of the time, agreed to support him in his theological education on condition that he would afterwards serve where the Guild might determine. The Academy of Geneva was then attracting many young Dutch Protestants and to Geneva Arminius went.

Calvin had been dead for seventeen years, and Beza, his able pupil and associate, was at the height of his career. Arminius was unfavorable to the Aristotelian logic expounded in the Academy, having felt the influence of that able anti-Aristotelian Frenchman, Peter Ramus, who had perished in the massacre of St. Bartholomew, 1572. Some friction over this point resulted in his going to Basel; but he later spent three years (1583-1586) at Geneva, imbibing the teaching of Beza. With another Dutchman he then made a tour of Italy, pausing at Padua and Rome; and thus exposing himself to the later insinuations of opponents that he had come under the influence of the Jesuits. Late in 1587 he was back in Amsterdam; and early in 1588 he began his preaching and pastoral ministry there.

The Dutch Republic was still in a state of insecurity. William the Silent had been assassinated in 1584; his son, Maurice, and John Oldenbarnevelt were the leaders to whom the emerging nation looked. The strain of politics was now relieved by England's defeat of the Spanish Armada. But under the tolerant regime of Oldenbarnevelt theological controversies were arising, the bitterness of which he tried to allay by appointing a commission to draw up a form of government for the church, 1591. Arminius and his close friend Utenbogaert were members of this commission; but its work was not completed because of the criticism of extremists.

Arminius was now deep in controversy. Dirck Coornhert, in the spirit of Erasmus, had assailed the high Calvinist doctrine of predestination, with such force that his opponents had conceded that the "supralapsarian" doctrine of the decrees of God was erroneous. This was the view advanced by Beza (as a logical enlargement of Calvin's conception of the decrees) that the decree of salvation preceded the fall of man and contemplated man's fallen state as part of the plan of God. The opposing view, called "sub-" or "infralapsarian," represented God as decreeing the salvation of the elect after the fact of the fall. Arminius attempted to prepare a defense of Beza's supralapsarianism; but found himself leaning in the other direction. His thought went beyond the infralapsarian position, to one in which salvation rested not upon the decrees alone, but in part also upon the coöperation of the will of the elect individual.

It was about 1590 that Arminius came to this position. He did not conceal his views, but regarded them as more or less tentative and was in no haste to publish them. He was a busy pastor, and in 1594 was entrusted with the added task of reforming the school system of Amsterdam. In 1597 he engaged in a controversial, though not unfriendly, correspondence with Francis Junius, Professor of Theology at Leiden. In 1598 he wrote a refutation of the treatise on Predestination of William Perkins of Cambridge, an outstanding exponent of Calvinism. The opposition to Arminius found able leadership in Francis Gomarus, his colleague at Leiden and brother-in-law of Francis Junius whom Arminius had succeeded.

The atmosphere of controversy, and the labors entailed in defending his views, wore down the health of Arminius. In 1608 he wrote a *Declaration*, complaining of misrepresentation, and setting forth his real positions. He was charged with Socinianism for his view of the Trinity, but was able to show that his position was that of the fourth century orthodox theologians. With Utenbogaert he petitioned the States General for a synod in which to discuss the points of difference. This was refused, but he and Gomarus were summoned before the Great Council of the States. The members of the Council were favorable to Arminius, who was conciliatory; but Gomarus could not be satisfied or silenced. Oldenbarnevelt was seeking peace with Spain, and Arminius was accused of Spanish sympathies and pro-Roman designs. He wrote a condemnation of the Papacy, which made certain exceptions in favor of a possible good pope,—an attitude too moderate for his opponents. He was charged with Pelagianism which, in the sense that man can of himself fulfil God's law, he repudiated, quoting "without me ye can do nothing." His ability to turn the point of every accusation was held by Gomarus to be culpable subtlety, tinged by Jesuitism.

With declining strength Arminius defended himself in tract after tract. His disease was pulmonary consumption. Like other victims of this malady, at intervals he felt assured of recovery. His loss of the use of his left eye was regarded by his enemies as a divine punishment for his heresy. A new discussion with Gomarus before the Council at The Hague took place in August 1609. In the midst of it Arminius collapsed; he was taken to Leiden where he died, October 19. His staunch and able friend, Utenbogaert, and his pupil, Simon Episcopius, were to carry on his work. Episcopius, indeed, was the formulator of Arminianism, but the materials of the system had come from Arminius himself.

Arminius made a brave attempt to unshackle Dutch Calvinism from the scholastic confessionalism which men like Junius and Gomarus wished to fasten upon it. He does not repudiate predestination, but condemns supralapsarianism as subversive of the gospel and injurious to the glory of God and the honor of Christ. He modifies the infralapsarian position by making the decree of election apply only to those who repent, believe and persevere, and the decree of reprobation to the impenitent only. For this view he claimed the assent of the majority of Christians in all times. The modern reader of his *Declaration* will find himself in an atmosphere that would not be regarded as particularly liberal today. But the significance of Arminius is far greater than that which his mere revision of predestination would suggest. He asserted the liberal and conciliatory side of Calvinism. He stands to Calvin somewhat as Melanchthon does to Luther. H. D. Foster has drawn numerous quotations from Calvin which go to show the truth of the remark of that Calvinist puritan, John Goodwin, that "Calvin himself had many pangs of Arminianism upon him." The absorption of certain Calvinists in the doctrine of predestination was due less to Calvin than to his successor Theodore Beza and those under Beza's influence. Arminius praised the work of Calvin, particularly his *Commentaries*, which were prescribed reading for his own students; and his followers, the Remonstrants, claimed to be good Calvinists. The Synod of Dort (1518-1519) which condemned the Arminian doctrines, gave an increased explicitness to the doctrine of predestination, and so imparted to Calvinism a narrowing trend, where Arminius would have liberalized it.

In his advocacy of church unity Arminius was a true disciple of Calvin, who once wrote that he would "cross ten seas" to bring about the unity of the church. In 1606 Arminius delivered a long oration "On Reconciling the Dissensions Among Christians." After a masterly analysis of the causes of dissension, he rejects the methods of conciliation proposed by Rome, and elaborates a project for a general council whose members will be "men burning with zeal for God and . . . inflamed with love of truth and peace."

In these words he was describing himself. His love of truth, indeed, shattered his own peace; but it was a light to guide many good men of later days.

Gottfried Wilhelm Leibniz

It is not likely that the seventeenth century deserves better than others to be called "the century of genius," but if the reference is to philosophy alone the name is not misapplied. In England, Bacon, Hobbes, Locke and Newton stand out from the throng of lesser philosophers of the age, in whose company are included such unforgotten thinkers as Herbert of Cherbury, Milton, Boyle and Clarke. On the Continent philosophy flourished chiefly in the Netherlands, the native land of Grotius and the inspired Jew, Spinoza, and the adopted home of the Frenchmen, Descartes and Bayle. Pascal and the Cartesian Malebranche in France, and Vico in Italy, shared with these the empire of thought. Modern Germany before Leibniz had no philosophical genius; in him German philosophy rose at once to maturity.

Leibniz has been called, with pardonable generosity, the Plato of the modern age, and his mind had some of Plato's capaciousness and poise. Yet pure philosophy was not his sole, scarcely even his major, concern in life. He carried into metaphysics a fundamental interest in the problems of religion; he projected and actively sought the reunion of the churches; he labored for the advancement of science; he gave a vast amount of time to detailed historical research, and through his service to princes and contacts with men of state he exerted a beneficent influence upon public affairs.

Gottfried Wilhelm Leibniz was born at Leipzig July 1, 1646. His father, Friedrich Leibniz, then sixty-five years old, had been trained in law but held the chair in moral philosophy in the university. He had a fine library which after his death in 1652 was kept intact for his son's use. Gottfried was the child of Friedrich's third wife, Catherine, née Schmuck, the daughter of a professor of law. She was a gifted woman who combined Lutheran piety with a spirit of tolerance, and seems to have devoted herself to the education of her brilliant son.

Young Leibniz was a child-prodigy. At an age when most children today are in kindergarten he was learning Latin and Greek. At eight he was given the key to his father's library and began an extensive course of reading in the Latin classics. In his old age he could recite the Æneid, which he had memorized before entering his teens. Once initiated, he had little need of tutors. Systematically he traversed virtually the whole field of Western literature. The church fathers, the medieval scholastics, the Reformation theologians and some of the contemporary scientific and philosophical writers, were devoured while he was in his early teens. He had already acquired the habit of reading judicially both sides of a controversy. He used to go from his solitary study for solitary walks in the woods, reflecting on the contrasts between Aristotle and Democritus. When at fifteen he entered the university of Leipzig he found the lectures too elementary for his requirements.

It was inevitable that the young genius should respond to the stimulus of Descartes, who, as Renan remarks, "had refreshed philosophy with his plain, sober rationalism." The fascinating clarity of Descartes was the result of his mathematical method. Leibniz, applying himself to mathematics, found his professor in that subject incompetent; when asked to explain a problem he could only say: "This is the rule." In the summer semester of 1663, Leibniz sought abler instruction at Jena, where Erhard Weigel was able to satisfy his mathematical interests, while he also applied himself to history and law. Returning to Leipzig he published a book on the principle of individuation (1663); this was soon followed by a treatise on the philosophy of law (1664). He was awarded the master's degree, but in 1666 was refused the doctorate on account of his youth.

He left Leipzig in displeasure, and at Altdorf took the

degree of Doctor of Laws; but he declined the professorship to which he was invited and went to reside in Nürnberg. Here he became secretary of a branch of that famous society of alchemists, the Rosicrucian order,—a post which gave him opportunities for chemical experiments. Becoming acquainted with the enlightened statesman Boineburg, he was led into the service of the Elector of Mainz, for whose use he wrote a number of his works on law and politics, and of whose supreme court of law he became a member. In this period he wrote a work on the disputed Polish royal election, which gave him a wide reputation. Several brilliant political works were devoted to the problem of Franco-German relations. Leibniz conceived a project for the French conquest of Egypt as an outlet for Louis XIV's aggressiveness and a means of shattering Turkish power. He took the plan to Paris; it was rejected, but its author remained to form philosophical and political friendships (1672-1676). He finally entered the service of the Duke of Hanover, and Hanover became, except for occasional absences, his permanent home (1676-1716). He had already been twice in London, where he had met Boyle, Oldenburg and other members of the Royal Society; and at Amsterdam he had visited Spinoza who impressed him greatly and whose thought is reflected in the mature works of Leibniz. At Hanover he had charge of the court library, but this task absorbed only a small portion of his inexhaustible mental energy. Under both the Roman Catholic prince, John Frederick, and his Lutheran brother and successor, Ernest Augustus, Leibniz enjoyed complete freedom of utterance, and formed friendly relations with leading European personages in church and state.

The breadth of his learning, and of his acquaintance with

the learned, is reflected in the catholicity of his thought. He remarked that there were few people and few books that had nothing to teach him. Yet he possessed an original, independent and powerfully synthetic mind, so that, out of parts provided by thinkers of all ages, he wrought a substantially consistent philosophy. It was not a finished system: he was continually amending the details. We may not here attempt even an outline of its fundamental elements. Suffice it to say that his world is a world of harmonious multiplicity in unity, moved by an energy that is immaterial. It is a world of active immaterial beings called *monads,* created by the Supreme Monad, God, and proceeding from him by continual radiation ("*fulguration*"). This concept naturally recalls the "emanation" idea of Neoplatonic and Gnostic speculation. But his affinities are really with the thinkers of our own century. His emphasis upon vitalism as opposed to mechanism dissociates him from both Cartesian and Darwinian principles, and makes him a forerunner of Einstein and Whitehead. He compares the smallest particle of matter to a garden full of plants or a pond full of fishes, and declares that there is "nothing sterile, nothing dead in the universe."

The thought of Leibniz is characterized by a profound philosophical optimism which has often been severely criticized. To him the universe, while imperfect in detail, is filled with the beneficent activity of God, and, "by a contrivance of the Divine foresight," coördinated into a harmonious whole. Not by mechanical cause and effect, but by a "preëstablished harmony" of nature and grace, the physical and the moral, the world is unified and made comprehensible. Descartes, the exponent of a mechanistic world-order, had, in Leibniz' view, at one point narrowly missed this happy philosophical discovery, and so had remained "in the antechamber of truth." The true City of God is "the assemblage of all rational minds," in which alone the glory of God is manifested. We live in "the best of all possible worlds," in which "everything works for the success of the good," that is, of those wise and virtuous persons who conform their lives to what appears to be the will of God.

Voltaire, the ardent champion of Locke and Newton against Leibniz, wondered why in the best of all possible worlds there was so much cutting of throats; just as he wondered how the hunchback poet Pope could write "Whatever is is right," when God might have made him with a straight spine. Similarly Albert Schweitzer says he has never been able to understand how Leibniz could think the world the "best possible." But whatever objections may be taken to the comfortable phrase, Leibniz assuredly did not mean to paralyze efforts to improve the conditions of human life. He was not, it is true, an apostle like Schweitzer or a crusader like Voltaire, but like them he desired to banish the world's brutality. He was looking upon the world in its ultimate nature, not in its temporary modes, and thinking of the possible as contained within the real world. The actual world was not perfect, but it was capable of infinite improvement; and every individual was a potential co-worker in the betterment of its temporal state. He declines to assert a dogma of continual, necessary progress, but sees everywhere a limitless opportunity for scientific and ethical advance. In this light his teaching is a source not of social complacency but of social hope, and a challenge to progress and reform. We are to accept the past, but we are to build the future. "We ought," he says, "to be content with the order of the past, because it is in conformity with the absolute will of God, but we must try to make the future . . . in conformity with the presumptive will of God."

As a religious philosopher Leibniz had much in common with the great scholastics; but he quite escaped their dogmatism. In the freedom he claimed for thinking he was the heir of the Renaissance; and he was a prime inspirer of the Enlightenment with its enthronement of reason and its vision of human betterment.

In the ecclesiastical sphere he was a zealous progressive. He espoused the cause of the union of the churches, which had been the life-devotion of the Alsatian, Martin Bucer, in the sixteenth century, and of the indomitable Scot, John Dury, and numerous others in the seventeenth. A recent author regards Leibniz as the most distinguished supporter of church union in history. He became the central figure in a series of negotiations, begun by others, for reunion between the Roman Catholic and the Lutheran churches, and drew up an elaborate plan of union (1691) which was dropped from consideration in Rome only because of more pressing issues between France and the Papacy. Leibniz also engaged in correspondence on the subject with the great French Gallican prelate, Bossuet. When these efforts proved disappointing he labored to establish relations between the Russian and the Western churches. In this and in other matters, he exercised considerable influence on Peter the Great. He also attempted to bring together Anglican, Reformed, and Lutheran churches, and this effort was maintained virtually to the end of his life. He had the support of some prominent princes and numerous churchmen, but his indifference to creedal minutiae was out of accord with the spirit of the majority, and the political conditions of the period of the Wars of the Austrian Succession precluded the success of a vast scheme of unification.

Leibniz based his hopes upon the employment of the old conciliar principle. He aimed to pledge the negotiating groups to accept the decisions of a free ecumenical council. It was essentially the proposal not only of the late medieval conciliarists, but of Luther, Calvin, Bucer, Arminius and Dury. It should be said that Leibniz approached the problem in a spirit of fairness and conciliation rarely equaled in the history of such transactions. Though a Lutheran by tradition, his attitude was more that of an arbiter than that of the representative of a party.

In one other respect Leibniz notably anticipated modern interests and attitudes. He was one of the few Protestants of his time to take a sincere interest in foreign missions. He conferred in Rome, and afterwards corresponded, with Jesuit missionaries to China. Against their Jansenist critics, he defended their use of the Chinese classics, and he urged Protestant leaders to undertake comparable missionary enterprises. His conception of missions approached that of modern liberalism. He looked upon the task in terms of cultural and social enrichment rather than of the rescue of perishing souls. Under his influence the Prussian Academy, of which he was the chief founder (1700), pledged itself to the propagation of Christianity. His letters to A. H. Francke apparently aroused the Pietist leader to undertake his epoch-making promotion of missions.

Leibniz, in Bacon's phrase, took all knowledge for his province, and is the last of those universal geniuses of whom such a statement can justly be made. Yet the variety of his practical interests almost matched the extent of his knowledge. He died little appreciated and little understood, and with some of his best work unpublished. There was too much in his mind for one generation to receive. He never built up a school of disciples or a fraternity of associates. He remained unmarried; he labored in solitude, neglectful of sleep and meals. The oddities of his person—the large head, broad, hollow chest, bent back, bowed legs, and high-pitched voice—may have constituted a social handicap. He was charged with an undue regard for money and for fame; but he distinguished himself by a noble generosity toward those from whom he differed in opinion. It was his misfortune that England took his Elector to be its first Hanoverian King (1714); as a consequence he spent his last days in reduced circumstances, lacking princely favor. He died November 14, 1716, and was buried "more like a robber than what he really was, the ornament of his country,"—his admiring secretary being his only mourner. The greatly gifted man, whose superior genius made Diderot feel that he ought to run away and hide, was as lonely as he was great. Posterity was slow to appreciate him. It is only our own age, with its new vitalism in philosophy, its enthusiasm for science, its interest in missions and in Christian unity, that can appreciate the creative power that was generated under his midnight lamp.

CHAPTER IX

INSPIRERS OF MODERN PIETY

In the Renaissance the Papacy forfeited the moral leadership of Europe; in the Reformation it suffered irreparable loss of power. Its nadir of humiliation was reached in the sack of Rome, 1527, when, as Dr. William Barry has written, "a Medici pope and a Catholic emperor delivered the capital of Christendom into Lutheran hands." The policies of Pope Clement VII (1523-34) had vastly more to do with politics than with religion, and he shrank from every suggestion of reform. Only with the early days of Paul III (1534-49) did any hope of the recovery of greatness begin to hearten the depressed adherents of Rome.

The revival of the Roman church which marks the history of the later sixteenth century, took its origin not from the efforts of this reforming pope, but from a fresh stimulation of medieval piety, which found expression in a number of organizations, chiefly in Italy. The Oratory of Divine Love, a sodality devoted to the reform of worship; the Theatines and Barnabites, who actively sought the reform of the clergy; and the Capuchins, or reformed Franciscans, who preached effectively to the masses, through religious revival instituted an ecclesiastical resurrection. Spain, too, was to make a highly significant contribution to papal reform.

The Pyrenees have made the Spanish peninsula culturally an island. Medieval culture there was largely Moslem; and while it contributed immeasurably to the mental awakening of the Christian West, it received no enrichment in return. Spanish Christianity was militant and uncompromising. When finally victorious it inherited little from the Moslem civilization which it displaced; and the Inquisition kept the Spanish Renaissance well in check. Under the strong hand of that gifted scholar and ruthless disciplinarian, Francisco Ximenes (d. 1517), clerical reform was vigorously promoted. The firm discipline of the Spanish church was a great factor in the survival and rescue of the Papacy. But Spain's chief contribution to Rome in her hour of need was to be the service of a little, limping saint, whom war-wounds had turned from soldiering to prayer.

Ignatius Loyola

Ignatius Loyola was the son of a nobleman of Azpeitia in the little province of Guipuscoa on the Bay of Biscay adjoining Navarre. His aristocratic lineage is suggested by his father's ponderous name: Don Beltran Yanez de Onaz Y Loyola; his mother, Maria, boasted a name equally formidable and respectable. He was baptized "Inigo," but when he left Spain he called himself by the elsewhere more familiar "Ignatius" or "Ignacio."

A member of a family of thirteen, Inigo received in youth only a very poor scholastic education. He grew up somewhat lax in morals and highly interested in sports and shows. He once fell foul of the law by some prank or other in which his brother, a priest, was implicated. His mind fed upon erotic romances. But there emerged in him a strong military ambition; and his military conduct shows that he possessed in a high degree the proud sense of honor which was the ideal of the Spanish soldier.

The French were seeking the extension of their Navarre territory. In May 1521 they besieged Pamplona. Ignatius was an officer of the garrison. He insisted, against the wish of the others, on resistance, but the French cannon soon shattered the walls of the citadel. Ignatius was severely wounded in the leg by a cannon ball. When the wound healed a broken bone protruded; he insisted on an operation to remove this unsightly blemish, and bore the pain with amazing composure. During convalescence he asked for copies of some favorite romances. They brought him instead two famous books of religion: Ludolf of Saxony's *Life of Christ*, and the *Golden Legend* of Jacopo de Voragine, both in Spanish translation. The former is the most elaborate of medieval books about Jesus, and contains much edifying comment and devotional suggestion. The latter is a collection of lives of the saints, perhaps the most popular of all medieval books. Ignatius was filled with enthusiasm, especially for Francis and Dominic, and desired to imitate them. Elements of Ludolf's piety were also to enter into his own. Rival pictures of fair ladies he had known came before his active imagination; but he found himself happier when he dwelt upon "the holy wish to imitate saintly men." In reflecting upon these experiences he began to cultivate the habit of detailed self-analysis. A vision of the Virgin and Child seems to have been the definite beginning of his commitment to a saintly course of life. He planned a pilgrimage to Jerusalem, and he began to scourge himself. The piety of Luther began in the desire to save his own soul. The piety of Ignatius began in the ambition to become a great saint. It was a maimed soldier's sublimation of the motive of military distinction.

Riding from Loyola to Montserrat he encountered a baptized Moor who debated with him against the perpetual virginity of Mary and then rode off and left him. He felt inclined to pursue and slay the heretic, but decided to leave the decision to his mule. At a cross-road the beast left the road followed by the Moor, and thus prevented a lapse from sainthood at its beginning. At the famous church of Montserrat after a vigil like that of a knight's initiation, he hung his sword on the altar of the Virgin, obtained a confessor, for whom he wrote in three days the history of his sins, and took vows of chastity and poverty.

On foot, in pilgrim garb, he went to Manresa and entered on a course of merciless self-castigation. He mixed ashes with his food, wore a hair shirt and a chain, and daily prayed seven hours and flogged himself thrice. The torture and humiliation which he inflicted on his body did not save him from agony of soul. Like Luther, he was troubled with scruples. He was particularly worried because he became aware that his confession had not included all his sins. Memories of long-forgotten offenses came to his mind. His depressions brought even suggestions of suicide. He wanted to leap to death from the window of his cell. He went to a secluded cave, and intensified his inhuman austerities. He was a student of his own states of mind, but interpreted them in terms of medieval supernaturalism. He gained the ability to distinguish the promptings of the devil from those of God; and at last he concluded that all his anxiety about his confession of sins was prompted by the devil. This comforted him greatly. Happy visions and suggestions now predominated in his experience. Sitting one day on the bank of a river, he envisioned the future Society of Jesus. This was followed by a period of ecstatic visions of things divine.

Ignatius, in his ambition to be a saint, had won through to a positive standing ground. He had learned to discipline his own thoughts. Henceforth his struggle was to be less with himself and more with the wills and motives of other men. He had learned a technique, where Luther had discovered a faith, yet he too was in an exalted religious state. He made a beginning of the writing of his *Spiritual Exercises* in which he sets forth the way to control the impulses and imagination so as to attain holiness. The book presents a most exacting four-weeks program of exercises in devotion, involving concentration upon the sufferings of Christ and the development of a method of prayer. He now determined on a pilgrimage to Jerusalem. This purpose was born of Ludolf's references to Jerusalem and the record of Francis' efforts to convert the Saracens.

The harbor of Barcelona was closed on account of the plague and there he waited till a ship would sail, visiting the sick and performing other works of mercy, and discoursing on religion to admiring ladies. He declined provisions offered him, and begged for food in the streets. Wretched after a stormy passage he arrived in Rome. Pope Adrian VI blessed him; he gave to beggars the gold pieces thrust into his hands. Though he was once arrested as a spy, he was generally regarded as either a saint or a harmless idiot. His manifest holiness procured for him favors in Venice, and he got on board a good ship for Jaffa. Some well-to-do traveler was always moved to pay for his necessities on the way to Jerusalem. So impressed was he by his visit to the holy places that he wished to remain permanently in Jerusalem. But the Franciscan provincial ordered him to return to the West, and citing papal authority, overcame his protest. He returned in disappointment by the way he had come. Renaissance Italy did not attract him, nor

His ignorance of Latin had no doubt proved an inconvenience during his journey. He now began the task of acquiring the language of the church. He was not a natural academician, and it was only by force of will, accompanied by prayers and vows, that he was able to hold himself to the task. He made fair progress, and was given Erasmus' *Enchiridion* as a text. But he found it, he said, benumbing to his soul. Perhaps the inadequacy of his Latin was one reason for this. But he had not the slightest sympathy for the type of piety represented by that marvelous book. He now went to the university of Alcalá, which Ximenes had founded. His studies in philosophy and theology were interrupted by his conversations on religion with inquirers, chiefly women of the artisan class. Some students attached themselves to him, and a religious agitation, with emotional phenomena, was engendered. The Inquisition, ever watchful, investigated. Loyola was ordered to give up wearing sackcloth and going barefoot. There were, however, a number of later investigations. They revealed that group meetings had been held, given chiefly to simple medieval teachings about the sins and virtues, and advice to go to confession. His ministries had been attended, however, by fainting and unconscious fits on the part of a number of women disciples. In April 1527 Loyola was put in prison. He had been charged with advising women to go on pilgrimages, and making others swoon. He was now forbidden for three years to teach or hold meetings. The Archbishop of Toledo advised him to go to the university of Salamanca. Here again he got into trouble for giving instruction. His answers to the inquisitors were non-committal and he was put in fetters, but his saintly behavior soon won him release. Yet he was forbidden to give explanations of the difference between mortal and venial sins.

He resolved to leave his native land for its hostile neighbor, France. He took the journey alone. On March 3, 1528, he wrote from Paris to a lady who had befriended him in Barcelona: "I mean to stay here and study till the Lord bids me do something else." He had arrived a month earlier. He entered the famed College de Montaigu about the time young Calvin left it with his degree. He had brought from Spain a little money, but a rascal got it from him, and he had to beg far and wide for the means of subsistence. Except for trips to Flanders and England to procure funds, he settled down to study. Not knowing French, he could not advise the women of Paris about the sins and virtues anyway. He later changed to the College de Ste. Barbe, where the Scottish humanist, George Buchanan was one of his teachers. He took the master's degree (1534), but never completed the course in theology. But even at Paris he soon began to allow his studies to be interrupted by religion, and became the religious leader and master of a group of students.

At Ste. Barbe he had two room-mates, one of whom, Peter Faber (Lefèvre), a Savoyard, was a good Aristotelian scholar. The other was Francis Xavier, a gay young gentleman from Navarre, less than five feet tall, who kept late hours in the Latin Quarter. Xavier at first detested the saint, who was constantly harping on the saving of souls. Both men were finally subjected to his overpowering will, and he administered to them the Spiritual Exercises. Laynez, of Jewish descent, and Salmeron, both from Alcalá, the Castilian, Bobadilla, and Rodriguez, a Portuguese, were soon added to the intimate group who were to form the nucleus of the Society of Jesus. Many others were brought in some measure under his influence. Of the interesting stories told of his student days, one of the best is that in which he challenged a doctor of theology to a game of billiards, on the condition that if Ignatius should win, the doctor would take the Spiritual Exercises.

In 1535, in broken health, he left Paris. Just before leaving he was again made to answer to an inquisitor. He showed this official his now completed *Spiritual Exercises*, and was commended and certified to be free from heresy. He mounted a little horse and returned to Spain. He preached to thousands in his home town, assailed the married priests, and induced the magistrates to prohibit gambling. He visited the birthplaces of his Spanish associates. He went to Italy, and gave the *Exercises* to a number in Venice including the great Contarini, newly made a cardinal. His companions came by agreement to Venice, early in 1538. They went on, without their leader, to Rome, and Paul III showed them favor by permitting them all to be ordained as priests. At Vicenza Ignatius and Faber engaged in a Mission. Ignatius was now a priest, but he postponed the celebration of the mass for over a year; reassured by a vision he said his first mass in the Roman church of St. Maria Maggiore, Christmas Eve 1539. Members of the group labored in various parts of Italy. Ignatius, whose work began with women of the low orders, now instructed his disciples to "avoid all relations with women except those of the highest rank." They attempted in vain the conversion of Renée of Ferrara, but were more successful with Victoria Colonna, one of Italy's greatest women of intellect, who was won away from Protestant influences. Through the good offices of Contarini, Ignatius procured from the Pope the bull *Regimini*, establishing the

Society of Jesus, September 27, 1540. The *Spiritual Exercises* was approved only in 1548, and printed by Ignatius in August of that year. Its general circulation was prevented by the fact that Jesuits alone were at first permitted to use it.

In his petition for the recognition of the order, Ignatius referred to its intended objects:—"to advance souls, to propagate the faith, to give the Spiritual Exercises, to do works of charity, to instruct children and uneducated persons, and to hear confessions." Its members were to regard themselves as soldiers of God, fighting under orders of the pope. They volunteered to go wherever sent by the Vicar of Christ, whether to the Turks or to the "regions called India" or to the lands of heretics. Soon two Jesuits made a wild-goose journey to Ireland by way of Scotland, and Xavier began his mission to India. Characteristic was Xavier's reply to Ignatius' sudden and unexpected command to go thither: "Father, I am ready." Even before his election as General, Ignatius authoritatively gave commands to his converts.

At Easter 1541 Ignatius was elected General of the Order. He professed surprise, and entered upon his work with all the evidence of great humility. He drew up a simple code of rules, stressing obedience to superiors as to God himself, and devotion to the salvation of sinners. This more than military emphasis on obedience is the burden of a statement prepared by Ignatius just before his death. "I ought to desire to be ruled by a superior who endeavors to subjugate my judgment and subdue my understanding." "I ought to be like a corpse, which has neither will nor understanding." The *Constitutions of the Order*, drawn up about 1541, guards against any attempt to mold the decisions of the superior, whose will is to be regarded as the will of God. Ignatius also forbade all "friendships," or special attachments, between members of the Order.

With masterly efficiency Ignatius now guided from Rome the development of the Society. In Rome he also aided in the care of the famine-stricken, and initiated a campaign against prostitution. His late years were full of struggle and business. It was not easy to control even men pledged to obedience, and Ignatius was at times hasty and autocratic. One disobedient brother was expelled and turned away in a rainstorm. For some trifling matter Ignatius berated the loyal Laynez till he wept. He seldom spoke except formally and coolly to Polanco, his devoted aide and secretary. Yet such was the charm of the man's holiness that he continued to command the highest esteem of his associates.

In all his activity there is very little evidence of direct hostility to the Reformation on the part of Ignatius himself, prominent as this phase is in the work of his order. His critics and slanderers were priests, monks, or laymen of his own church. He had no more pronounced enemy than John Peter Caraffa, Pope Paul IV. Yet he set in motion a great power for the revival of religion in the Roman church, making it fit to cope with the determined forces of Protestantism.

Ignatius Loyola, more than any Stoic, excelled in self-mastery. In him the will gained complete control over the emotions. For this reason his motives are difficult to know and easy to misjudge. A self-controlled man is a concealed man; something remains inscrutable in his character. Loyola was not, in his relations with others, a confiding saint. "It is profitable to listen quietly," he wrote to the Jesuits at the Council of Trent, "in order to understand the minds of others." To listen quietly and avoid self-revelation was a lesson that he had learned well. It was, and remains, part of the secret of his power.

John Wesley

The conflict between Anglicanism and Puritanism was spent by the opening of the eighteenth century. A sturdy remnant of the Puritans had resisted the repressive laws of the later Stuarts, and taken advantage of the tolerant system of William III to form Presbyterian, Congregationalist and Baptist churches. New issues were arising within both Nonconformity and Anglicanism. Calvinism survived, in declining esteem. It was no longer an order of life and thought, but in the main merely the rigid principle of predestinationism set forth in answer to Arminianism. Socinianism was favored by a few, and was beginning to take shape ecclesiastically in England in Unitarian churches. A powerful leaven of liberalism was introduced by the Deists, with their appreciation of non-Christian religions, their conception of a world of law devoid of miracle, and their significant, if crude, suggestions toward biblical criticism. The works of the Deists are said to have been the favorite reading of a large element of the clergy. The prevailing profligacy and intemperance were attributed by the orthodox to the relaxing influence of the new thought. But the political bondage of the church rather than the thought tendencies of the age may have been responsible for the spread of irreligion. The established church was increasingly controlled by the government. Deprived even of its Convocation (1718) it lacked the organs of motion, and sank into the arms of the politicians. The bishops were Whigs, the lower clergy Tories; and few of either class were selected for religious qualifications. The social life of the laity was marked by coarseness. Profanity was an art, and crime, vice and cruelty were common. Philosophers in the church, like Joseph Butler and George Berkeley, might powerfully confute the arguments of the free thinkers; and devout believers might feed their piety on Taylor's *Holy Living,* Allestree's *Whole Duty of Man* or Law's *Serious Call;* but not before Whitefield and Wesley was the life of the common people stirred by a profound religious impulse.

John Wesley was born June 17, 1703, in the rectory of Epworth, an obscure village in the then marshy strip of Lincolnshire lying west of the Trent. The people were poor, uncultured, surly and vicious. Samuel Wesley, John's father, the rector of Epworth parish, was a stern, courageous, odd little man, who had been educated in one of the dissenting academies, but had become an ardent high churchman. His Toryism and severity were so much resented by his half-savage parishioners that they maimed his cattle and his dog, and burned his barn and his house. Susannah Wesley, the mother of the household, was the twenty-fifth child of Samuel Annesley, a distinguished nonconformist, but had also turned with conviction to the national church. Brilliant, capable and highly educated, she managed to feed and clothe her nineteen children on a sadly meager income, despite her husband's weakness for contracting debts, and to impart to the eight of her offspring who lived to grow up a fund of religious knowledge and unusual graces of character. Poverty that would have blighted other households became a means of useful discipline to the high-minded Wesleys. When Samuel and Susannah quarreled it was not over their pennies but over their politics. Indeed, John Wesley might not have been born if William III had not died in 1702; for the rector had left his wife because of her refusal to say "Amen" to the Prayer for the King, and only returned on the succession of Queen Anne. Fifteen months later John, the fifteenth child and second son was born. In 1709 at midnight in midwinter the boy narrowly escaped death in the burning rectory, the thatched roof of which fiendish enemies had fired. Some men formed a human ladder, and "poor Jackie leaped" from the window to their arms. In remembrance of the scene, he used to call himself "a brand plucked from the burning." His parents thereafter looked upon him as a child of destiny.

In his eleventh year he entered the Charterhouse School, London. His brother, Samuel, a capable, correct, and unoriginal minister, having finished at Oxford was now at Westminster, and kept an eye on the lad. For exercise John methodically ran round the garden three times each morning. He was moderately religious, read somewhat freely in non-religious authors, studied with good success Latin and Greek, to which he had been introduced by his mother, and even applied himself to Hebrew. At seventeen he went up to Oxford. He describes himself as "a very little fellow" at that time; and he never grew much taller. But he possessed a strong, athletic body, which was to bear an enormous strain triumphantly to old age. He has been called, for his physical qualities, "a human gamecock."

Oxford was academically at one of the lowest points of her history. Professors and fellows lived comfortably and lazily, and examinations were without terror. Serious students were few; the vast majority spent their time in pleasures neither intellectual nor innocent. Wesley played a little tennis, and wrote some frivolous verses, but pursued learning not only from a sense of duty but also from sheer delight. About 1725 an austere religion became dominant in Wesley. He began to read the classics of piety, and to keep a diary in which he laments such sins as boasting and intemperate sleep, and resolves "to avoid idleness, freedom with women, and high-seasoned meats," and to begin every important work with prayer. By progressive manipulation of an alarm clock he schooled himself to rise at four o'clock every morning.

His college was Christ Church; but in 1726 he became a fellow of Lincoln, then the best college in the university. "Leisure and I," he wrote to his mother, "have parted company." They had never companioned together much! That autumn his younger brother, Charles, came up to Christ Church. John had occasion to rebuke the youth's innocent gaieties. He was already seeking the spiritual reclamation of other students.

In 1728 William Law issued his challenging affirmation of piety, *A Serious Call to a Devout and Holy Life*. Wesley read the book and answered the challenge: it accentuated his austere and rather self-centered devotion. In July 1728, he was ordained a priest. He spent some months before and after his ordination in assisting his father at Epworth and Wroote, but returned permanently to Oxford in November 1729. The eager and companionable Charles had already formed a group of three earnest students for prayer and the visiting of jails. The group now added John and numerous others to its membership, and met in John's rooms. George Whitefield was one of the last of the two dozen admitted to the society and the only one besides the

Wesleys to attain to distinction. Students in derision applied nicknames to the group,—"Holy Club," "Bible Moths," "Methodists." Of these it was justly the last mentioned that stuck. Wesley was aware that the students who applied the name were recalling the Methodist school of physicians of the ancient world; but its applicability lay in the fact that the quest of holiness had never been more methodical than in the exercises of his group. There is a flavor of monasticism about the rules which John Wesley prepared for the society, though the avowed model was the practice of the primitive church. "My one aim in life," he wrote to his father, who had implored him to come and relieve him at Epworth, "is to secure personal holiness"; hence he could not leave Oxford where he was "screened from all the frivolous importunities of the world." Wesley's "conversion" was from this to a more unselfish devotion.

His father died in April 1735, and in October with Charles and two others, he went, at Governor Oglethorpe's invitation, as a missionary to Georgia. At sea a dangerous storm gave him heart-searchings. A company of Moravians nurtured in the simple faith of that communion then recently revived by Count Zinzendorf, sang hymns with unperturbed confidence during the tempest. Wesley was impressed, and took his first lessons in the school of Moravian piety. Charles Wesley soon returned from Georgia; John remained till December 1737. He had gained no success in his religious work, had made enemies by his stiff high-churchmanship, had been disillusioned about the "noble" Indians, whom he had found to be thieves and liars, and had been through a distressing love affair. He reached England in February, in a state of personal deflation; he was apparently looking forward to a sheltered academic career.

But the Moravians attracted him. They had really, he

felt, found the secret of the "devout and holy life," though their holiness was of a pattern at variance from his own. One of their young inspirers, Peter Böhler, then in London on his way to Georgia, conferred with Wesley. In a Latin conversation—they had no modern language in common—he said: "My brother, that philosophy of yours must be cleansed away by fire (excoquenda est)." His reference was to the "philosophy" of ritual and good works. Böhler had been trained a Lutheran, and he coupled with Moravian trustfulness Luther's doctrine of salvation by faith alone.

For some weeks Wesley was under a new religious excitement. On the twenty-fourth of May 1738, he attended an evening meeting of a newly formed religious society in a house in Aldersgate street, London. "There," he writes, "while someone was reading Luther's preface to Romans, about a quarter before nine, I felt my heart strangely warmed." The warmth came from a new assurance that Christ had taken away his sins. It was a definitive psychological release. In different circumstances, though also under Moravian influence, Charles had reached the same ground three days earlier.

Wesley's old "philosophy" was not really "cleansed away." It was essentially retained, though subordinated to the new impulse of faith. He followed still his old exacting rules, and they were to form the foundation of the Methodist discipline as the conversion experience formed the foundation of the Methodist enthusiasm. The unique ability to combine stern discipline with emotional fervor makes Wesley supreme among modern religious founders and evangelists.

Determined to extract all the honey from the Moravian hive, Wesley paid a visit to the centers of the Moravians at Marienborn and Herrnhut. His admiration was not uncritical, and he was a little repelled by the lordly ways of Count Zinzendorf, their pious patron. Some time afterward, embarrassed by the quietistic tendencies in Moravianism, and out of favor with their London leader, he withdrew from their company in Fetter Lane (1740), taking with him nearly a score of followers who joined the Methodist society of the Foundry which he had instituted a few months earlier.

On account of the "enthusiasm" which Wesley's new assurance had imparted to his preaching, he was excluded from numerous Anglican pulpits. Meanwhile George Whitefield, an innkeeper's son who had earned his way through Oxford, had become a brilliant preacher. He had a vivid and florid imagination, a voice for oratory comparable to Caruso's for song, and rare perfection of gesture and dramatic delivery. He had learned the art of arousing the emotions of massed congregations. Some months in a mission to Georgia had added to his fame and pulpit power. Having on his return suffered exclusion from the London churches, he boldly pioneered a way to evangelistic success by an open-air preaching campaign centered at Kingswood, a newly populated mining area near Bristol whose people were ignorant and degraded and neglected by the church. About to leave for London and America, he invited Wesley to take his place; and Wesley decided the question by lot! On April 2, 1739, overcoming great reluctance at so novel a procedure, he began his real career, when he preached in a brickyard beside Bristol to 3,000 sooty miners, from the text: "The spirit of the Lord is upon me, because he hath anointed me to preach the gospel to the poor." It was the beginning of a national, indeed a world-wide, mission to the forgotten man.

Whitefield accomplished much before his death (1770), but to compare him with Wesley is like comparing a meteor to a planet. Not his least service to the great revival was that of finding for Wesley his true function.

Wesley, though by habit reserved and scholarly, strangely proved even more effective than his forerunner in stirring the emotions of his hearers. He was surprised and perplexed by the nervous agonies into which men and women of all classes were often thrown. But he was more tolerant of their outcries than his brother Charles who at Newcastle sent certain "unstill sisters" to a far corner of the room, and thereafter obtained a quiet hearing. Even the reading of one of Wesley's sermons could bring a staid layman to cry out against the devil, and hurl himself repeatedly on the ground. It was not Wesley's use of hell-fire imagery that made them roll and rave; for he seldom referred to hell, but glowingly proclaimed the love of God. Yet he thought their sufferings due to "Satan tearing them as they were coming to Christ"; and their own presuppositions supplied a strong sense of violent conflict with demonic powers. In time Wesley found the opposition of demons wane, while that of humans became serious.

The mob violence so often threatened and inflicted on the early Methodists, and so often encountered by Wesley himself, was due to the incitement of interested persons and the prevalent brutality of the age. As a traveling evangelist he was regarded by many of the clergy as a dangerous interloper, while his discipline was resented by the liquor and theatrical interests. Wesley was the victim of malicious false reports. He was charged with sedition and with Romanism. During the rebellion of the Forty-five, a Cornish mob, supposing him an agent of the Young Pretender, howled for his blood. Coolness itself, he managed to get a hearing, and made them all his friends. Not infrequently he went straight to one who seemed to lead the persecution, and "after a few sentences, the lion became a lamb." "I will knock the first man down that touches him," said one suddenly converted bully. "Sir, I will spend my life for you," said another. In many such adventures, he never suffered more than slight injuries. He was invariably self-possessed, good-natured, and devoid of fear. If he feared anything it was mud-stains and the disheveling of his garments, for he liked to be neat and immaculate. Horace Walpole once remarked that Wesley was "wondrous clean."

Cotton Mather's maxim for ministers: "The saddle is the seat of health," was vindicated in the case of Wesley, "the Lord's horseman." He probably held the world's record for mileage on horseback until it was broken by his disciple, Francis Asbury, in a more spacious land. Most of his 250,000 miles of travel were taken in the saddle. He records many interesting facts about his numerous mounts, whose qualities he could well appreciate. He preached more than 40,000 sermons, not all of them good, but some of them great. At eighty-three he said: "I am never tired," but at eighty-five he complained that he could no longer preach more than twice a day. His benevolent face and slight figure, his long hair—so worn to avoid the expense and inconvenience of the then fashionable wig—now turned from black to white, and his clear, far-reaching voice had become familiar to countless thousands of Englishmen, and to many in Scotland and Ireland. He paid about fifty visits to Ireland (1747-89), for whose scenery and people he had a discriminating appreciation, and made some thousands of converts there. Scotland he visited twenty-two times (1751-90).

"Everyone here at least loves to hear the Word of God," he said; and again, with that penetrating wit which came easily to his pen: "I admire this people, so decent, so serious, so perfectly unconcerned." Whitefield, the Calvinist, had stirred the Scots to emotional demonstration. Wesley, the Arminian, found them attentive but undemonstrative. It is probable that his message became a pervasive influence in the Kirk, in which Moderates and Evangelicals were then in conflict.

The areas in which he chiefly labored were the scenes of England's rising industrialism. It was there that he found, in their neediest state, his beloved poor. He trusted the poor, and distrusted the rich. He wrote to a nobleman: "I do not desire intercourse with persons of quality." He prayed that if the Lord wanted to save the rich he would choose other missionaries; "I would rather continue to preach the gospel to the poor." The trouble was that, under his instruction in providence and frugality, the poor began to grow rich! He then faced the old vicious cycle of religion and property. "The Methodists," he said, "grow diligent and frugal; consequently they increase in goods. Hence they proportionately increase in pride," and other major sins. His solution of the puzzle was expressed in the immortal economic triangle: "Gain all you can; save all you can; give all you can."

Wesley was in fact more concerned with the behavior of his converts than with their theology. Revolting from the predestinarian presuppositions of Thomas à Kempis, he had early pitched his tent with the Arminians; and when the issue was forced upon him he assailed the degenerate Calvinists with crushing satire—and with indefensible use of an opponent's materials. Yet it has been cogently argued by Dr. Cell that he was in substantial agreement with the

Calvinism of John Calvin himself. If he preached forgiveness and love with more emphasis than did the Genevan reformer, he also greatly stressed the Reformation doctrine of justification, on which he declared his accord with Calvin. He obviously resembled Calvin rather than Luther in the activism of his ethics, his proclamation of a social Christianity and his espousal of social reform. Though a well-read theologian, he was impatient of the refinements of dogma. Generally he avoided the "hot disputes" of theology as more "subversive" of religion than the error of reprobation.

He was a tolerant, open-eyed truth-seeker with a tendency to skepticism and a strong bent toward both pure and applied science. He was one of the first Englishmen to appreciate the importance of electricity, which he began to study in 1747. "What an amazing scene is here opened for after years to improve upon," he remarked. He was a disciple of the scientific scholars who partly anticipated in that age the Darwinian account of the evolution of life. Notwithstanding some remarkable survivals of superstition in his brain, Wesley was a man of the Enlightenment.

But more than all else; he was a saint, a man completely consecrated to an unworldly aim. His biographers reveal to us his scientific interests, his political prejudices, his pathetic if amusing love affairs and unfortunate marriage experience, his autocratic rule of his subordinates; but all these matters are peripheral to his personality. An inward glow of pure devotion burned all waste out of his life and made possible his amazing career as a saint and an apostle. There were always those who opposed and defamed him; but the masses learned to appreciate his deep sincerity and high consecration, and they made a great response to his proclamation of the love of God. Stirred by religious zeal,

they were marshaled into a disciplined army which meant ten times more for the good of England than all the overseas expansion of his lifetime. When he died, there were 8,000 groups of them in England and in Wales, under as many class leaders; while 2,000 local preachers and 200 traveling preachers multiplied his power; and in America the Methodist Episcopal Church was in full operation.
the Methodist Episcopal Church was in full operation.

The bishops having declined his repeated appeals to ordain ministers for America, Wesley, who had long believed presbyterial ordination justifiable, with other presbyters of the church ordained the needed ministers. He always professed and felt a deep loyalty to Anglican principles; but his followers, recruited largely from classes neglected by, and unfamiliar with, the church, had less hesitation in severing Methodism from Anglicanism.

Though Wesley, perhaps largely because of the importance of saving time, ruled his followers with something like autocratic power, he so organized them in societies as to give them an invaluable training for civic and political affairs. His work has justly been held largely responsible for that revival of the sense of humanitarianism and civic duty which lies behind the whole series of English nineteenth century reform laws. A lover of his fellowmen, it was fitting that his last letter was an exhortation to Wilberforce, the crusader against slavery, to "go on in the name of God." He died March 2, 1791, and on the day following was "borne to his grave by six poor men, leaving a library, a well-worn gown, a much abused reputation and the Methodist Church." To many besides the 40,000,000 Methodists of today, Wesley has left an incalculable legacy. He brought to Protestantism a new social optimism, and vastly helped to make it less dogmatic and more benevolent and humane.

Friedrich Daniel Ernst Schleiermacher

The world into which Friedrich Schleiermacher was ushered November 21, 1768, was astir with religious and social conflict. Eighteenth century German Protestantism exhibited a definite cleavage between two tendencies which had been inherent in the Reformation and were then manifest as Rationalism and Pietism. English Deism and Free Thought insisted on the subjection of dogma to rational inquiry; and this spirit bore fruit on the Continent in Voltaire's brilliant assault upon traditional Christianity, and in the more solid genius of Lessing, in whom the German Enlightenment reached its summit. Of Lessing Goethe said: "Only one equally great could understand him: to mediocrity he was dangerous." Mediocrity ever prevails however: and the Enlightenment left the majority in spiritual perplexity. Schleiermacher's father confessed to his son that he had preached for twelve years doctrines which he did not believe, justifying himself on the basis of the theory of "accommodation" employed by Lessing to interpret the history of revelation. If God "accommodated" revelation to the undeveloped understanding of early ages, the preacher might accommodate his teaching to the viewpoints of his hearers. No wonder that many were anticipating the dissolution of Christianity.

The decisive importance of Immanuel Kant's *Critique of Pure Reason*, 1781, came slowly to recognition. Without the slightest reaction to scholastic dogmatism, Kant led philosophy away from the worldly optimism of the Enlightenment. "God, freedom, and immortality," he affirmed,—not indeed as rationally demonstrable but as postulates of the moral order, necessary in a moral world. Kant furnished to Schleiermacher's generation a new philosophical orientation, and offered a fresh if somewhat ambiguous support to Christianity. At the same time Romanticism, with its varied literary expression, was reviving the emotional life of the age. Under its impulse John Gottfried Herder, friend of Goethe, Claudius, Richter and Schiller directed religious thought away from dogmatic conflict to "humanity," and stressed with warmth of emotion the imagery and poetry of the Bible.

If between Leibniz and Kant religion had derived small comfort from philosophy, it had received fresh practical affirmation in Pietism. Specifically this was a group movement instituted about 1675 by Philipp Jakob Spener and later developed at Halle under the leadership of August Hermann Francke. Count Zinzendorf, the organizer of the revived Moravian Church, drank deep of the biblical and mystical piety of Halle. Francke promoted missions and religious education, but lapsed into a new evangelical dogmatism, while the Moravians exhibited a unique communal piety. Schleiermacher, like Wesley, owed a religious debt to the Moravians; like Wesley, too, he found their interests too narrow for the expansive life that called him. But in his case Moravianism exerted its influence in childhood, since it colored the religion of his parents. To them he owed the dominant note of spirituality in his character.

He himself said that piety was the maternal womb of his soul. "I can recall its first stirrings," he adds, "it was during a walk with my father." Scarcely less potent was the influence of his devout and gifted mother. Both parents were from families of Reformed (Calvinist) Church ministers. Daniel Schleiermacher, eloquent preacher of Elberfeld, was so far an experimenter in religion as to become involved with an extravagant apocalyptic sect, and to be charged by enemies with witchcraft. Gottlieb, his son, Friedrich's father, in his training for the ministry left his early fanaticism behind and was intellectually well equipped, but there remained in him "something undisciplined, passionate, restless, divided." Alive to the currents of rationalism, he nevertheless used a Moravian handbook for the instruction of his children. He was a military chaplain, and his frequent absence from the home circle left the care of the children largely to his wife. She was the daughter of a preacher of repute, and the sister of Samuel E. T. Stubenrauch, for some years professor in the theological faculty at Halle. Friedrich was the second member of the family. His sister Charlotte let him fall from her arms in babyhood, with the result that his shoulder remained slightly deformed. Charlotte exercised a gracious influence over him in his boyhood; at seventeen she devoted herself to service with the Moravians. A younger son, Carl, whom the father playfully called "our savage," became a business man. "Fritz is all spirit and Carl all body," wrote the mother when Fritz was twelve. He grew to manhood slender and far from robust, studious and short-sighted, but with a noble countenance, captivating voice, and rapid gait.

From Breslau, his birthplace, he was taken in his tenth year to Pless. His schooling was not intensive: he had time for his own thoughts. Doubts about the affirmations alike of historians and of dogmatists occasioned "manifold internal conflicts," in which his young powers were given useful exercise. He was now (1783) sent to a Moravian school which was presently removed to Niesky. Clearly the school was chosen for reasons of religion. His mother lived to rejoice in his admission to communion with the Brethren; he was fifteen when she died. Two years later he passed to a theological seminary at Barby. Here he became conscious that his pious teachers were shielding their pupils from the best learning of the age, and he fell into a mood of sorrowful doubt and denial. In no small degree his depression was due to the anticipated and later realized shock and disappointment of his father over his apostasy. His plea now was to be allowed to go to Halle, where Rationalism had long since replaced Pietism and studies were free.

At Halle, 1787-89, Schleiermacher lived with his wise and generous uncle. He regained the full confidence of his father, who now in correspondence acquiesced in, and aided, the son's quest of truth. He read widely in philosophy, and it was Kant who chiefly fascinated him. He neglected the lectures of his professors, but passed their examination and was graduated licentiate in theology (1790).

On leaving Halle Schleiermacher entered a period of frequent changes of location in which he came to know Germany and to experience the intellectual forces of the time. He was in turn tutor to the family of an East Prussian count, teacher in an orphanage and at the same time in a teacher-training school in Berlin, assistant pastor at Landsberg, chaplain in a Berlin hospital, and court preacher at Stolpe on the Baltic. His powers matured under the influence of the French Revolution, Romanticism, and the Kantian philosophy. In Berlin he read Goethe and Shakespeare, and studied Italian, in the literary circle of the gifted

Jewess, Henrietta Herz, and formed a brief but significant friendship with Friedrich Schlegel. Schlegel drew him deeper into Romanticism, and urged him to write, but also aroused in him a certain resistance that led him to assert his own genius. Schleiermacher formed at this period a chivalrous attachment to Eleanore Grunow, who, fortunately for his career, finally declined to free herself from a wretched marriage in order to become his wife.

He returned to Halle in 1804 as university preacher and *Professor Extraordinarius* in theology; but after the Battle of Jena, 1806, the university was dispersed. At this period he first gave distinguished leadership to the cause of German patriotism against Napoleon. In 1809 he formed a happy marriage with Henrietta Willich, who was twenty years his junior, the widow of a clerical friend. In that year, too, he took up his permanent residence in Berlin, where he occupied a post of great importance for the nation. He made the pulpit of Trinity Church a national oracle in the cause of resistance to Napoleon and in advocacy of internal reform and religious revival. He helped to found the university of Berlin (1810) and occupied in it the chair in Theology. He was engaged in countless public duties, and embraced in the circle of his personal influence and affection many persons of varied type and social rank.

As an inspirer of patriotism he was not surpassed even by Fichte; but in contrast to Fichte he rejected the state's infringement on the self-government of the church. In the struggle induced by King Frederick William III's attempted Prussian Church Union of 1817, he stood for unity against the sectarian Lutheranism of Claus Harms, yet stoutly opposed the King's policy of coercion. He wished to substitute the common name "Evangelical" for both "Lutheran" and "Reformed," and sought what he called "a well-organized Christian presbyterian system" in which freely elected elders would coöperate with the ministers in governing synods.

During his life-time Schleiermacher's influence was largely confined to Germany. He wrote in terms of scorn of the religion of the "proud Islanders" and of the French. But after his death (February 12, 1834) his writings came to exercise an ever growing influence upon Protestant thought and life in all lands.

Schleiermacher spoke more easily and more expertly than he wrote; yet his writings impress us as works of genius. This is especially true of the early works, the *Speeches on Religion*, 1799, and the *Soliloquies*, 1800, both first published anonymously. The former was addressed to the "cultured despisers" of religion. In a sense it marks for Protestantism that religious appropriation of the emotional force of Romanticism which Chateaubriand's romances and *Genius of Christianity*, 1802, less successfully achieved for Roman Catholicism. Religion for Schleiermacher has its roots in feeling, not in thinking; and theology is thinking about feeling. He studies religion not from the framework of theology but from "the interior of a pious soul." "A longing for love, ever satisfied and ever again renewed, forthwith becomes religion." Religion is a sister of Art. He calls it "a sense and taste for the infinite," but criticism led him to drop this phrase in his second edition. His fellow ministers were shocked by the Spinozist pantheistic tendency which they found in the *Speeches*. The "cultured despisers" on their part offered faint praise, but in large degree ceased to "despise"; for Schleiermacher had shown reasons, more valid to Romanticists than to theologians, for placing religion at the very heart of culture. In the *Soliloquies* he lays a foundation for morality in the inner life, and eloquently celebrates the experience of liberation and exaltation which he has himself attained in spiritual introspection. Thus in two short, surprising books, religion and morality were reclaimed from the territory of dogmatists and academicians and established among the fundamental urges of life. With like literary impressiveness he wrote *Christmas Eve*, 1806, in the form of a report of the charming conversation of a group of friends bound together in an unforced and truth-seeking piety.

In the later works inspiration largely yields to logic and erudition, though without the loss of originality. In 1807 he made his first and most important contribution to biblical criticism in an essay in which he exhaustively disproved Paul's authorship of I Timothy. This study gives him a place of eminence among the founders of historical criticism. Ably critical, too, are his introductions to the several Dialogues of Plato, in the translation of which he filled spare moments for over twenty years, and his *Outline of a Critique of Previous Ethical Theory*, a polemic against all moralists except Plato and Spinoza for their failure to recognize the individual. His own ethical system was never completed, though he published various essays in the field, and two treatises, *Philosophical Ethics* and *Christian Ethics*, appeared after his death. He builds his ethical thought about the concept of freedom, as he builds his theology about the principle of dependence. In ethics he is indebted to Kant, and a Kantian vitamin of moral earnestness is recognizable in most of his works. He is best known to students for his elaborate theological work, *The Christian*

Faith, 1821-22. His *Brief Outline of the Study of Theology*, 1811, contained "philosophical," "historical" and "practical" sections, and *The Christian Faith* is an expansion of the first of these. "Christian doctrines," says Schleiermacher, "are accounts of the Christian religious affections set forth in speech," and "where these [affections] do not exist the doctrines cannot arise." Thus theology becomes an explication of the religious emotions; external revelation gives place to emotional experience, and theological science is turned upside down.

Schleiermacher had the boldness to write to a friend in 1822: "With my dogmatics a new epoch will begin . . . in the whole of theological science." The judgment has been substantially repeated in countless later estimates. The work was not simply a superior work of the familiar class of dogmatic *summæ*, or reasoned catalogues of beliefs. Through all his carefully systematized categories runs the conception that nothing in theology is static or lifeless. All is vital with the life of the changing church and the inner experience of its members. As in philosophy he seeks to mediate between rationalism and idealism, in theology he affirms at once individualism and fellowship. For this he has been charged with inconsistency. But it should be remembered that his Christian individualism has no relation to the harshness of the separatist. Any such tendency is corrected by the fundamental piety from which the structure of his thought arises, with its concept of religion as a feeling of dependence upon God. Jesus, the perfectly God-conscious man, is central to the church, through which he continues to impart to its members the salvation which is the attainment, in the degree possible, of his own God-consciousness. The Christian life is marked by "spontaneous activity in living fellowship with Christ." As God is the unifying principle of the universe, the consciousness of God is the fundamental unifying element and constitutive principle of the church. In the *Speeches on Religion* he had glowingly described the "superabundant life of the City of God" as manifested in the worshiping congregation in which "every man is a priest in so far as he draws others to himself in the field he has made his own," and in which the pious speak and listen, give and receive. Here he argues that the church as a whole, disengaged from the world, "takes shape through the coming together of regenerate individuals to form a system of mutual interaction and coöperation."

Schleiermacher does not labor over rational proofs of the existence of God. For him the recognition of the universality of the "feeling of dependence" renders such proofs needless. If it is claimed that some individuals have not this feeling, he explains the lack of it in terms of arrested development. Like his forerunner, the "God-intoxicated" Spinoza, he leaves some vagueness in his definition of God. In the second of the *Speeches* he describes God as "exalted above all personality, the universal, productive, connecting necessity of all thought and existence." In the *Christian Faith,* while he moves so far to the right as to present a catalogue of the divine attributes—eternity, omnipresence, omnipotence, omniscience—these terms are held to signify merely something special in the manner in which the feeling of dependence is related to God.

As we read the "romanticist-theologian" there comes to mind the maxim of the Elizabethan soldier-sonneteer: "Look in thine heart and write!" He has been censured for his undue emphasis upon emotion. One may question for example whether curiosity about the universe is not as elemental as the sense of dependence upon it. But in his case certainly "it is the heart that makes the theologian." However he may have called to his aid his well-loved Plato, or Spinoza or Kant or other masters of thought, his theology was primarily a projection of his emotional piety, the product of an energic force generated in his own personal life. That force was great enough to liberate him from dogmatism, and make him the chief modern liberator of theology. Almost all later Protestant thought before the emergence of the Barthian school bore reference to his work, and Roman Catholic Modernism has obviously, if indirectly, felt his influence. Modern psychology too may be said to have empirically verified much that he intuitively discerned. But he was not concerned with theology merely as an intellectual pursuit. As in the case of other great theologians, his main concern was with religion as a primal fact of human experience and with Christianity as its highest form. Accordingly the measure of his greatness lies in the increment and revival that he brought to Christianity. He was even more an inspirer than an interpreter. He not only revived theology; for many he restored religion itself, and his life and writings stand as a challenge to every generation of its "cultured despisers." An eager herald of future spiritual progress, he held, like many of the greater poets, conscious fellowship with posterity. "I am," he writes in the *Soliloquies*, "a prophet-citizen of a later world, drawn thither by vital imagination and strong faith. . . . All who like myself belong to the future are drawing toward each other in love and hope, and each in his every word and act cements and extends a spiritual bond by which we are pledged to better times."

SELECTED BIBLIOGRAPHY

(Revised, 1964)

Church Histories:

Baker, A. G., Editor, *A Short History of Christianity*. University of Chicago Press, 1940; Fourth printing, 1947.

Gifford, W. A., *The Story of the Faith. A Survey of Christian History for the Undogmatic*. New York: Macmillan, 1946.

Latourette, K. S., *A History of Christianity*. New York: Harper & Brothers, 1953.

Lortz, J., *History of the Church*. Translated and adapted from the fourth German edition by Edwin G. Kaiser. Milwaukee: Bruce, 1938.

Sohm, R., *Outlines of Church History*. Translated by M. Sinclair with a preface by H. M. Gwatkin. Introduction by J. L. Adams. Boston: Beacon Press, 1958.

Walker, W., *History of the Christian Church*. Revised by C. C. Richardson and Others. New York: Scribner, 1959.

Biographical:

Baring-Gould, S., *Lives of the Saints*. Revised Edition, 16 vols. Edinburgh, 1914.

Britt, A., *The Great Biographers*. London: Whittlesey House; New York: McGraw-Hill, 1936.

Dunn, W. H., *English Biography*. London and New York, 1916.

Garraty, J. A., *The Nature of Biography*. New York: Knopf, 1957.

Johnson, J. C., Biography, *The Literature of Personality*, with an Introduction by Gamaliel Bradford. New York and London, 1927.

Lee, Sir Sidney, *Principles of Biography*. Cambridge, 1911.

Maurois, A., *Aspects of Biography*. Translated from the French by S. C. Roberts. New York, 1929.

Stuart, D. R., *Epochs of Greek and Roman Biography*. Berkeley, California, 1928.

Thayer, W. B., *The Art of Biography*, New York, 1920.
Walker, W., *Great Men of the Christian Church.* 2nd. impression, Chicago, 1910.
Watt, H., *Representative Churchmen of Twenty Centuries.* London and New York, 1929.
Williamson, C., *Great Catholics.* New York: Macmillan, 1943.

Chapter I

Alfred the Great

Asser's Life of Alfred. Translated with Introduction and Notes by L. C. Jane. London, 1908.
Besant, W., *The Story of King Alfred.* 2nd. Edition. New York, 1913.
Duckett, E. S., *Alfred the Great, King of England, 849-901.* University of Chicago Press, 1956.

Nicholas the Great

Burn-Murdoch, H., *The Development of the Papacy.* London: Faber, 1954.
Duchesne, L., *The Beginnings of the Temporal Sovereignty of the Popes, 754-1073.* Translated from the second French edition by A. H. Matthew. London. 1908.
Howells, T. B., *The Chair of St. Peter.* London: Independent Press, 1935.
Mann, H. K., *Lives of the Popes* Vol. III. London, 1925.
Roy, J., *St. Nicholas I.* Translated from the French by M. Maitland. London, 1901.
Ullman, W., *Medieval Papalism.* London: Methuen & Co., 1949.

Chapter II

Odo of Cluny

Evans, J., *Monastic Life at Cluny*, 910-1157. London, 1931.
Smith, L. M., *The Early History of the Monastery of Cluny.* Oxford, 1920.
Thompson, J. W., *Feudal Germany.* Chicago, 1928. Chapter II.

Sitwell, Dom G. Editor and Translator, *St. Odo of Cluny: Life of St. Odo by John of Salerno,* London and New York: Sheed and Ward, 1938.

Bernard of Clairvaux

The Complete Works of St. Bernard, Abbot of Clairvaux. Translated from Mabillon's edition (1690) by S. J. Eales. 5 vols. London, 1889-1896.

Coulton, G. G., *Five Centuries of Religion,* Vol. I. Cambridge University Press, 1923.

James, B. S., *St. Bernard of Clarvaux as seen through his selected letters.* Chicago and New York: Regnery, 1953.

Storrs, R. S., *Bernard of Clairvaux: The Times, The Man and His Work.* New York, 1892. Reprinted, 1901.

Williams, W. W., *St. Bernard, Abbot of Clairvaux.* Manchester University Press, 1935.

Norbert of Xanten

Anderson, L. T., *St. Norbert of Xanten, a Second St. Paul.* Dublin: Gill, 1955.

Gendens, M., *Life of St. Norbert.* London, 1886.

Maire, E., *Saint Norbert, 1082-1134.* 2nd Edition, Paris 1922.

Zak, A., *Der heilige Norbert. Ein Lebensbild nach der Kirchen- und Profanengeschichte entworfen.* Vienna, 1930.

Chapter III

Hildebrand

Emerton, E., *The Correspondence of Pope Gregory VII.* [Records of Civilization XIV] New York: Columbia, 1932.

Fliche, A., *Saint Grégoire VII.* 3rd Edition, Paris, 1920.

Macdonald, A. J., *Hildebrand, a Life of Gregory VII.* London: Methuen, 1932.

Whitney, J. P., *Hildebrandine Essays.* Cambridge University Press; New York: Macmillan, 1932.

Innocent III

Binns, L. E., *Innocent III.* London, 1931.

Cheney, C. R., and W. H., Semple, Editors, *Innocent III. Select Letters concerning England,* (Latin and English

Text), Oxford, Medieval Text Series. 1955. Milwaukee: Bruce, 1940.
Packard, S. R., *Europe and the Church under Innocent III*, New York, 1927.
Sedgwick, H. D., *Italy in the Thirteenth Century.* 2 vols. New York, 1912.

Chapter IV

Lambert the Stammerer

Callaey, F. "Lambert li Beges et les beguines." *Revue d'histoire ecclesiastique. XXIII*, 1927, 254-259.
Greven, J., *Der Ursprung des Beginenswesens. Eine Auseinandersetzung mit Godefroid Kurth.* Munster, 1914.
Kurth, G., *La cité de Liége au moyen âge, II.* Brussels, 1910.
Loch, C. S., *Charity and Social Life.* London, 1910. (For the background of this chapter.)
Phillips, D., *Beguines in Medieval Strasburg.* Palo Alto: Stanford University, 1941.

Francis of Assisi

Boase, T. S. R., *St. Francis of Assisi.* London: Duckworth, 1930.
Engelbert, O., *St. Francis of Assisi, a Biography.* Translated and Edited by E. Hatton. London: Longmans, 1950.
The Little Flowers and the Life of St. Francis, with the Mirror of Perfection [Everyman's Library]. London, 1910.
Moorman, J. R. H., *The Sources of the Life of Francis of Assisi.* Manchester University Press, 1940.
Petry, R. C., *St. Francis of Assisi, Apostle of Poverty.* Durham, N. C.: Duke University Press, 1941.
Sabatier, P., *The Life of Francis of Assisi.* Translated from the French by L. S. Houghton. London, 1894.
Scudder, V. D., *The Franciscan Adventure.* London: Dent; New York: Dutton, 1931.
Seton, W. W., *St. Francis of Assisi; Essays in Commemoration.* London, 1926.

Elizabeth of Thuringia

Canton, W. E., *The Story of Elizabeth of Hungary.* London: Harrap, 1932.

De Roebeck, N., *St. Elizabeth of Hungary.* Milwaukee: Bruce, 1954.

Kingsley, C., *The Saint's Tragedy.* (Drama). London, 1948.

Montalembert, C. F. R. de, *The Life of St. Elizabeth of Hungary, Duchess of Thuringia.* (1836.) Translated from the French by F. D. Hoyt. New York, 1904.

Catherine of Siena

The Dialogue of the Seraphic Virgin, Catherine of Siena. Translated from the Italian by A. Thorold. London, 1907.

Fraigneux, M., *Sainte Catherine de Sienne, Mystique et diplomat.* Paris, La Colombe, 1950.

Gardner, E. C., *St. Catherine of Siena. A Study in the Religion, Literature and History of the Fourteenth Century in Italy.* London, 1907.

Gillet, M. S., *The Mission of St. Catherine.* London and St. Louis: Herder, 1955.

Jorgenson, J., *St. Catherine of Siena.* Translated from Danish by I. Lund. New York: Longmans, 1938.

Chapter V

John Scotus Erigena

Bett, H., *Johannes Scotus Erigena. A Study in Medieval Philosophy.* Cambridge, 1925.

Joannes Scotus Erigena, On the Division of Nature. Translated by C. Schwarz [Classics of St. John's Program] Book I. Annapolis: St. John's Bookstore, 1940.

Cappuyns, Dom M., *Jean Scot Érigène, sa vie, son oeuvre, sa pensée.* Louvain: Abbaye du Mont Cesar; Paris: Desclee, 1933.

Poole, R. L., *Illustrations of the History of Medieval Thought.* 2nd Edition. London, 1910.

Anselm of Canterbury

St. Anselm of Canterbury: *Proslogium; Monologium; an Appendix in Behalf of the Fool by Gaunilon; and Cur Deus Homo.* Translated by S. N. Deane, with an Introduction, etc. Chicago, 1930.

Church, R. W., *Saint Anselm.* New York: Macmillan, 1937.

Clayton, J., *Saint Anselm. A Critical Biography.* Milwaukee: Bruce, 1933.

MacIntire, J., *St. Anselm and His Critics: a Reinterpretation of Cur Deus Homo.* Glasgow: Oliver and Boyd, 1954.

Peter Abailard

Abailard's Ethics. Translated with an Introduction by J. R. McCallum. Oxford, 1935.

Historia Calamitatum, the Autobiography of Peter Abelard. Translated by H. A. Bellows. Minneapolis, 1922.

The Letters of Abelard and Heloise. Translated by C. K. S. Moncrief. New York: Knopf, 1933.

Gilson, E. H., *Heloise and Abelard.* Chicago: Regnery, 1951.

McCollum, J. R., *Abélard's Christian Theology.* London: Blackwell; New York: Macmillan, 1949.

Sikes, J. G., *Peter Abailard.* Cambridge University Press, New York: Macmillan, 1932.

Thomas Aquinas

Fairweather, A. M., Editor, *Nature and Grace; Selections from the Summa Theologica of Thomas Aquinas* [Library of Christian Classics XI] Philadelphia: Westminster Press; London: S.C.M. Press, 1954.

Pegis, A. C., Editor, *Basic Writings of St. Thomas Aquinas.* 2 vols. New York: Random House, 1945.

Grabmann, M., *Thomas Aquinas, His Personality and Thought.* Translated from the German by V. Michel. New York and London, 1928. (Harper Torchbook edition in process.)

Maritain, J., *The Angelic Doctor; the Life and Thought of Thomas Aquinas.* Translated from the French by T. Scanlon. New York: Sheed and Ward, 1931.

McCormick, J. F., *St. Thomas and the Life of Learning.* Milwaukee: Marquette University Press, 1937.

Pegis, A. C., *Introduction to Thomas Aquinas.* New York: Random House, 1948.

Desiderius Erasmus

Allen, P. S., *The Age of Erasmus.* Oxford, 1914.

Allen, P. S., *Erasmus; Lectures and Wayfaring Sketches.* Oxford: Clarendon Press, 1934.

Binns, L. E., *Erasmus the Reformer.* London, 1923.

Huizinga, J., *Erasmus of Rotterdam, with a selection from the Letters of Erasmus.* Translated by B. Flower. London: Phaidon Press, 1952. Reprinted as *Erasmus and the Age of the Reformation*, New York: Harper Torchbooks, 1957.

Hyma, A., *Erasmus and the Humanists.* New York, 1930.

Seebohm, F., *The Oxford Reformers of 1498 . . . John Colet, Erasmus and More.* London, 1867.

CHAPTER VI

Peter Waldo

Jalla, P., *Pierre Valdo*, Paris: Editions "Je Sers;" Geneva: Editions "Labor et Fides," 1934.

Newman, L. I., *Jewish Influence on Christian Reform Movements.* New York, 1925.

Vedder, H. C., "Origin and Early Teaching of the Waldenses" *American Journal of Theology* IV (1900), 465-489.

Marsiglio of Padua

Emerton, E., *The Defensor Pacis of Marsiglio of Padua.* Cambridge, Massachusetts, 1920.

Flick, A., *The Decline of the Medieval Church.* Vol. I. New York, 1930.

Gewirth, A., Editor, *Marsilius of Padua, Defender of Peace.* 2 vols. New York: Columbia University Press, Oxford University Press, 1951, 1957.

Poole, R. L., *Illustrations of the History of Medieval Thought.* 2nd Edition. London, 1920.

Previté-Orton, C. W., *The Defensor Pacis of Marsilius of Padua* (Critical Text and Introduction). Cambridge, 1928; Oxford: Oxford University Press, 1936.

John Wyclif

Deanesly, M., *The Lollard Bible and other Medieval Biblical Versions.* Cambridge, 1920.

MacFarlane, H. B., *Wycliffe and the Beginning of English Non-conformity.* London: English Universities Press, New York: Macmillan, 1953.

Spinka, M., editor, *Advocates of Reform from Wyclif to Erasmus.* [Library of Christian Classics XIV] Philadelphia: Westminster Press: London: S.C.M. Press, 1953, pp. 13-88.

Trevelyan, G. M., *England in the Age of Wycliffe.* London, 1899, 4th Edition 1909. Reprinted 1929. New York: Harper Torchbooks, 1963.

Workman, H. B., *John Wyclif; A Study of the English Medieval Church.* 2 vols., Oxford, 1926.

John Hus

The Letters of John Hus, with Introduction and Explanatory Notes. Translated and edited by H. B. Workman and R. M. Pope. London, 1904.

Kitts, E. J., *Pope John XXIII and Master John Huss of Bohemia.* London, 1910.

Schaff, D. S., *John Huss. His Life Teachings and Death.* New York, 1915.

Spinka, M., *John Hus and Czech Reform.* University of Chicago Press, 1941.

Spinka, M., Editor, *Advocates of Reform from Wyclif to Erasmus.* [Library, Christian Classics XIV] Philadelphia: Westminster Press; London: S.C.M. Press, 1953, pp. 137-278.

Chapter VII

Martin Luther

Bainton, R. H., *Here I Stand, A Life of Martin Luther.* New York and Nashville: Abingdon-Cokesbury, 1950.

Schwiebert, E. G., *Luther and his Times.* St. Louis: Concordia Publishing House, 1950.

Mackinnon, J., *Luther and the Reformation.* 4 vols., London, 1925-1930.

Luther's Works. Edited by J. Pelikan. (Series projected in 55 vols.) St. Louis: Concordia Publishing House, 1957.

Works of Martin Luther with Introductions and Notes. (By a group of Lutheran Scholars.) 6 vols. Philadelphia: Muhlenberg Press, 1915-1932.

Rupp, G., *Luther's Progress to the Diet of Worms, 1521.*

London: S.C.M. Press, 1951. New York: Harper Torchbooks, 1964.

Tappert, T. G., Editor, *Luther: Letters of Spiritual Counsel.* [Library of Christian Classics XVIII] Philadelphia: Westminster Press; London: S.C.M. Press, 1955.

John Calvin

Breen, Q., *John Calvin: a Study in French Humanism.* Grand Rapids: Eerdmaus, 1932.

Fuhrmann, P. T., *Instruction in Faith (1537) by John Calvin.* Philadelphia: Westminster Press, 1949.

Haroutunian, J., Editor, *Calvin: Commentaries.* [Library of Christian Classics, XXIII] Philadelphia: Westminster Press; London: S.C.M. Press, 1958.

Hunt, R. N. C., *Calvin.* London: Bles, 1933, 1935.

McNeill, J. T., Editor, *John Calvin on the Christian Faith: Selections from the Institutes, Commentaries and Tracts.* (Library of Liberal Arts, 93) New York: Bobbs-Merrill, 1964.

McNeill, J. T., *The History and Character of Calvinism.* New York: Oxford University Press, 1954.

Parker, T. H. L., *Portrait of Calvin.* London: S.C.M. Press, 1954; Philadelphia: Westminster Press, 1955.

Reid, J. K. S., Editor, *Calvin: Theological Treatises.* [Library of Christian Classics XXII]. London: S.C.M. Press; Philadelphia: Westminster Press, 1954.

Thomas Cranmer

Bromiley, G. W., *Thomas Cranmer, Archbishop and Martyr.* London: Church Book Room Press, 1956.

Hutchinson, F. F., *Cranmer and the English Reformation.* London and New York: Macmillan, 1950.

Smythe, C. H., *Cranmer and the Reformation under Edward VI.* Cambridge, 1926.

Strype, J., *Memorials of Thomas Cranmer, Archbishop of Canterbury.* 3rd Edition, 2 vols. London, 1853.

John Knox

Brown, P. H., *John Knox, a Biography.* 2 vols. London, 1895.

Burleigh, J. H. S., *A Church History of Scotland.* London: Oxford University Press, 1960.

Dickinson, W. C., *Andrew Lang, John Knox, and Scottish Presbyterianism.* Edinburgh: Nelson, 1952.

Dickinson, W. C., Editor. *The History of the Reformation in Scotland by John Knox.* 2 vols. London: Nelson; New York: Philosophical Library, 1950.

Fleming, D. H., *The Scottish Reformation: Causes, Characteristics, Consequences.* London, 1900.

MacGregor, G., *The Thundering Scot, a Portrait of John Knox.* Philadelphia: Westminster Press, 1957.

Chapter VIII

Faustus Socinus

Cory, D. M., *Faustus Socinus.* Boston: American Unitarian Association, 1932.

Kot, S., *Socinianism in Poland.* Translated by E. M. Wilbur. Boston: Beacon Press, 1957.

Wilbur, E. M., *A History of Unitarianism: Socinianism and its Antecedents.* Cambridge, Massachusetts: Harvard University Press, 1945.

Jacob Arminius

The Works of James Arminius . . . Translated from the Latin, to which is added Brandt's Life of the Author. by James Nichols. 3 vols. 1825-1875; *Reprinted as The Writings of James Arminius by James Nichols and W. R. Bagnall with a Sketch of the True Life of the Author.* Grand Rapids: Baker, 1956.

Harrison, A. W., *The Beginnings of Arminianism to the Synod of Dort.* London, 1926.

Hoenderdaaf, G. J., "The Life and Thought of Jacob Arminius." *Religion in Life XXIX*, 1960, 540-555.

Gottfried Wilhelm Leibniz

Leibniz, G. W., *Discourses on Metaphysics; Correspondence with Arnauld; Monodology.* Translated by G. R. Montgomery, Chicago, 1902. Reprinted Chicago, 1931.

Leibniz, G. W., *Selections*. Edited by P. P. Wiener. New York: Scribner, 1951.

Russel, B. A. W., *Critical Exposition of the Philosophy of Leibniz*. London: Allen, 1937; New York: Humanities Press, 1951.

Carr, H. W., *Leibniz*. London, 1929.

Jordan, G. J., *The Reunion of the Churches. A Study of Leibniz and His Great Attempt*. London, 1927.

Mellone, S. F. F., *The Dawn of Modern Thought: Descartes, Spinoza, Leibniz*. London, 1930.

Chapter IX

Ignatius Loyola

The Autobiography of St. Ignatius. Edited by J. F. X. O'Connor. New York, 1900.

The Spiritual Exercises of Ignatius Loyola. A New Translation by L. J. Puhl. Westminster, Maryland: Newman Press, 1951.

St. Ignatius and the Ratio Studiorum. Edited by E. A. Fitzpatrick. New York and London: McGraw, Hill, 1933.

Dudon, P., *St. Ignatius of Loyola*. Translated by W. J. Young. Milwaukee: Bruce, 1949.

Harvey, Q., *Ignatius Loyola*. Milwaukee: Bruce, Toronto: Ryerson Press, 1936.

Sedgwick, H. D., *Ignatius Loyola, an Attempt at an Impartial Biography*. New York, 1923.

Van Dyke, P., *Ignatius Loyola, the Founder of the Jesuits*. New York, 1926.

John Wesley

The Journal of the Reverend John Wesley. Edited by N. Curnock. 8 vols. London, 1909-1916. Reprinted, London: Epworth Press, 1938.

Selections from the Journal of John Wesley. Edited by H. Martin. London: S.C.M. Press, 1955.

Cell, G. C., *The Rediscovery of John Wesley*. New York: Holt, 1934.

Deschner, J. W., *John Wesley's Christianity*. Dallas: Southern Methodist University Press, 1960.

Edwards, M. L., *John Wesley and the Eighteenth Century: A Study of His Social and Political Influence.* London: Allen; New York: Abingdon, 1933.

Harrison, G. G., *Son to Susanna.* Nashville: Cokesbury, 1938.

Lee, U., *The Lord's Horseman.* New York, 1938.

McNeill, J. T., *Books of Faith and Power.* New York: Harper & Brothers, 1947. Chapter vi.

Vulliamy, C. E., *John Wesley.* London: Bles, 1931; New York: Scribner, 1932.

Whitley, A. S., *Wesley's England.* London: Epworth Press, 1938.

Herbert, T. W., *John Wesley as Editor and Author.* Princeton University Press, 1940.

Friedrich Daniel Ernst Schleiermacher

Drummond, A. L., *German Protestantism since Luther.* London: Epworth, 1951.

Friess, H. L., Editor, *Schleiermacher's Soliloquies: An English Translation of his Monologen with a Critical Introduction and Appendix.* Chicago, 1920.

Rowan, F., *The Life of Schleiermacher as Unfolded in his Autobiography and Letters.* London, 1860.

Schleiermacher, F., *The Christian Faith.* English Translation of the second German edition. Edited by H. R. Macintosh and J. S. Stewart. Edinburgh, 1928. Harper Torchbook edition, with Introduction by Richard R. Niebuhr, 1963.

Schleiermacher, F., *On Religion. Speeches to its Cultured Despisers.* Translated by John Oman. London, 1893. Harper Torchbook edition, with an Introduction by Rudolf Otto, 1958.

Selbie, W., *Schleiermacher, A Critical and Historical Study.* London, 1913.

INDEX

Revised August, 1964

harper torchbooks

HUMANITIES AND SOCIAL SCIENCES

American Studies

JOHN R. ALDEN: The American Revolution, 1775-1783.† *Illus.* TB/3011

RAY STANNARD BAKER: Following the Color Line: *American Negro Citizenship in the Progressive Era.‡ Illus. Edited by Dewey W. Grantham, Jr.* TB/3053

RAY A. BILLINGTON: The Far Western Frontier, 1830-1860.† *Illus.* TB/3012

JOSEPH L. BLAU, Ed.: Cornerstones of Religious Freedom in America. *Selected Basic Documents, Court Decisions and Public Statements. Enlarged and revised edition with new Intro. by Editor* TB/118

RANDOLPH S. BOURNE: War and the Intellectuals: *Collected Essays, 1915-1919.‡ Edited by Carl Resek* TB/3043

A. RUSSELL BUCHANAN: The United States and World War II. † *Illus.* Volume I TB/3044 Volume II TB/3045

ABRAHAM CAHAN: The Rise of David Levinsky: *a novel. Introduction by John Higham* TB/1028

JOSEPH CHARLES: The Origins of the American Party System TB/1049

THOMAS C. COCHRAN: The Inner Revolution: *Essays on the Social Sciences in History* TB/1140

T. C. COCHRAN & WILLIAM MILLER: The Age of Enterprise: *A Social History of Industrial America* TB/1054

EDWARD S. CORWIN: American Constitutional History: *Essays edited by Alpheus T. Mason and Gerald Garvey* TB/1136

FOSTER RHEA DULLES: America's Rise to World Power, 1898-1954.† *Illus.* TB/3021

W. A. DUNNING: Reconstruction, Political and Economic, 1865-1877 TB/1073

A. HUNTER DUPREE: Science in the Federal Government: *A History of Policies and Activities to 1940* TB/573

CLEMENT EATON: The Growth of Southern Civilization, 1790-1860.† *Illus.* TB/3040

HAROLD U. FAULKNER: Politics, Reform and Expansion, 1890-1900.† *Illus.* TB/3020

LOUIS FILLER: The Crusade against Slavery, 1830-1860.† *Illus.* TB/3029

EDITORS OF FORTUNE: America in the Sixties: *the Economy and the Society. Two-color charts* TB/1015

LAWRENCE HENRY GIPSON: The Coming of the Revolution, 1763-1775.† *Illus.* TB/3007

FRANCIS J. GRUND: Aristocracy in America: *Jacksonian Democracy* TB/1001

ALEXANDER HAMILTON: The Reports of Alexander Hamilton.‡ *Edited by Jacob E. Cooke* TB/3060

OSCAR HANDLIN, Editor: This Was America: *As Recorded by European Travelers to the Western Shore in the Eighteenth, Nineteenth, and Twentieth Centuries. Illus.* TB/1119

MARCUS LEE HANSEN: The Atlantic Migration: 1607-1860. *Edited by Arthur M. Schlesinger; Introduction by Oscar Handlin* TB/1052

MARCUS LEE HANSEN: The Immigrant in American History. *Edited with a Foreword by Arthur Schlesinger, Sr.* TB/1120

JOHN D. HICKS: Republican Ascendancy, 1921-1933.† *Illus.* TB/3041

JOHN HIGHAM, Ed.: The Reconstruction of American History TB/1068

DANIEL R. HUNDLEY: Social Relations in our Southern States.‡ *Edited by William R. Taylor* TB/3058

ROBERT H. JACKSON: The Supreme Court in the American System of Government TB/1106

THOMAS JEFFERSON: Notes on the State of Virginia.‡ *Edited by Thomas Perkins Abernethy* TB/3052

WILLIAM L. LANGER & S. EVERETT GLEASON: The Challenge to Isolation: *The World Crisis of 1937-1940 and American Foreign Policy* Volume I TB/3054 Volume II TB/3055

WILLIAM E. LEUCHTENBURG: Franklin D. Roosevelt and the New Deal, 1932-1940.† *Illus.* TB/3025

LEONARD W. LEVY: Freedom of Speech and Press in Early American History: *Legacy of Suppression* TB/1109

ARTHUR S. LINK: Woodrow Wilson and the Progressive Era, 1910-1917.† *Illus.* TB/3023

ROBERT GREEN McCLOSKEY: American Conservatism in the Age of Enterprise, 1865-1910 TB/1137

BERNARD MAYO: Myths and Men: *Patrick Henry, George Washington, Thomas Jefferson* TB/1108

JOHN C. MILLER: Alexander Hamilton and the Growth of the New Nation TB/3057

JOHN C. MILLER: The Federalist Era, 1789-1801.† *Illus.* TB/3027

† The New American Nation Series, edited by Henry Steele Commager and Richard B. Morris.

‡ American Perspectives series, edited by Bernard Wishy and William E. Leuchtenburg.

* The Rise of Modern Europe series, edited by William L. Langer.

‖ Researches in the Social, Cultural, and Behavioral Sciences, edited by Benjamin Nelson.

§ The Library of Religion and Culture, edited by Benjamin Nelson.

Σ Harper Modern Science Series, edited by James R. Newman.

° Not for sale in Canada.